BEST BIR
SITES IN T
HIGHLANDS

by
Gordon Hamlett

For Chris,
who can light up the world with her smile

BUCKINGHAM PRESS LTD

in association with

SWAROVSKI
O P T I K

Published in 2005 by:
Buckingham Press Ltd, 55 Thorpe Park Road, Peterborough
Cambridgeshire PE3 6LJ, United Kingdom
Tel/fax: 01733 561739
e-mail: buck.press@btinternet.com

© Buckingham Press 2005

ISBN 0 9533840 98
ISSN 0144-364 X

Editor: David Cromack
Design and maps: Hilary Cromack
Publisher: Hilary Cromack

About the author: Gordon Hamlett, a freelance writer, is a regular contributor to *Bird Watching* magazine, both as a reviewer of books, DVDs and computer software and also as sub-editor of the UK Bird Sightings section. Gordon has visited the Scottish Highlands every year since the mid-1980s and used his first-hand knowledge of the area to write this book.

Cover illustration: Golden Eagle by Andrew Hutchinson
Andrew Hutchinson was born in North Yorkshire but from 1991 he and his wife Louise lived in the Highlands of Scotland where he had always found inspiration in the dramatic and unspoilt beauty of the Cairngorms. He has undertaken many commissions, and can count The Duke of Edinburgh among his customers.

The cover image *Golden Eagle* may be produced as a limited edition print. For details of this and future exhibitions please contact Andrew Hutchinson at Dulnain House, Marton, Sinnington York YO62 6RD Telephone 01751 430637 e-mail andrew-hutchinson@tesco.net
To see further images go to www.giclee-art.co.uk

Black and white illustrations: All by Dan Powell
Dan is a well-established bird and wildlife artist who lives in the south of England. In 1995 he won the Artists for Nature Foundation award which resulted in a field trip to the Pyrennees and an exhibition in Barcelona. He has also won the *British Birds'* Bird Illustrator of the Year title.

Dan is best known for his fieldguide *The Dragonflies of Great Britain* that he wrote, designed and illustrated. His work has appeared in numerous wildlife books and publications. He can be contacted on: dan.powell@care4free.net

Printed and bound in Great Britain by:
Cambridge University Press, Cambridge UK.

CONTENTS

CONTENTS

MESSAGE FROM OUR SPONSOR

THE GRANDEUR of the landscape and its tranquillity makes the Scottish Highlands an irresistible magnet for visitors from all parts of the globe. Among them are thousands of birdwatchers excited at the prospect of seeing Golden and White-tailed Eagles, Capercaillies and Black Grouse, Ptarmigan and Dotterel, Crested Tits and Scottish Crossbill, of course.

The supporting cast of birds and mammals is just as impressive, but with so many glens, lochs and coastal bays to explore, an accurate and up-to-date guide is an essential tool for trip planning. *Best Birdwatching Sites in the Scottish Highlands* is the result of intensive research and field trips conducted by author Gordon Hamlett and the level of detail he brings to each route is unprecedented.

Here at Swarovski Optik, we are delighted to once again be associated with a quality publication from Buckingham Press that we are sure will enhance the growing reputation of its *Best Birdwatching Sites* series.

The two companies have a shared commitment to producing products that are innovative and that bring genuine benefits to the birdwatching community within Britain and further afield. We trust you will have many happy hours exploring all that Scotland has to offer.

John Brinkley
Managing Director, Swarovski Optik

INTRODUCTION

THERE ARE many reasons to go birding in the Highlands. Chief among them is that you get birds here that occur nowhere else in Britain, from the tiny Crested Tit to the mighty turkey-like Capercaillie.

There is a fine supporting cast too, from the massive seabird colonies to eagles patrolling hidden glens. For anyone from England, Ireland and Wales, a great attraction is to see birds such as resplendent divers and Slavonian Grebes that are only normally seen in drab winter plumage.

Exciting birds need a spectacular backdrop and they certainly get it here, with the best scenery in Britain bar none. Then there is a whole host of history, from prehistoric stone circles, through the strange and mysterious Picts to the romantic tales and bloody battles of the Jacobite rebellions.

There are castles aplenty to visit and all those whisky distilleries as well. No wonder some people claim to have seen strange monsters in the lochs. This is a very special place and it doesn't take long for the magic to enter your soul.

For us, it was a quarter to five on a Saturday afternoon when we arrived at our destination in the Highlands for the first time. Pulling in to the driveway of our cottage in Nethy Bridge, we were greeted by a stunning male Siskin feeding on nuts no more than three feet above our heads. By the time we had got out of the car, the second feeder had produced a Crested Tit and red squirrel.

Rushing inside for the football results, I was just in time to hear them being announced – in Gaelic for teams I had never heard of. Somehow, it didn't matter. It was the only time I had never cared how big a defeat my beloved Manchester City had suffered.

Quickly unpacking, we headed straight down to Loch Garten, just in case all the Ospreys in Scotland decided to desert overnight. They hadn't and the magic continued. It has never left.

Wildlife highlights

Over the years, there have been many highlights, such as Black-throated Divers, looking as if they have come straight from a Paris fashion house; Hen Harriers displaying over the car; our first otter and pine marten.

The view of snow-dusted Cairngorms at dawn from the bridge over the Spey at Boat of Garten will live forever in our memory, as will a White-tailed Eagle having its tail tweaked by a Hooded Crow. Being dive bombed by skuas was as memorable as watching 30 bottle-nosed dolphins leaping out of the sea, but the sensations were very different.

On one occasion we had a Golden Eagle heading straight at us as it tried to avoid the attention of three Buzzards and five Ravens and then there was the time we were scared witless by 'Mad George', a rogue Capercaillie famed for his attacks on human visitors.

I hope these examples are beginning to whet your appetite. Pay a visit and you may enjoy, as we did, the sight of three young red squirrels, beautifully backlit, playing tag on the road or a mini fall of Spotted Flycatchers with 14 birds in the same tree.

Regional differences

The Highlands can be roughly divided into three main areas. To the east is Deeside. This is the area to explore if you are into history, castles and royal connections. The downside of this is that it attracts huge numbers of tourists and you can find the best known spots get very busy – not conducive to great birding. Better by far to find your own quiet bit of countryside. There's plenty to go round.

Speyside is the bit in the middle and is the centre for all sorts of activity holidays – mountain biking, windsurfing, pony-trekking etc. The main attraction for birders is that all the Scottish specialities can be found here and the area makes a great centre for day tripping with easy access to the rest of the Highlands.

The west coast is where you find the most dramatic scenery with stunning vistas of mountains and lochs at every twist and turn of the road. The tourists don't seem to venture much further north than Fort William and by the time you get past Ullapool, you can find whole roads, valleys and beaches to yourself.

Set the right pace

You may find it takes a bit of time to get used to birding in the Highlands. If you are used to birding at English hotspots such as RSPB Titchwell or Minsmere and ticking off 60-70 species in an hour or so, you will find sites such as Insh Marshes very different. Comments get written in the logbook such as 'Boring. I've been here half an hour and only seen six species.'

Well, to start with, I reckon these critics weren't looking properly. And secondly, what did they expect? The density of birds up here is relatively low, but the interest is high. Birding in the Highlands is like that other prime Scottish product, a fine malt whisky: something to take your time over and savour, not rush.

A fortnight's holiday in spring or summer, taking in a good range of habitats, and actively chasing the birds, should produce 120-140 species or so. But equally, you could spend an entire day exploring mountain and moorland and come back with a day list of less than 20 species.

When I consider what makes the Highlands so special I come up with different theories every time, but one recurring factor is that because there are so few people exploring, whatever wildlife you see tends to be a very personal experience; just you and the birds and animals, often in extreme close up. Little wonder that the memories get permanently etched.

All these trips in this book are designed to take you through some prime birding areas and habitats, covering all the speciality birds. You may see all the birds, you may not, but at the end of the day, it doesn't really matter. You are sure to want to come back again. This book is for those who enjoy their birding, but who also want to savour the whole Highland experience.

DRIVING in the Highlands should be a doddle with all those wide-open spaces and precious little traffic to worry about. It's not quite that simple.

Many of the designated A-roads are only single-track roads with passing places, so you can imagine what some of the B-roads are like. In the remoter areas, it's a good unclassified road that doesn't have grass growing down the middle. When you add in a selection of twists and turns, blind bends, summits and unfenced roads with a big drop on one side, they can make for some challenging driving.

If you are not used to driving on single-track roads, then Glen Affric offers a gentle introduction. The roads to avoid if you lack confidence are at Applecross, the Wee Mad Road in Inverpolly, the stretch of Glen Quoich approaching Loch Hourn, the Farr Road in the Findhorn Valley and the return leg after you come off Handa.

Another problem is the scenery. It's gorgeous and there is a great tendency to slow down and look at everything. There is a very good reason why the locals talk about 'Highland miles'. You will find that journeys take a lot longer than you anticipate. By the time you get onto the steep, twisty minor roads, scanning for birds as you go, you will be lucky to average 10-15mph.

My advice if you are travelling to one of the tours in this book, is to ignore as much as you can on the way there, enjoy your birding at the recommended hotspots and then, if you have any time left over, drive slowly back, taking in all those bits you missed on the way out.

Single-track roads

Anticipation is the key to using passing places. If you see another car coming towards you, pull in to a passing place if there is one on your side of the road or stop opposite one if it is on the other side. Don't keep going to determine how far the two cars can close before one of you has to get out of the way. If a car flashes its lights, it generally means that it has stopped for you and it is safe to continue.

Similarly, if you have someone behind you, pull in and let them pass. Remember that not everyone is a tourist. Just imagine that you have a doctor behind you en route to an urgent case. He doesn't want to be held up as you dawdle along looking for Wheatears, so get out of his way.

Most local drivers tend to drive on full beam headlights when it is dark and you may have to flash them several times to get them to dip their lights. If you get a reluctant dipper, get off the road as quickly as possible. Being dazzled and steep hills with no crash barriers do not make a good combination.

By all means stop to scan for birds from your passing place, but don't leave your car unattended unless you are sure that there is plenty of room for other traffic to get past. There is nothing worse than having to reverse for half a mile round bends and up hills just because of someone else's inconsiderate parking.

Courtesy

It is customary to wave your thanks to anyone who pulls in for you. Both drivers usually wave, regardless of who stops. It is a nice friendly gesture, doesn't cost anything and believe me, you will quickly get angry when someone fails to acknowledge your gesture.

Strange as it sounds, you get different types of wave depending on which part of the Highlands you are visiting. In Speyside, you normally get a full wave of the hand and a nod of the head. On the west coast, you get the 'west coast finger', an almost grudging lift of the index finger from the steering wheel.

The strangest gesture I've seen was on Skye when a lorry came down a hill towards us. We pulled off and the driver promptly took both hands off the wheel in a sort of one-man Mexican wave. Scary.

Snow blocks many roads during the winter, including many of the main routes. If this is the case, don't even think of trying to drive into the mountains. The authorities have enough trouble looking after the main roads. Minor roads just get ignored.

The A9 and other major roads

Even on major roads, you should drive with consideration for other drivers. If you are taking your time and enjoying the view, hang back from the car in front so that other cars can overtake more easily. Remember, it is often the second car in a queue that is causing a jam.

The A9, the main road through Speyside to Caithness, is largely single carriageway with the occasional stretch of dual carriageway to allow overtaking.

Slowly moving lorries and caravans lead to drivers getting very frustrated, especially on the stretch from Perth to Speyside, and there are many accidents caused by a combination of poor road courtesy and bad overtaking. If you see a queue building up behind you, pull over and let the traffic clear.

Conversely, when the road is clear, avoid the temptation to put your foot down. The Highlands police are very keen on deterring speeding and often have radar traps in operation. There are many twitchers who still rue the night they rushed to view the Wandering Tattler which turned up in the Moray Firth!

Concern for animals

In your neighbourhood rabbits may have learned to avoid cars, but this survival instinct is not common up north. We drove from Nethy Bridge to Grantown at 4 a.m. one day, a distance of some five or six miles. It took us 45 minutes as scores of rabbits and deer just stood their ground in the road and looked at us. I ended up walking in front of the car trying to shoo them away.

Sheep are the main problem, especially when they have young lambs. The lambs will leave it until the very last second before rushing across the road to the safety of their mother's side. Assume that all sheep are like random bombs, waiting to go off. There is no doubt that they are in league with the devil and have contracts with all the local garage owners. Drive slowly past them.

Deer can do serious damage to your car if you collide. When one animal runs across the road in front of you, the rest of the herd usually follows. Reports from the police suggest that motorists usually manage to miss the first deer, but it is the second one that impacts on the vehicle.

While you can usually see the deer coming during the day, they are potentially more dangerous at night. Returning from Insh Marshes after dark, half a dozen roe deer suddenly bounded out of the woods in front of us. All that we could see was six pairs of eyes, shining bright green in the headlights, bouncing across our path.

Fuel supplies

For those of you used to the luxury of all-night garages and supermarket price wars, buying fuel in the Highlands can come as a bit of a shock. Not only are garages few and far between away from the major towns, but they also tend to keep 9-5 hours and are not open on Sundays. In the more remote areas, prices can also be 15-20% higher than in the cities.

The obvious solution to this is to make sure that you have a full tank of petrol before you set out on a trip and to check your petrol gauge every time you pass a garage. Anything less than a quarter of a tank and I would definitely take the opportunity to fill up.

The cheapest petrol tends to be in the Nairn-Elgin area of Moray. If you are going through Inverness, there is a large Tesco's just along the A96 Aberdeen road that is both reasonable and open all hours.

GETTING TO GRIPS WITH GAELIC

THERE comes a moment every birdwatcher dreads up in the Highlands. You know how it is; you meet another birder and the conversation starts off: 'What have you seen?' 'Oh,' comes the reply, 'I've just had a so-and-so.' 'Great,' you say, 'where?'

And that's where the problem starts for the place name is in Gaelic. Now Gaelic is an oral rather than a written language. It might be a beautiful, musical and poetic language, but to a non-native, it is surely one of the least intuitive languages ever, especially when you see it printed out. To make matters worse, dialects and pronunciations seem to change from village to village.

So what do you do? You can try pronouncing it as written, knowing that you will be way off beam, but at least giving your opposite number a fighting chance.

Or you can have a bash at trying a 'proper' pronunciation, from whatever bits of knowledge you have picked up. This is probably the least effective option as it guarantees that the person you are talking to will have little idea of what you mean. By far the simplest solution is to get a map out of the car and point!

A T LONG LAST, the day of your holiday dawns. Naturally, you can't wait to arrive at your chosen cottage or hotel, but for many visitors from south of the border, it is a long drive – remember, London to Speyside is about 500 miles. So how about a bit of birding en route? If you are going to make several stops, you might as well pick places that just happen to have a few interesting birds to see rather than the back end of a service station.

There are two basic routes that you are likely to take. The A9 takes you right into the heart of Speyside, before continuing up through Inverness and into Caithness. If you are heading towards the west coast, then you will almost certainly be taking the A82 alongside Loch Lomond, through Glencoe and up towards Fort William.

Let's take the west coast route first. This is a very slow road to drive, especially round Loch Lomond which seems to be undergoing a major series of road repairs. To be honest, the birding isn't great along this route. You may spot a few common waterbirds at one of the Loch Lomond visitor centres and a few moorland species with possibly your first glimpse of a Golden Eagle at the Glencoe visitor centre, but otherwise there isn't a great deal to see en route. You are better advised to continue to your destination and then start exploring those remote valleys and wonderful coastline.

If however you are travelling along the A9, then there are several places worth a stop. For anyone coming via the Forth Bridge in Edinburgh, then Vane Farm RSPB (see map on page 12) is a must. Only a couple of miles off the M90, this is one of the RSPB's flagship reserves, complete with shop, café and toilets.

Anyone coming via Glasgow will miss out on Vane Farm, but all the rest of the stops are ideal. A word of warning here. There are no shops or petrol stations on the A9 itself. You will need to visit one of the local towns if you have to fill up with petrol. Also note that the police are very keen on catching speeding motorists here so take care. See page 9 for extra details.

A couple of miles off the A9 at Dunkeld is the Scottish Wildlife Trust's reserve of Loch of the Lowes (see page 26), excellent for watching Ospreys at the nest in summer. Just beyond Dunkeld is the Scottish National Trust's reserve at the Hermitage (see page 25), ideal if you want to stretch your legs on a walk through some beautiful woodland.

If you are in need of food and petrol, then Pitlochry is the next major town and from here, you can explore the River Tummel (see page 30) for woodland and river species and there is always a chance of seeing a salmon using the fish ladder.

Continuing north for another few miles, there is another Scottish National Trust centre of Killiecrankie (see page 31), which has a café and toilet facilities as well as being the best place to see Wood Warblers in spring.

You are now only about 40 miles from Speyside. It always looks as if this stretch of road should be good for birds, but apart from Oystercatchers, Buzzards and Common Gulls, we have only ever seen a few Wheatears, one Peregrine, one Merlin and one

Short-eared Owl. There might be a temptation to visit Insh Marshes RSPB reserve (see page 86), but it really deserves more of your time.

Aviemore has shops, petrol and toilets and you can explore the woods at Craigellachie (see page 80) from here, hoping to see the resident Peregrines. Continuing north, the RSPB's Loch Garten site (see page 76) is well signposted if you want a quick look for Ospreys and Crested Tit.

Longman Point (see page 152) is worth a look if you are stopping in Inverness and if you are heading much further north on the A9, then the best site for your picnic without a shadow of a doubt is Loch Fleet (see page 195).

And after all these brief stops, it's time for some serious birding.

Vane Farm
Background information

VANE FARM OFFERS a good range of habitats and you should get your holiday list off to a good start here. Common woodland birds enjoy the pickings from the feeders round the visitor centre and you could see a Siskin on the nuts.

The woods behind the centre, accessed by two nature trails, climb quite steeply giving superb views over the loch. Summer migrants such as Willow Warbler and Tree Pipit are easy to see here. Scan the mountain ridges above the woods for Buzzards and Peregrines.

Renowned for its internationally important numbers of winter wildfowl, a few geese – mostly Pink-footed – hang on until May and you could pick out the occasional Bean Goose among them. Waders frequent the pools, some staying to breed, while others, such as Black-tailed Godwits, pass through. There is always a good selection of wildfowl present. Ospreys fish

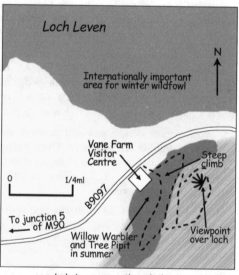

regularly in summer, though the views tend to be distant.

Viewing is either from the comfort of the visitor centre, coffee on hand and telescopes provided, or from a couple of hides that get you closer to the action, but without quite the same degree of luxury!

The reserve is well signed. Leave the M90 at Junction 5 and head east for three miles along the B9097.

Centre open 10am-5pm April to December and 10am-4pm January to March. Admission fee payable for non-members. Reserve telephone number 01577 862 355. Disabled access to visitor centre.

**Redstarts breed in many of the
Highlands oak woodlands.**

WHILE THERE are no bad times to visit the Highlands, here are a few highlights to help you choose when to time your visit. Without a shadow of doubt, mid-May is my personal favourite time as all the summer migrants have arrived, everything is still in its breeding finery, the woods are alive with song and there are no midges to worry about!

April also has a lot to offer. You might miss a few late-arriving migrants, but you gain by catching up with a lot of wintering species. For any bird heading to the Arctic, the north Scottish coast is the last bit of land before they have to cross the North Sea, so birds linger and feed up before migrating.

For many though, the longer hours of daylight and better weather in June and July make that the perfect time to visit. There is always plenty of bird activity with the parents constantly bringing food to the nest, followed by all the young taking to the wing for the first time. Or how about the autumn migration when all the colours start to turn and the valleys echo to the roar of red deer?

I also know many hardier souls who prefer the joys of a winter trip when huge snow falls change the appearance of the landscape yet again. They revel in the huge flocks of seaducks, thousands of geese, the chance of Waxwings, Great Grey Shrikes or a few white-winged gulls. This time also gives them the chance to view the region's bird specialities without having to cope with non-birding tourists.

13

YOUR BIRDING YEAR IN SCOTLAND

ALL YEAR

Many of the sought-after Scottish specialities are present throughout the year. Crested Tits and Capercaillie can be found in suitable woodland, mostly around Speyside. The same woods hold Scottish Crossbills, though in varying numbers.

Golden Eagles and Ptarmigan remain on the mountains, with Red Grouse on the moors. White-tailed Eagles remain, by and large, on the west coast though some juveniles do wander. Findhorn Valley regularly gets sightings along with all the other raptors there. Species such as Rock Dove and Twite are ever-present, but start to flock in winter.

JANUARY

Check flocks of finches for Bramblings and buntings. Tit flocks may contain Goldcrests and Treecreepers. Any fishing village and harbour is worth checking for Glaucous and Iceland Gulls – Ross's or Ivory Gull if you are really lucky.

Ptarmigan, in their winter white, can often be seen really well at the big ski centre car parks without having to get out of your car.

FEBRUARY

Raptors will start displaying on fine days towards the end of the month. It is possible to see Buzzards and Sparrowhawks soaring over suitable woods as well as the spectacular sky-dancing of Golden Eagles. Some species, such as Ravens, are already on eggs.

The Beauly and Cromarty Firths will still be full of seaducks. The first tentative songs from resident species such as Mistle Thrushes will be heard.

MARCH

Wintering wildfowl start to head north and seaducks reach their peak numbers, while divers and grebes round the coast start to acquire their summer finery.

Waders such as Lapwings and Oystercatchers start arriving back on territory. By the end of the month, the first few migrant Sand Martins and Wheatears arrive. An early Osprey could turn up, too.

APRIL

This is a dynamic month, with migration in full flow, both in and out. Parties of wintering birds, such as geese and thrushes, are heading back north. The volume of song in the woods increases dramatically as birds set up territories and try to attract mates. Black Grouse leks are particularly active.

Moors come to life after their bird-free winter desolation and Ring Ouzels arrive back. April is a good time to check wader flocks on the coast for something unusual. Slavonian Grebes move back to Loch Ruthven and Black and Red-throated Divers to northern lochs.

14

YOUR BIRDING YEAR IN SCOTLAND

MAY

This is the month of maximum all-round activity. The last migrants – Swifts and Spotted Flycatchers arrive. The woods are still full of song and frenzied activity as the parents collect food for newly-hatched young.

Periods of easterly winds could bring vagrants to the east coast. On the west and north coast, the last of the wintering Great Northern Divers depart and this is your best chance to find all three diver species in their breeding plumage.

Seabird cliffs start to fill up. Dotterel are back on the high tops. Waders are displaying with Snipe, Curlews, Redshanks and Lapwings all active. Listen out at dusk for Spotted Crakes (Insh Marshes) and Corn Crakes (north coast and Skye).

JUNE

Not quite 24-hour birding but not far off it. The long, summer days see plenty of young birds around with the adults on continuous feeding forays. This is the best month to visit the mountain tops.

Seabird cliffs are at their most spectacular, with those on the extreme north coast attracting the attention of breeding Arctic and Great Skuas. For many birders, this is the month when the Highlands are at their best, enhanced by wildflowers, butterflies and young deer.

JULY

Waders start moving down from the moors to the coast and some migrants such as Cuckoos will prove very tricky to find. Woodland song is replaced by a whole spectrum of strange squeaks and twitters as young birds leave their nests and start exploring their surroundings.

Young Ospreys are on the wing, so a visit to a popular feeding area such as the Inverdruie Fish Farm, Findhorn Bay or Spey Bay should be worthwhile. This is the last month when you can guarantee seeing species such as Dotterel and Puffin.

AUGUST

Local waders are now joined on the coast by incoming migrants from the High Arctic. Seabirds begin to move and a trip to a headland with winds in the north should prove rewarding with views of skuas and shearwaters.

Small birds start to slip away and you can expect to see family parties turning up in unusual habitats as they move south. Ospreys also start to move, the adults quite happy to leave the young to fend for themselves. This is an excellent month, together with September, for watching raptors. The Findhorn Valley is usually the most popular choice of venue.

15

YOUR BIRDING YEAR

SEPTEMBER

Any remaining summer visitors start moving south and the vanguard of the winter visitors arrive, possibly including Barnacle Geese on the west coast. Wildfowl that have bred on freshwater lochs start moving to sea lochs for winter. Wader passage on the east coast could produce Curlew Sandpiper and Little Stint, as well as something rarer.

Seawatching should be worthwhile from coastal headlands with seabird passage at its best. Movements of tens of thousands of birds are possible. Your chances of finding the elusive Capercaillie improve as young are now on the wing. Calm days on the west coast should produce whale sightings.

OCTOBER

Though the hills echo to the sound of red deer rutting, many of the birds have moved away to more suitable lowland habitats for the winter. Thrushes start pouring in from Scandinavia and small birds start to flock. Suitable winds are guaranteed to bring in a scattering of rare birds, so head to the east coast and check any bushes that offer potential shelter.

Parties of Greylag Geese and Whooper Swans arrive. Numbers of wintering waders start to increase and with so many birds on the coast, there is a good chance of finding a hunting Peregrine or Merlin.

NOVEMBER

The mountains and moors are largely deserted now with only the grouse and Golden Eagles remaining. Insh Marshes will give you good views of Whooper Swans, plus a Hen Harrier roost at dusk. Check out the larger lochs for geese and gulls coming in to roost at dusk. Plenty more Fieldfares and Redwings arrive.

Little Auks might move along the coast in gales and it is always worthwhile checking sheltered bays and harbours after strong storms for any manner of birds taking refuge from the wind. Look for good numbers of Slavonian Grebes on the sea.

DECEMBER

Check the east coast for sea ducks. There's a pretty good chance of something scarce among them - American Wigeon, Black Duck, Green-winged Teal or King Eider could all be found together with Surf Scoters mixed in with their Common and Velvet cousins. On the west coast, the most likely rarity is a White-billed Diver. Look for Snow Buntings in areas of dunes and Purple Sandpipers round harbours or on rocky outcrops.

THIS BOOK, the third in a series from Buckingham Press, is somewhat different from other birdwatching 'where to watch' guides. The vast distances of the Highlands means you need a car to get the most out of your visit, as public transport and the wilds of the Scottish Highlands aren't the closest of cousins.

Most site guides feature individual nature reserves, but in this region they are not necessarily easy to work. For instance, Inverpolly measures roughly 12 miles by 15, so where about in the 180 square miles do you start looking for birds and wildlife? As it happens, most of the interior is totally inaccessible to all but the hardiest of walkers, so you just drive slowly round the edge, stopping occasionally and seeing what you can.

To facilitate this, *Best Birdwatching Sites in the Scottish Highlands* is organised into a series of suggested day trips or road tours. One of the benefits of arranging the book this way is that many of the areas described don't lend themselves to a simple 'here is the reserve, now go and explore' approach. If you are driving down a 14-mile valley, you might want to stop briefly in several spots, to watch a family of Wheatears, a Merlin on a post or a soaring Golden Eagle, but there is no single defining spot where you can say 'stop here and watch'.

The drives are circular wherever possible and have been selected to take in as many habitat types as possible – moorland, loch, wood, mountain and sea. You won't have time in a single day to attempt every site mentioned, especially if you decide to get out and climb a mountain, so pick and choose whichever bits appeal. Don't expect to see everything in just one visit.

I've used my own direct experience to recommend routes that take in the most interesting roads and best scenery. Places of interest to non-birders are also mentioned. Speyside and Deeside are good for distilleries, castles and more recent history. Sutherland and Caithness are great for ancient history and sites of archaeological interest.

Most of the roads are minor and fairly quiet so you should be able to stop easily if something interesting hops up in front of you, but please study the chapter on driving etiquette on page 9. Because the roads chosen are obscure, they often make for challenging driving and those of a nervous disposition might like to skip some of the more minor valleys. Remember to keep checking your fuel levels as service stations are not common.

Being car-based, many of the suggested routes give great value to wheelchair-users or frail birdwatchers who are unable to walk long distances. Many places can be watched directly from the roadside and you will be able to see a good range of species with minimum effort. It should be pointed out though that disabled facilities at reserves are few and far between.

HOW TO USE THIS BOOK

Here are typical page layouts of the tour pages. Once familiar with the layout, you will be able to extract the information you need quickly and easily.

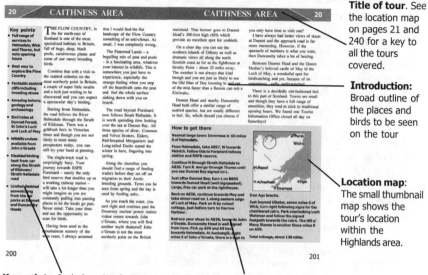

Title of tour. See the location map on pages 21 and 240 for a key to all the tours covered.

Introduction: Broad outline of the places and birds to be seen on the tour

Location map: The small thumbnail map shows the tour's location within the Highlands area.

Key points: Includes what facilities are available and where, whether there are hides, information on likely terrain, suitability for wheelchairs as well as other useful info and tips.

How to get there: Directions to find your way to the different sites covered in the tour, the nearest large town and the overall mileage of the tour.

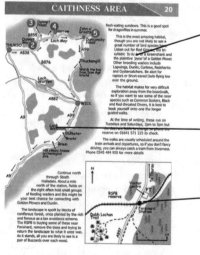

Background information: This section will cover each individual site on the tour in more detail. It may contain more information on points which have been briefly mentioned in previous sections.

Tour map: For each site there is a large map covering the tour and showing the main towns, places of interest and stopping off points. Small arrows show recommended route of travel.

Site map: Each significant site on the tour will have a more detailed map showing trails, hides and other key features for the site. The scale shown is in miles.

Seasonal approach

Most of the trips described cover the periods from spring through to autumn, simply because that is when most people visit. Where there are interesting birds to be seen in winter, these are mentioned in the site accounts.

Remember though that many roads can get closed because of snow in winter and driving conditions can be particularly treacherous. In addition, many of the valleys are relatively bird-free zones and all the seabird cliffs will be deserted, so pick and choose your trip accordingly.

Planning your time wisely

All the basic tours can be done easily in a day. How you decide to allocate your time at each site to you is up to you. If your mountain watching produces an eagle within ten minutes, you might decide to move on straight away. Or you might be there for several hours before a bird shows. Wherever possible, I've given rough estimates for the time it will take to climb a particular mountain, or walk round a wood.

A simple rule of thumb is, whatever you do (both driving and birding) will always take a lot longer than you think, partly because the roads do not encourage speed, but also because you tend to stop to look at every loch and scan every mountain ridge for birds.

Though it is tempting to stop frequently, resist the urge and listen to the voice of bitter experience. The places to stop mentioned in the book have all proved to be the most productive over the years. Decide beforehand which sites you want to visit, stick rigidly to your plan and then use any time left at the end of the day for the more 'suck it and see' approach.

Sensitive information

A quick word here about what isn't in this book. There are no display sites mentioned for Capercaillie and Black Grouse, apart from those that are properly controlled. If you are looking for these birds away from well-known sites, such as the Capercaillie watch at Loch Garten, then please read the the Capercaillie Code of Conduct (on page 20) and act in ways that will not disturb these thereatened species.

There are a lot of Schedule 1 breeding birds up in Scotland and unfortunately, there is still a small group of egg collectors determined to plunder their nests. Please be very careful about disclosing nest site information to others and report any suspicious behaviour to the police (ask for the wildlife liaison officer) or the RSPB. To the best of my knowledge, all the sites mentioned in this book are already in the public domain and offer no new information to eggers.

CAPERCAILLIE CODE OF CONDUCT

- The Capercaillie is listed on Schedule 1 of the Wildlife & Countryside Act 1981. This makes it illegal to intentionally disturb birds when nesting.

- The RSPB provides opportunities to watch Capercaillies lekking from its Osprey Centre at RSPB Abernethy Forest nature reserve, Strathspey, during April and May. Telephone 01479 821409. Away from here, Capercaillie leks should not be visited at all during the crucial April-May period.

- Capercaillies can be easier to see in autumn (from September), as there are usually more birds once juveniles have fledged.

- Capercaillies are less disturbed by vehicles than by walkers; if you have vehicular access to a forest, remain inside with the engine switched off and observe birds quietly until they have moved back into the forest.

- Use well-defined tracks and paths, to which birds will often come in search of grit. Do not wander in heather and blaeberry/bilberry, especially between May and August when nesting hens and young birds may be present. Flushing them can split up broods, exposing them to predators, or cause birds to fly into fences every year, deer fences kill an estimated quarter of juvenile Capercaillies.

- For the best chance of seeing Capercaillies, book with a reputable Scottish wildlife tour company, which may have special arrangements with private estates and experience of showing Capercaillies to visitors.

BLACK GROUSE CODE OF CONDUCT

- Avoid looking for Black Grouse after heavy snowfalls, when birds are under stress.

- View leks from a vehicle. Black Grouse pay little attention to stationary vehicles that are at least 100 metres away. Ensure that you do not block access and that your presence will not disturb nearby residents. Avoid approaching a lek on foot, which usually disturbs the birds.

- Arrive before daybreak. A vehicle stopping once it is light can disturb the birds. Stay in your vehicle and watch quietly through binoculars and telescopes. Get the flask of coffee from the boot before your vigil! Don't start the engine until after lekking has wound down, usually about two hours after dawn. Alternatively, consider watching a lek in the evening.

- Keep to footpaths, especially in June and July, when there may be nesting females and young birds present. Do not go looking for Black Grouse in heather or thick field vegetation, especially in woodland (birds may fly into deer fences, with lethal consequences, if flushed).

- Do not bring dogs into the field when you're watching grouse.

HAVE YOUR SAY

Experience gained over many years has gone into the content of this book, but inevitably, you will have favourite places of your own, not mentioned in the book. I'd be delighted to hear from readers willing to share information and to receive updates on sites change and new access details, together with your suggestions and corrections.

Feel free to write to Gordon Hamlett, c/o Buckingham Press, 55 Thorpe Park Road, Longthorpe, Peterborough PE3 6LJ or email me at admin@buckinghampress.com

The publishers' goal is to bring out new editions on a regular basis so that information can be kept as up to date as possible.

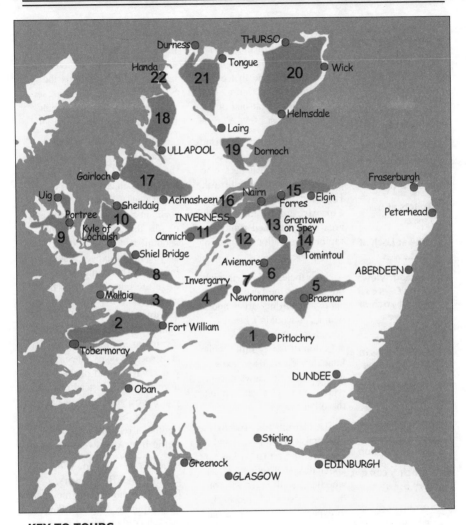

KEY TO TOURS

1. Perthshire Tour
2. Ardnamurchan Tour
3. Loch Arkaig Tour
4. Loch Laggan Tour
5. Upper Deeside Tour
6. Speyside Area
7. Insh Marshes
8. Loch Hourn Tours
9. Isle of Skye Tours
10. Applecross Peninsula
11. Inverness Glens
12. Findhorn Valley Tour
13. Lochindorb Tour
14. Glenlivet Estate
15. Moray Firth Tour
16. The Black Isle Tour
17. Beinn Eighe Tour
18. Inverpolly Tour
19. Loch Fleet Tour
20. Caithness Tour
21. Lairg and Tongue Tour
22. Handa Tour

Key points

- **Full facilities (food, toilets, petrol) in Pitlochry, Dunkeld and Aberfeldy.**

- **No facilities on the A9 itself – you have to visit a town.**

- **Toilets at Ben Lawers**

- **Hide at Loch of the Lowes**

- **Fantastic views of the Osprey nest at Loch of the Lowes**

- **Spectacular dawn chorus in the Hermitage**

- **Limited passing places and parking along Glen Quaich and possible long-term disruption**

- **Pitlochry can get very busy**

- **Terrain and driving generally easy.**

- **Wear suitable gear for the climb at Ben Lawers**

TREES SEEM TO BE the focal point of this tour, starting with Britain's tallest, continuing via one that comes complete with an Osprey nest and finishing up at one of Europe's oldest.

For some reason, Perthshire seems to be totally ignored among wildlife watchers who prefer to continue north to the Highlands. There are many expensive grouse moors in the area and continued rumours of raptor persecution do nothing to help the cause.

Nevertheless, this trip picks out some of the best beauty spots and birding areas and of course, it wouldn't be complete without a good selection of twisty little, white-knuckle ride roads to explore, giving fantastic views except when you meet a car coming the other way.

The Hermitage is run by the National Trust for Scotland. The first thing that strikes you about this enchanting woodland walk is the size of the trees. Now it's reasonable to expect trees in a wood but these are huge. One Douglas fir was measured nearly ten years ago at 212 feet (65 metres) – the tallest in Britain.

Robins and Chaffinches demand feeding in the car park from where a well-

marked path leads you along the River Braan to a waterfall and folly – Ossian's Cave, built back in 1758. Nearby is the Scottish Wildlife Trust's reserve at Loch of the Lowes, which offers fantastic views into an Osprey nest.

The narrow, twisty little road though Glen Quaich and past Loch Freuchie is known as being one of the most scenic roads in Scotland. It winds and climbs through prime 'huntin', shootin' and fishin' country' so, as you might expect, game birds are abundant. However, there are currently plans being considered for a wind farm in the area. If these get the green light, then expect considerable disruption in the area while construction takes place. As you reach the end of the road, if you turn left instead of right, you almost immediately come across the Scottish Crannog Centre, a reconstruction of a Celtic Iron Age dwelling.

Locals were so upset to discover that Ben Lawers, Britain's tenth highest mountain didn't quite reach the 4,000ft mark, that they built a cairn on the top so as to reach the magical mark. As it happens, the cairn has now been removed and wouldn't have counted anyway.

The National Trust for Scotland owns the whole area

and runs the visitor centre. It is free at the moment but they are considering charging a small admission fee. One of the major problems here is erosion and replacing the path is an expensive job.

The centre has assorted multimedia exhibits, illustrating the nature and geology of the area. Have a go at identifying the bird songs; there are a few tricky ones. There are toilet facilities and disabled access to the visitor centre.

A climb to the top of Ben Lawers starting from the centre will take 5-6 hours. If you attempt the climb, make sure that you are properly equipped.

Also know as the 'Crooked Glen of Stones', Glen Lyon is the longest enclosed glen in Scotland, stretching for some 34 miles. As always with glens like this, the further you get into them, the quieter they tend to be and the better chance you have of seeing wildlife.

Continues on page 24

How to get there

Nearest large town: Pitlochry is 28 miles N of Perth.

From Pitlochry, head S on A9. The Hermitage is on R just before you get to Dunkeld. Look for the National Trust for Scotland signs.

Continue S on A9 towards Dunkeld. Loch of the Lowes is well signposted off on L, following A923 towards Blairgowrie and then taking a minor road R.

Retrace your steps back to A9 and head straight across on A822 towards Crieff. About two miles after the junction with A826, turn R in Amulree on a minor road towards Kenmore. At the bottom of the road, turn R and then L almost immediately on A827, following the north shore of Loch Tay.

Stay on A827 for about 12 miles until you see a minor road on R signposted to Ben Lawers. Follow this road up to the Visitor Centre – there is a large car park on R.

Continue on this minor road until you

come to a junction. Turn L and follow the minor road along the River Lyon into the glen, stopping wherever you want or when the road ends.

To return to Pitlochry, retrace your steps along Glen Lyon, ignoring the turn off for Ben Lawers. Fortingall is about 12 miles along the glen after the Ben Lawers junction. From there, continue till you reach B846, turn L towards Tummel Bridge and turn R there along B8019 back to Pitlochry.

Length of route as written is approximately 120 miles.

Key points

- **Disabled access to Loch of the Lowes and the visitor centre at Ben Lawers**

- **Some disabled access at the Hermitage. Much of the rest of the trip can be viewed from the car**

From page 23

It doesn't always work though. On our last visit, we reached the end of the road only to meet a professional film company. They looked through my telescope at a pair of Peregrines and a Dipper feeding a youngster and in turn, I was photographed as a bit of local Scottish colour to help sell £900 handbags for an Italian fashion

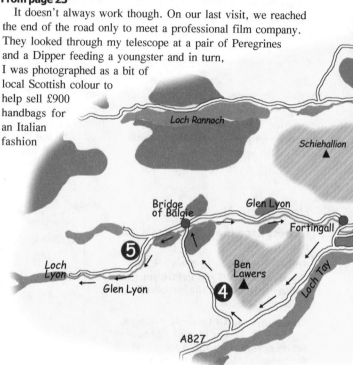

shoot. Anyone who knows me will realise just how unlikely this is.

As you come out of the valley, it is worth a quick stop at the village of Fortingall. Not only is it supposed to be the birthplace of Pontius Pilate, unlikely as that sounds, but it also boasts one of the oldest living trees in Europe, variously estimated at between 3-5,000 years old.

Heading north on the B846, you will see the conical shape of Schiehallion on your left. Such is the regularity of shape of this mountain, that in 1774-6, Neville Maskelyne, astronomer royal and magician, used it to determine the weight of the Earth from its gravitational pull.

Head back towards Pitlochry along the edge of Loch Tummel. This is a good place for fishing Ospreys. Queen Victoria made

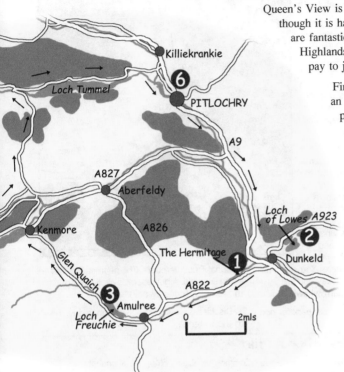

the area famous back in the 1840s and the Queen's View is a popular tourist spot though it is hard to see why. There are fantastic views all round the Highlands; you don't have to pay to join the crowds.

Finish back at Pitlochry, an excellent if somewhat popular holiday centre. As well as the wildlife here, there are plenty of other attractions including music and theatre festivals, a distillery and lots of history – Killiecrankie and Blair Atholl are just up the road.

Spring and summer are the best times to visit for birds, autumn for the colours.

❶ The Hermitage
Background information

THOUGH THE WALK is delightful at any time, an early morning in spring when the birds are in full voice is the best time to visit. Species include all the typical woodland birds – Green and Great Spotted Woodpeckers, tits, finches, Siskins, Redpolls, Goldcrests and Treecreepers. There are Grey Wagtails and Dippers along the river. Spring sees the arrival of warblers. Listen out for Garden Warblers and Blackcaps as well as the three *Phylloscopus* warblers, Willow Warbler, Wood Warbler and Chiffchaff. Though their range is spreading, Chiffchaffs become decidedly localised north of here and you might

struggle to find them if you are heading up to Speyside.

The cleared scrubby area at the far end of the trail holds Tree Pipits, Whinchats, Redstarts and Whitethroats in spring and summer. There is the occasional Capercaillie in the coniferous plantations, with Black Grouse on the woodland fringes though a sighting of either bird is unlikely.

Red squirrels are common and a visit towards dusk could produce Daubenton's bats hunting over the river or a roding Woodcock. Long-

25

eared and pipistrelle bats are also present. Wildflowers are plentiful with carpets of bluebells in spring.

Raptors in the area include Kestrel, Sparrowhawk, Buzzard and Osprey. There are Goshawks in some of the surrounding coniferous woods. These are best seen on fine days in February through to March when they display high over the woods but there is always the chance of an unexpected encounter.

One flew low across a road in front of our car near here. Woodland came right to the edge of the road but the Goshawk just stood on its tail and climbed vertically without missing a wing beat, the most exciting and powerful bit of flying I have ever encountered. They say that when it comes to separating Buzzards and Golden Eagles, you know when you see an eagle. It's the same here. You see that sort of power and there is no way you are going to confuse it with a Sparrowhawk.

There is a fee payable in the car park for non

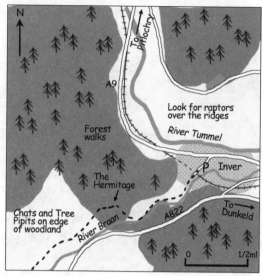

National Trust members. The nearest facilities are in Dunkeld. A guidebook is available from the car park (honesty box).

Disabled drivers have permission to drive up to the waterfall.

Likely bird species/other fauna

All year		Common woodland birds	Whinchat
Black Grouse	Green Woodpecker		Blackcap
Capercaillie	Great Spotted Woodpecker	*Summer*	Garden Warbler
Buzzard	Grey Wagtail	Goosander	Whitethroat
Goshawk	Dipper	Osprey	Chiffchaff
Sparrowhawk	Goldcrest	Tree Pipit	Willow Warbler
Woodcock	Lesser Redpoll	Redstart	Wood Warbler
	Siskin		

❷ Loch of the Lowes
Background information

THIS PICTURESQUE reserve has had a pair of breeding Ospreys for some years now and the hide has good views looking right into the nest - much better views than at Loch Garten, where you can just about see the top of a bird's head if you are lucky.

Other birds on the loch itself include Great Crested Grebe, Wigeon, Goosander, Mallard, Teal, Tufted Duck and Coot. Goldeneye and Red-breasted Merganser are possible with winter seeing a large influx of wildfowl including up to 3,000 Greylag Geese. Reed Buntings flit through the reeds and you might hear the scratchy sound of a Sedge Warbler.

There is no real access to the woods here, but you can watch from the edge for a variety of common species, including Jay, coupled with migrants such as Redstart and Spotted Flycatcher. The species list is similar to that of the Hermitage or Pitlochry Woods.

Otters are increasingly seen. Stoats and weasels are present and the area is something of a squirrel battleground as the bigger, butcher grey squirrels have moved in to threaten their smaller red cousins. Roe and fallow deer can often be seen from the hide.

The double-decker hide is open all year, with the lower level suitable for wheelchair access.

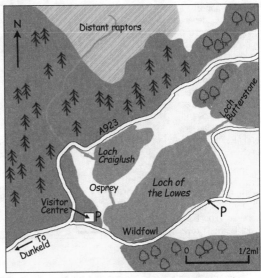

The visitor centre is open roughly when the Ospreys are present, ie. April to September, 10am to 5pm (6pm from mid-July to mid-August). A fee is requested for entrance to the visitor centre for non-Scottish Wildlife Trust members.

Likely bird species/other fauna

All year		*Redstart*	*Other wildlife*
Great Crested Grebe	Goldeneye	Redstart	Otter
Wigeon	Goosander	Sedge Warbler	Fallow and roe deer
Mallard	Jay	Spotted Flycatcher	
Teal	Reed Bunting		
Tufted Duck		*Winter*	
Red-breasted Merganser	*Summer*	Greylag Goose	
	Osprey	Wildfowl (large numbers)	

❸ Glen Quaich and Loch Freuchie
Background information

GAME BIRDS ARE plentiful with Pheasants, Grey and Red-legged Partridges, Snipe, Woodcock and Red Grouse in the area. There are Black Grouse around too, but if you see them, stay in your car and use that as a hide.

The loch holds Great Crested Grebes among

the commoner wildfowl. Curlews and Oystercatchers are widespread. As the road climbs to the top of the hill, scan the moorland for the likes of Ring Ouzels, Cuckoos, Wheatears, Meadow Pipits and chats. Hen Harriers and Merlins hunt the area.

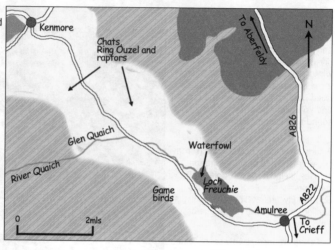

There are Hooded Crows here but you are in the middle of the hybridisation zone so expect pure black Carrion Crows and birds suggesting mixed parentage too.

Likely bird species

All year			
Great Crested Grebe	Snipe	Hooded Crow	Cuckoo
Red Grouse	Woodcock	Hooded Crow hybrids	Whinchat
Black Grouse	Stonechat		Wheatear
Grey Partridge	Whinchat	*Summer*	Ring Ouzel
Red-legged Partridge	Wheatear	Hen Harrier	
	Crow	Merlin	

---

❹ Ben Lawers
Background information

A WALK IN SPRING or summer will produce Red Grouse and Curlews on the ascent with Ptarmigan present as you reach the higher reaches. Listen out for Ravens at the top too. Dotterel are seen only occasionally.

Kestrels and Buzzards are common and there is a chance of Peregrine, especially on the upper slopes, Merlin and Short-eared Owl. Golden Eagles are sometimes seen though you will have a better chance in Glen Lyon.

Wheatears, Meadow Pipits and Sky Larks are common and you will hear if not see Cuckoo. Check gullies for Ring Ouzels and burns for Dippers and Grey Wagtails.

There is a nature trail, which takes 1-2 hours if you don't fancy the whole walk. This concentrates more on the alpine plants. You should see some of the birds mentioned above, though not the ones of the upper reaches.

Other wildlife includes palmate newts,

viviparous lizards, small pearl-bordered fritillary, small mountain ringlet and small heath butterflies. The botany is fantastic. Seventeen species of mammal have been recorded including plenty of mountain hares.

There are some stunning views as the road drops down to Glen Lyon and it is worth stopping and scanning the mountain ridges for raptors. Look out too for the occasional Whinchat or Stonechat.

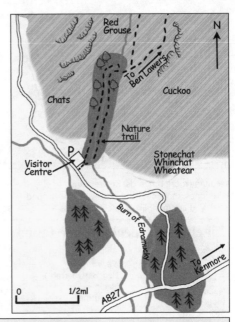

Likely bird species/other flora and fauna

All year	Grey Wagtail	*Summer*	Whinchat
Red Grouse	Dipper	Merlin	Ring Ouzel
Ptarmigan	Stonechat	Peregrine	
Buzzard	Raven	Short-eared Owl	*Other wildlife*
Golden Eagle		Curlew	Mountain hare
Sky Lark	*Spring*	Cuckoo	Amphibians
Meadow Pipit	Dotterel (rare)	Wheatear	Alpine plants

❺ Glen Lyon
Background information

THE GLEN HAS a good range of habitats to explore. Listen for the shimmering song of Wood Warblers in any wooded areas. Further exploration of the woods should produce other summer migrants including Redstart, Tree Pipit and Willow Warbler. Swallows, martins and, from the last week in May, Swifts can be encountered anywhere along the length of the valley.

The river holds Common Sandpiper, Dipper and Grey Wagtail with the chance of a Goosander. There are plenty of Wheatears, Stonechats, Whinchats, Ring Ouzels and Curlews on the open moorland but as always, it is likely to be the raptors that are of most interest. Find a spot with a good, all-round panoramic view and scan the ridges.

Golden Eagles are present though you will

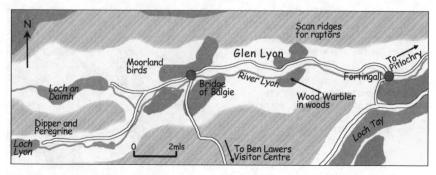

see many more Buzzards. Kestrels and Peregrines show over the ridges too. At ground level, you are more likely to come across a Merlin or Short-eared Owl. Hen Harriers are supposed to be in the area though I've never seen one here. Red and roe deer are present.

Likely bird species/other fauna

All year	Raven	Common Sandpiper	Willow Warbler
Buzzard		Short-eared Owl	Wood Warbler
Golden Eagle	*Summer*	Tree Pipit	
Grey Wagtail	Hen Harrier (rare)	Wheatear	*Other wildlife*
Meadow Pipit	Merlin	Whinchat	Red and roe deer
Dipper	Peregrine	Redstart	
Stonechat	Curlew	Ring Ouzel	

❻ Pitlochry and area
Background information

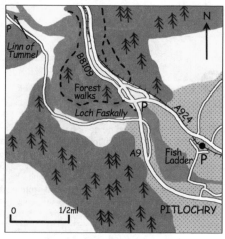

THE RIVERS GARRY and Tummel have their confluence in the town, creating a much loved beauty spot – Linn of Tummel - complete with waterfalls and shingle islands, all in a mixed woodland setting. Another popular destination is the fish ladder, where you can see salmon using this artificial aid to get them past the dam here. Salmon can also be seen leaping in the River Tummel itself.

Any walk along the rivers, or round Loch Faskally, should provide a good selection of species, starting with Dipper, Grey Wagtail and Common Sandpiper, all bobbing in their individual manner as they search for insects above, on and under the water. Other waterfowl could include the striking Goosander and Red-breasted Merganser. Oystercatchers and Common Gulls use the islands to breed.

The woods contain a good selection of summer migrants to complement the resident birds such as Green and Great Spotted Woodpeckers, Siskin, Redpoll, Treecreeper and Goldcrest. This is an excellent area to find Garden Warbler. There always seems to be at least one Buzzard in the sky and it wouldn't be a surprise to see at least a half a dozen if you get yourself a good vantage spot. Ravens fly over occasionally. All these sites and walks are just a couple of minutes away from the town centre. They are well signed and there is plenty of parking.

Just north of Pitlochry is the National Trust for Scotland's site at Killiecrankie (well signed from the A9, car parking fee for non-members). As well as the visitor centre's display about the battle in 1689, a path leads from there to Soldier's Leap, a rock jutting out over the river where a Government soldier jumped over the river to avoid Bonnie Dundee's pursuing Highland troops. History aside, this is one of the best and easiest places I know to find Wood Warbler.

The area to the left of the path is steeply banked so you get a chance to actually see the birds at something approaching eye level rather than the usual 'up the bum' shot, or if you prefer, a detailed study of the undertail coverts.

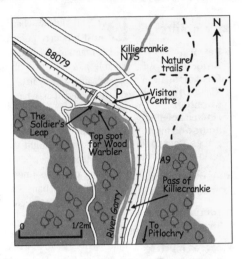

Birds normally arrive in the second week of May and if you time your visit right, you might encounter a small fall; the best we have managed is ten singing birds in the one small area.

Also in the woods are Redstarts, Pied and Spotted Flycatchers and red squirrels. The path drops down to the river and you can explore as far you want, looking for a similar range of species to those mentioned above.

Please note that the RSPB's lease at Killiecrankie (on the other side of the river from the NTS place) has now expired and this is no longer an RSPB reserve. At the time of writing, no details had emerged as to whether there will be any public access.

Likely bird species/other flora and fauna

All year	Siskin	Common Sandpiper	Spotted Flycatcher
Buzzard	Lesser Redpoll	Oystercatcher	
Green Woodpecker	Raven	Common Gull	*Other wildlife*
Great Spotted	Common woodland birds	Redstart	Salmon
Woodpecker		Blackcap	Red squirrel
Grey Wagtail	*Summer*	Garden Warbler	Otter
Dipper	Goosander	Willow Warbler	Pine marten
Goldcrest	Red-breasted Merganser	Wood Warbler	Pearl-bordered fritillary
Treecreeper	Osprey	Pied Flycatcher	

Key points

- **Petrol in Ardgour, Glenborrodale, Kilchoan and Strontian. Limited opening hours and high prices. Best to fill up in Fort William**

- **Plenty of places to eat en route**

- **Tourist office at Strontian**

- **Far too much to do in a day. Take a holiday here**

- **Spectacular views, birding and sunsets**

- **The roads, many single tracked, get surprisingly busy. Be prompt in using pull-ins**

- **Natural History Centre and Glenfinnan have café and toilets**

- **Better than usual chance of wildcat and pine marten at dusk but still slim**

DO YOU know what is the most westerly point of the British mainland? I once lost a sizeable jackpot in a pub quiz through this gap in my education and it has haunted me ever since.

After this traumatic experience, you might think I would harbour deep psychological resentment about Ardnamurchan - for that was the correct answer – but life's too short and besides, the peninsula is brilliant. You could easily spend a week in the area and still feel you have only seen a fraction of its treasures.

Birds just seem to fly in front of you as you drive: a Bullfinch here or a Redstart or Whinchat there. I have always managed to get bigger day lists here than just about anywhere else in the Highlands. Wind down the windows and Willow Warblers and Wood Warblers serenade you as you drive

through any belt of woodland. Buzzards soar, Meadow Pipits flit, Curlews bubble and you haven't even left your vehicle.

The area is made up of five separate districts – Ardgour, Sunart, Moidart, Morvern and Ardnamurchan, though most people just refer to the whole as the Ardnamurchan peninsula. Heading south from Fort William, from the moment you pull up at the car park for the ferry, taking you across Loch Linnhe, this tour is birding all the way. Though you can make detours (south into Morvern and the ferry for Mull, north into Moidart), this is essentially a 50-mile drive from the ferry to the lighthouse, stopping off wherever you please.

Much of the road is single track and the locals here seem less tolerant than most, so make sure that you are the first one to pull into the passing place. If you are only here for the day, keep your stops at places like Sallachan and the Garbh Eilean hide fairly short as you

Check the fast flowing streams in Ariundle oakwood for sightings of Dipper.

may run out of time. If the seawatching is slow, then bird more slowly on the way back.

A mile or so after getting off the ferry, you reach Sallachan Point, where the large bay is good for seals, waders and waterbirds. The road continues through Glen Tarbert, a good place for raptors, before coming to the small village of Strontian where local lead mines once produced the raw material for the bullets used by the Duke of Wellington's armies. The village, which means Point of the Fairies, also gave its name to the element Strontium which was discovered in the mines.

A minor road, leading north, takes you to the oakwoods of Ariundle National Nature Reserve and eventually to the shores of Loch Shiel. There are at least ten Golden Eagle territories within a 25-mile radius of Strontian, so your chances of seeing one are quite high.

The main road now follows the north shore of Loch Sunart. According to local legend, a Celtic chieftain once fell in love with a local girl, but his disapproving mother cast a spell and turned the girl into a swan, which the unfortunate prince then killed and ate. He fell on his sword so that they could lie under the loch for all eternity and to this day, no swan has ever been seen on Loch Sunart. And if you do see a wintering Whooper Swan, don't spoil the story. Just report it as an albino White-fronted Goose!

There are reckoned to be more than 1,400 otter holts here, the highest density outside Shetland, though they are not all in use at the same time. There are also

Continues on page 34

How to get there

Nearest large town: The tour begins at Fort William and is 65 miles to Ardnamurchan Point via the ferry.

From Fort William, head S down A82 for 13 miles. Cross Corran Ferry and turn L. Take A861 to Salen then B8007 and minor road to Ardnamurchan lighthouse. Retrace to Salen then turn L on A861 to Lochailort. Turn R on A830 back to Fort William stopping at Glenfinnan if required.

For Ariundle, turn R on minor road in Strontian. Reserve on R after a mile. The car park for the Garbh Eilean hide is on L, five miles W of Strontian. Car park for Glenborrodale RSPB is about eight miles W of Salen and Ben Hiant a further five miles W. For Kentra and area, continue N from Salen on A861

to Acharacle. Look for pier on R in Acharacle. Turn L on B8044 to Kentra. Road to Castle Tioram is on L, one mile N of B8044.

Length of route is approximately 150 miles

Key points

- **Very good chance of seeing otters**

- **Inland and coastal wildlife cruises available**

- **Telescope recommended at the hide and lighthouse**

- **Very limited disabled access to woods and Glenborrodale but much birding can be done from or near the car including the lighthouse area**

- **Full disabled access to hide**

From page 33

good numbers of wildcats and pine martens, though this doesn't make them any easier to see. With a powerful spotlight you can explore the roads from Strontian to Polloch and Glenborrodale to Kilchoan after dark. If you are staying in the area, it is worthwhile chatting up the locals to see if they know who is having their dustbins raided or is putting out jam sandwiches to attract pine martens.

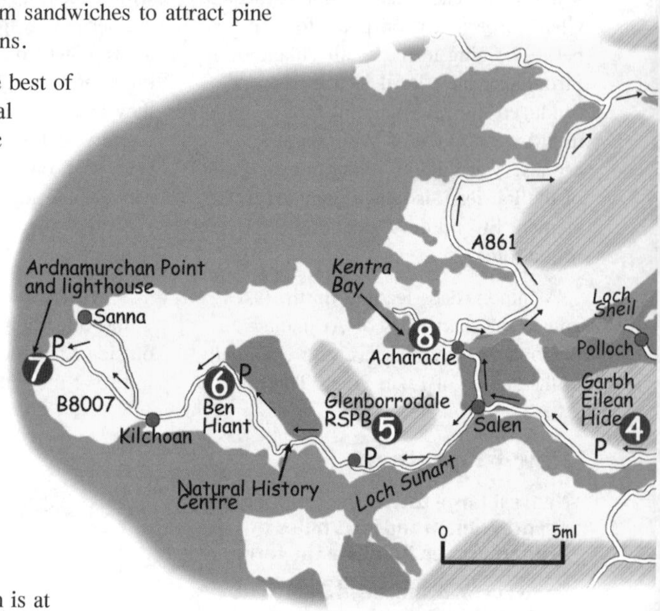

The best of several picnic sites

Ardnamurchan Point and lighthouse
Sanna
P
B8007
Kilchoan
Ben Hiant
Natural History Centre

A861
Kentra Bay
Acharacle
Loch Sheil
Polloch
Glenborrodale RSPB
Salen
Garbh Eilean Hide
Loch Sunart

0   5ml

along this stretch is at Ardery, complete with bird hide. At Salen, turn off onto the B8007, a very slow, 23-mile long single-track road through some fantastic countryside with any number of little bays off on your left and hills and moorland to your right.

There is an RSPB reserve at Glenborrodale and just beyond that, the Ardnamurchan Natural History Centre. As well as a coffee shop and toilets, there is an excellent interactive display (fee payable) of the local wildlife. The centre is open Mon-Sat 10.30-5.30, Sun 12noon–5.30. See www.anhc.co.uk for more details.

The road now skirts Ben Hiant and drops down to Kilchoan.

This area is particularly good for Twite and is the best place on the peninsula for orchids. There are a few iris beds here and sporadic reports of Corn Crakes calling, though there isn't any regular breeding.

Following signs to the Lighthouse, passing places disappear altogether so your progress is controlled by traffic lights! Ardnamurchan translates as Point of the Great Ocean and it is aptly named. There are fantastic views over to Mull, Coll and the Small Isles – born in Eigg, lived on Rhum and died in Muck as the locals say. There is a café, toilet facilities and shop here and you can pay to go in the lighthouse if you want. Sunsets can be spectacular.

You have to retrace your steps to Salen, but you can make a detour to Sanna Bay if you have the time for fantastic beaches, passage waders and wildcat (if you are very lucky). At Salen, you can either continue back to the ferry, birding at a few of the places you ignored on the way down, or continue north into Moidart.

Acharacle (pronounced A-ha-rackle, not Ack-a-rackle) is at the southern tip of Loch Shiel and the starting place for the inland wildlife cruise. You can also explore Kentra from here (see page 43).

The road continues past a couple of sealochs – Moidart and Ailort – and there are several places to stop and scan the bays and sea for the likes of Black Guillemot, Eider, divers, waders and Rock Pipits.

Eventually you join up with the Mallaig to Fort William Road to the Isles, passing the National Trust for Scotland's site at Glenfinnan. This is where Bonnie Prince Charlie first raised the Jacobite standard prior to the 1745 rebellion. There is a café and toilet facilities as well as a display and access to the monument (fee payable for non-members).

Continues on page 36

From page 35

If you are not birded out by now, then there are plenty of mountain ridges to scan for raptors and the north end of Loch Shiel just beyond the monument. For all the sites, spring, summer and autumn are likely to be the most productive times to visit.

Corran Ferry

Background information

FERRIES across Loch Linnhe, non-bookable, run frequently from 7am – 9.30pm in summer (see http:// www.lochabertransport.org.uk/ corranferry.html for full details). Crossings take about ten minutes. While you are waiting, a quick scan of Loch Linnhe should produce an assortment of gulls, Eiders, Red-breasted Mergansers and Black Guillemots.

Buzzards are common over woods and hills

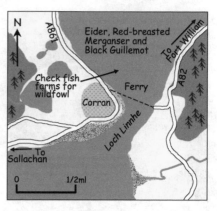

Likely bird species/ other fauna

All year
Eider
Red-breasted Merganser
Black Guillemot

Other wildlife
Harbour porpoise

and Golden Eagles occasional. There is a small school of harbour porpoises that swim up and down Lochs Linnhe and Eil. As you return from Ardnamurchan, it is worth checking the area next to the fish farms, which is usually the best place to see wildfowl.

Sallachan Point

Background information

A COUPLE of miles after the ferry dock, you see a big sandy bay on your left. Look for the display boards in the lay-by and park there. Grey and common seals are easy to

Likely bird species/other fauna

All year	*Winter*	Cuckoo
Eider	Great Northern Diver	Hirundines
Red-breasted Merganser	Goldeneye	
Ringed Plover		*Other wildlife*
Rock Pipit	*Summer*	Grey and common seals
	Common Sandpiper	

see on the rocks and the bay is a good place to find lingering Great Northern Divers and Goldeneyes, Eiders, Red-breasted Mergansers, Common Sandpipers, Oystercatchers, Ringed Plovers, Rock and Meadow Pipits etc.

Cuckoos and Willow Warblers can usually be heard and there are usually plenty of hirundines hawking for insects. Even if there is not a lot about, it allows the traffic behind you to clear, making it a lot easier to bird as you go.

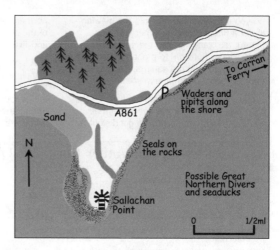

❸ Ariundle Oakwood

Background information

THERE ARE some splendid oakwoods all round Sunart. This one at Ariundle has a visitor centre/tea shop and is the best place to start. Despite the name, the woods contain a good variety of trees, including ash, elm, hazel, alder and birch. Most of the oaks are sessile oaks, which thrive in the acid soil.

As well as the common woodland species such as tits, Goldcrests, Great Spotted Woodpeckers, Treecreepers etc, spring brings several migrants and the stunning dawn chorus is enhanced by the likes of Wood and Willow Warblers, Redstarts and Tree Pipits. Spotted Flycatchers are usually the last birds to arrive, in mid to late May.

There are Dippers and Grey Wagtails on the fast-flowing streams

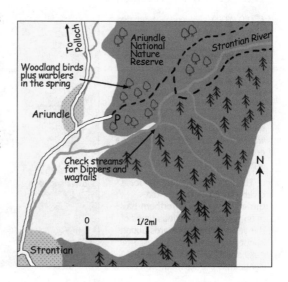

and you are never too far from the mewing calls of a Buzzard or two. Other wildlife is plentiful too, ranging from the scarce chequered skipper butterfly to a good assortment of mammals including red squirrel, red and roe deer, fox, badger and pine marten.

In warm weather, slow worms bask by the side of the track. Over 200 species of moth have been recorded and this a good sight for northern emerald dragonflies. This is also one of the best areas in Britain for mosses, lichen and liverworts.

A loop trail – about 2.5 miles long - complete with information boards leads round the reserve. A new woodland trail has been added, but involves some steep climbing. Spring and summer are best for the mixture of wildflowers and birdsong.

Likely bird species/other flora and fauna

All year	*Summer*	*Other wildlife*
Buzzard	Tree Pipit	Red squirrel
Grey Wagtail	Redstart	Pine marten
Dipper	Wood Warbler	Butterflies
Great Spotted Woodpecker	Spotted Flycatcher	Dragonflies
Treecreeper		Wildflowers
Goldcrest		

④ Garbh Eilean bird hide
Background information

SITUATED at Ardery, about five miles west of Strontian, this newly-built hide is designed to be as eco-friendly as possible. It overlooks Loch Sunart and the two main attractions are a heronry on one of the small islands and good numbers of seals – both common and grey – hauling themselves out onto the rocks where they are watched over by a dozen or so Oystercatchers. Otters are frequently reported.

The loch itself could produce a diver – Black-throated, Red-throated and Great Northern have been recorded at various times of the year. Teal and Mallards puddle about in the shallows and assorted gulls squabble for scavenging rights with the Hooded Crow

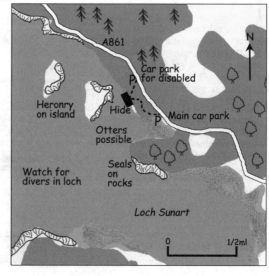

population. Look out too for Red-breasted Mergansers, Shags, the occasional auk or even something of a surprise. We had two Arctic Skuas flying up the loch on our last visit.

The oakwoods behind the hide produce a similar selection of species to Ariundle Oakwood. Scanning the mountain ridges could produce all sorts of raptors; both species of eagle have been reported here, along with Peregrine, Kestrel, Buzzard and Sparrowhawk.

The hide has full disabled access. There is a second car park just beyond the first, for the exclusive use of wheelchair users. Please don't park here otherwise. There is a half-mile walk from the car main park to the hide. Though the seals and Grey Herons can be seen well with binoculars, a telescope is recommended for watching the rest of the area.

Likely bird species/other fauna

All year
Red-breasted Merganser
Grey Heron
Golden Eagle
White-tailed Eagle (rare)
Common woodland birds

Winter
Great Northern Diver

Summer
Red-throated Diver
Black-throated Diver
Wood Warbler

Spotted Flycatcher

Other species
Common and grey seals
Otter

---

❺ RSPB Glenborrodale
Background information

A NEW CAR PARK (half a mile west of Glenborrodale Castle) has made access to one of the RSPB's lesser-known reserves a lot easier. Seals are common offshore and there is a good chance of an otter sighting here. In the woods, listen for Wood Warblers trilling away. Redstarts and Spotted Flycatchers are easy to find in summer. Look for Woodcocks at dusk.

The woods give way to moorland, complete with Wheatears, Stone-chats, Whinchats, Meadow Pipits and Sky Larks. Merlins hunt low over the heather, while the occasional Golden Eagle breaks the skyline. Ravens are usually fairly obvious on the cliffs. Look for red squirrels in the woods and red deer, basking lizards and slow worms on the hills.

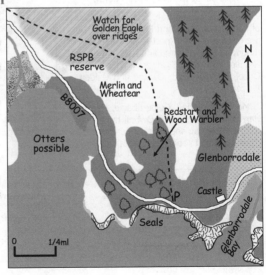

There is a two-mile circular nature trail, along a rough track, which takes two hours or so to walk round. There are regular guided walks, currently every Sunday from May to September at 2pm, but check with the RSPB or local tourist offices for up-to-date details.

Likely bird species/other fauna

All year	*Summer*		
Golden Eagle	Merlin	Wood Warbler	Red squirrel
Woodcock	Tree Pipit	Spotted Flycatcher	Red Deer
Stonechat	Whinchat		Lizards
Raven	Redstart	*Other wildlife*	
		Seals	
		Otters	

---

❻ Ben Hiant and Loch Mudle

Background information

THOUGH not high enough to be classed as a Munro, Ben Hiant is the tallest mountain in the area and still big enough to hold a few Ptarmigan on the top (the return trip takes about two and a half hours).

There are fairly distant, but scopable views of Loch Mudle here and Red-throated Divers are often present. Expect a good selection of moorland species, including Red and Black Grouse, Wheatear, Stonechat, Whinchat, Ring Ouzel, Meadow Pipit, Cuckoo and Golden Plover.

Merlin, Peregrine, Golden Eagle, Hen Harrier and Short-eared Owl all hunt. Look for the latter two species near conifer plantations up to about 12-15ft tall.

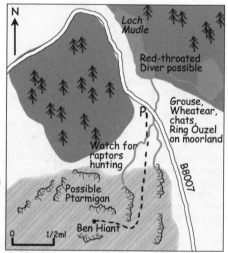

Likely bird species

All year	Stonechat	Hen Harrier	Cuckoo
Red Grouse	Raven	Merlin	Ring Ouzel
Black Grouse		Peregrine	Wheatear
Ptarmigan	*Summer*	Golden plover	Whinchat
Golden Eagle	Red-throated Diver	Short-eared Owl	

⑦ Ardnamurchan Point

Background information

A FANTASTIC place for seawatching, there are viewpoints all round the headland. The best place by far is to walk round the lighthouse to the viewing platform by the foghorn. Here, you have something like a 270° field of view.

Rock Pipits flit around in front of you. At sea, there is a constant movement of Shags, Guillemots and Razorbills as parties of birds fly to and from their feeding grounds. In calm conditions, you get large rafts of birds sitting on the sea and scoping these should produce a few Puffins too.

Black Guillemots tend to keep to themselves a bit more, but the white wing patches show up well and birds shouldn't be too difficult to find – check in front of any rocky outcrops. Eiders and Red-breasted Mergansers are the most likely wildfowl.

Oystercatchers are the commonest waders, with the occasional Ringed Plover adding variety. Spring and autumn can produce migrating birds, so look out for flocks of Whimbrel or Bar-tailed Godwits.

Divers are regularly seen on the sea. Black-throated and Red-throated Divers breed on the peninsula, but come to feed here. Great Northern Divers – sometimes in good numbers – overwinter all round the peninsula and are present from autumn through to late spring.

Manx Shearwaters are present, often in good numbers and can come very close if there are strong onshore winds. In calmer conditions though, you might just see the occasional distant bird flicking black and white as it lives up to its name and shears across the surface of the waves.

Other shearwaters are seen too, with Sooty Shearwater the most likely. Balearic Shearwaters are only occasionally recorded in the Highlands, usually a bird or two seen from the east coast in autumn

gales. However, a friend found a small flock here in spring 2004, a fantastic record but probably more of a testament to the place being totally underwatched rather than massive scarcity.

Other species that you can expect to see include Kittiwakes, Fulmars, Gannets, gulls, Common and Arctic Terns, Arctic and Great Skuas, Pomarine and Long-tailed Skuas (spring and autumn), the diminutive Storm Petrel and the much rarer Leach's Petrel (autumn).

Numbers are highly variable, but the likes of Gannets, auks and Kittiwakes can reach movements of many thousands of birds per hour in the right weather conditions, usually gales from the north or north-west in autumn.

It is not just seabirds that are of interest here. Look for Golden Eagles over the hills, or perhaps a visiting White-tailed Eagle drifting over from Mull or Rhum. The 'kronk' of a Raven might betray the presence of a patrolling Peregrine.

Even if the sea is like a millpond, there is still

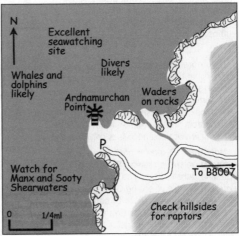

N

Excellent
seawatching
site

Whales and
dolphins
likely

Divers
likely

Ardnamurchan
Point

Waders
on rocks

P

Watch for
Manx and Sooty
Shearwaters

To B8007

Check hillsides
for raptors

0   1/4ml

plenty of interest. This is one of the best places on the mainland to look for whales, dolphins, porpoises and basking sharks. Minke whales are the most likely, seen throughout the summer and, especially, in the autumn though killer whales (orcas) are occasionally noted.

Look for frenzied feeding by the seabird flocks and you may get lucky and see a tail fluke. More likely is the appearance of a low, flat island, as the whale comes to the surface. Cetaceans normally appear a fair way out and you will almost certainly need a Telescope as well as a fair chunk of luck to be looking in the right place at the right time. Alternatively, take a wildlife cruise (see below).

Likely bird species/other fauna

All year	Raven	Arctic Tern	Bar-tailed Godwit
Eider		Common Tern	Long-tailed Skua
Red-breasted Merganser	*Spring/summer*	Puffin	Pomarine Skua
Shag	Black-throated Diver	Guillemot	
Golden Eagle	Red-throated Diver	Razorbill	*Winter*
White-tailed Eagle (rare)	Manx Shearwater		Great Northern Diver
Peregrine	Fulmar	*Autumn*	*Other species*
Ringed Plover	Gannet	Sooty Shearwater	Cetaceans
Gulls	Great Skua	Storm Petrel	Otter
Black Guillemot	Arctic Skua	Leach's Petrel	Grey and common seals
Rock Pipit	Kittiwake	Whimbrel	

Wildlife Cruises

TWO COMPANIES offer wildlife cruises. If you are more interested in coastal birds and mammals, then Ardnamurchan Charters, operating out of Glenborrodale (Tel: 01972 500208, www.west-scotland-marine.com/) is the one to try.

It offers a range of trips from a two hour cruise looking for seals and otters, seabirds and both species of eagle, through visits to the Treshnish Isles off Mull, looking for Puffins, to whole day whale-watching trips.

If you prefer exploring the otherwise inaccessible hinterland, including a cottage at Gaskan where wildlife author Mike Tomkies lived for nearly 20 years, then take a look at Loch Shiel Cruises, operating out of Acharacle and Glenfinnan (Tel/Fax: 01687 470322, www.highlandcruises.co.uk).

More than 50 species of birds have been recorded on these cruises. Given their breeding density here, you have an excellent chance of seeing Golden Eagles over the mountains. Black-throated Divers are another possibility though views of Seilag, the Loch Shiel monster (think Nessie only smaller) are far from guaranteed!

Improve your chances of seeing diving Gannets by taking a boat trip

❽ Kentra Bay Area

Background information

THIS IS one of the best areas on the peninsula for passage waders and wintering wildfowl and waders. The bay can be explored from its southern or eastern edge, depending on the state of the tide.

Before you leave Acharacle, it is worth checking the southern tip of Loch Shiel for waterbirds (the pier makes an excellent vantage spot). As you head north, turn left onto the B8044. Almost immediately, look for a small lochan on your right and a pinewood with a small car park on your left. Park and check the wood for Crested Tits. Other possible species include Siskins, Redpolls and Goldcrests.

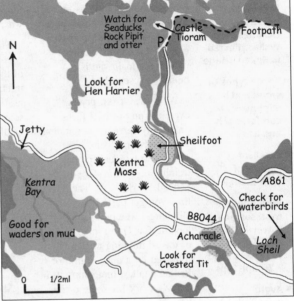

After half a mile, you come to some minor crossroads. Turn left here to explore the southern edge of the Bay or stay on the B8044 to explore the northern side, checking Kentra Moss, on either side of the road for possible Hen Harriers.

If you want to explore the coast in this area, then Castle Tioram, as featured in the films *Rob Roy* and *Highlander III*, offers an unbeatable combination of history, views, a fantastic beach and the wildlife with, in all probability, not another person in sight. Look for Eiders, Red-breasted Mergansers, Rock Pipits, otters etc. Access is signed from a minor road north of Acharacle.

Likely bird species/other fauna

All year	*Winter*		*Summer*
Eider	White-fronted Geese	Greenshank	Hen Harrier
Red-breasted	Waders	Dunlin	
Merganser		Curlew	*Other wildlife*
Rock Pipit	*Spring and autumn*	Whimbrel	Otter
Crested Tit	Bar-tailed Godwit	Grey Plover	
Woodland birds	Redshank	Sanderling	
		Golden Plover	

Key points

- **No facilities (petrol, food, toilets) en route. Full facilities in Fort William, limited in Spean Bridge**

- **Three types of woodland to explore – conifer, birch and ash**

- **Excellent chance of Golden Eagle**

- **Very uneven road surface towards its end. This is a very slow road – 20mph tops**

- **Avoid weekends if possible – that's when the locals visit**

- **Fantastic place for insects as well as birds**

- **Picnic sites at the falls and Allt Mhuic, but views are better further into valley**

THOSE BIRDWATCHERS who feel the western Highlands is Scotland's poor relation (especially if you remove the coastline as one of the major habitats), may have to revise their views if they embark on this drive, even though the main site is a butterfly reserve!

Well away from prying eyes, the mix of cliff faces, unfriendly terrain, mountains, woodlands and lochs was deemed to be ideal for the training of Commandos in the Second World War. The next time you get puffed out climbing a wee bit of a hill looking for Tree Pipits, think of the 18-mile jog to Ben Nevis followed by a quick climb of Britain's tallest mountain, all in a day's work for some of our bravest, and fittest, soldiers.

History takes another bow at the next stop, albeit the Hollywood version. The bridge at the Chia-aig waterfalls was used as one of the locations in Rob Roy where Liam Neeson has to leap into the swirling black torrents below. The area just before the falls is known as the Dark Mile and featured heavily in a book of the same name by DK Broster, set in the Jacobite revolutions of 1715 and 1745. Latterly, rope bridges and Tarzan swings

marked this out as another Commando training area. The woods have been thinned out recently and the area is no longer as brooding as it once was.

The road continues along the edge of Loch Arkaig, another of those great, twisty little tracks that litter the Highlands, leading right into the midst of some great wilderness. Where would we birders be without them?

If you want a break from birding, then how about a treasure hunt? In 1746, a consignment of gold to help fund Bonnie Prince Charlie, was buried somewhere near Loch Arkaig. It has never been found.

About halfway along the road lies the butterfly reserve of Allt Mhuic, home to a fabulous variety of insect life and one of the few places where it is possible to get good views of chequered skipper butterflies. Most of the key butterfly species are on the wing from mid-May to June and this is the best time to visit birdwise, though the drive is of interest from spring through to autumn.

As you climb the way-marked trail, vistas, which remain hidden from the road, suddenly open out in front of you, making this a fine place to scan for raptors as well as watching the woodland birds.

The return trip gives elevated views over the Caledonian Canal, together with some superb late evening views of Ben Nevis and finishing at a flight of eight locks on the canal, known locally as Neptune's Staircase. Back at Fort William, a quick scan of Lochs Eil and Linnhe could add a few seabirds to your list or maybe a mammal or two.

Most of the sites can be viewed from the road/car parks, though Allt Mhuic is not suitable for wheelchairs.

Key points

- **Amazing views towards the end of the road, ideal for raptor watching**

- **No disabled access to Allt Mhuic, otherwise watch from road/car parks**

How to get there

Nearest large town: Fort William is the start of the tour.

Both the A82 and A830 out of Fort William have many lay-bys from where you can scan the lochs.

From Fort William, head N on A82 to Spean Bridge (eight miles). In Spean Bridge, turn L at the T-junction, still on A82 towards Inverness. After a mile, turn L onto B8004 (signposted the Commando Memorial and Gairlochy). The memorial car park is immediately on L.

At Gairlochy turn R onto B8005 (signposted Clunes and the Clan Cameron museum). While travelling to the end of the road (18 miles), look for the waterfall and Allt Mhuic on R after approximately six and eight miles. The former is well signed, the latter not so.

Retrace your steps to Gairlochy and use B8004 back towards Fort William and finish at Neptune's Staircase, parking in a big car park on L at the end of the road.

Length of the route is approximately 65 miles.

❶ Fort William
Background information

FORT WILLIAM ITSELF lies at the junction of two lochs - Eil and Linnhe. Of these, Linnhe is the more productive and could produce species normally associated with the sea such as Eider, Red-breasted Merganser, Red-throated Diver, various gulls and Black Guillemot.

The area between Fort William and the Corran Ferry (seven miles to the south) is likely to be the most productive. Swifts arrive at the end of May and this is the best place in the area to see them.

There is a resident school of harbour porpoises, moving between both lochs and the best times to see them are on still days when the loch surfaces are totally smooth. Otters, best seen at dusk, often frequent the area around the pier in Fort William.

Look for raptors over mountain ridges

Likely bird species/ other fauna

All year

Red-throated Diver
Eider
Red-breasted Merganser
Black Guillemot

Other wildlife

Harbour porpoise
Otter

② The Commando Memorial
Background information

THE MOORLAND HERE holds a typical range of species including breeding Lapwings. Watch them in spring as they wheel and call in display over their nest site. They are among the most aggressive of parents, too and will fly up immediately to see off any Hooded Crow, Raven or Buzzard that wanders into their territory.

Other birds likely to be seen here are Meadow Pipit and Stonechat.

See main map for location

Likely bird species	
All year	Raven
Meadow Pipit	*Summer*
Stonechat	Lapwing

③ Chia-aig waterfalls
Background information

AS YOU HEAD out towards Loch Arkaig, you pass the bottom corner of Loch Lochy on your right. As with most huge lochs, it is too deep to hold much birdlife though you might see the occasional Mallard or Grey Heron feeding in the shallows.

Continue through Clunes until you come to the well-signed picnic site by the waterfalls (Cia-aig on some maps). You are in the middle of coniferous woods here, so look out for Sparrowhawks, Goldcrests, Crossbills, Siskins and Redpolls in the woods. Buzzards hunt above the woods and there is usually a Cuckoo or two calling in the distance.

As you drive on, the conifers give way to birch woods and even with the car windows shut, you should hear Chaffinches, Willow Warblers and Wood Warblers singing.

Likely bird species	
All year	*Summer*
Siskin	Wood Warbler
Redpoll	
Crossbill	

④ Allt Mhuic
Background information

THE TWO HARDEST parts about this fantastic little reserve is finding it in the first place and then pronouncing its name correctly (moo-ee). The reserve isn't signposted. Instead, you have to look out for a small car park and display boards, off on your right, about six miles west of Clunes. From the car park, a well-marked trail climbs the hill behind you and a full circuit should take about 90 minutes to two hours.

The open ash woods contain a range of common woodland species including Great Spotted Woodpecker.

As you start to climb, look out for Redstarts, Spotted Flycatchers and Pied Flycatchers. Tree Pipits, Stonechats and Whinchats are present and there are Grey Wagtails and Dippers on the burn.

The higher parts of the walk are excellent places to find raptors over the hills and mountains. Buzzards are common and this is a particularly good spot to see Golden Eagles.

The walk is excellent for butterflies. As well as

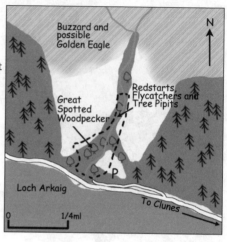

chequered skipper, look out for pearl-bordered fritillary, green hairstreak and Scotch argus. Dragonflies include azure hawker. Choose a warm, still day for maximum insect activity. Otters and pine martens are plentiful, dawn and dusk being the best chances of seeing one.

Likely bird species/other fauna

Summer		*Other wildlife*	
Tree Pipit	Spotted Flycatcher	Otter	Other butterflies,
Whinchat	*All year*	Pine marten	moths and dragonflies
Redstart	Golden Eagle	Chequered skipper	
Pied Flycatcher	Stonechat	Pearl-bordered fritillary	

⑤ Loch Arkaig
Background information

THE LOCH IS HUGE and continues past the reserve for another ten miles or so. This depth of water is normally bad news for waterfowl, but both Red and Black-throated

Divers come to feed and there are usually pairs of Goosander and Common Sandpipers along the edge.

Before their return to Speyside in the

1950s, the last pair of British Ospreys bred here in 1908. Now they are back in the area again and birds can sometimes be seen fishing in the loch.

As the woods disappear, the road opens out into moorland, complete with spectacular views of the nearby mountains. There are several places to scan the mountain ridges for more raptors including Golden Eagle, Peregrine, Kestrel and Buzzard. Just pick your favourite view and make sure that you don't block the road or completely take up a passing place.

There is a turning circle at the end of the road and whatever cars are in the valley - mostly belonging to walkers - tend to stop here. If you do head to the high tops, you will find Dotterel and Ptarmigan, but as ever, do go properly prepared.

Meadow Pipits and Sky Larks breed on the open ground and are hunted by Merlins. Cuckoos are widespread and you should also find Wheatears and Stonechats along the edge of the road. Check any gullies for Ring Ouzels. Red deer could turn up anywhere along the route.

After retracing your steps to Gairlochy, you can now take the back road through an area of farmland to Fort William. There are many places to stop and look down towards the Caledonian Canal.

The elevated position gives you the chance of getting some unusual views of birds, such as looking down on a Buzzard rather than looking up at it. Swallows, Sand Martins and House Martins are common along this stretch. One bird that you might glimpse here is the Woodpigeon – surprisingly shy in these parts, unlike the huge, overfed flocks further east and south.

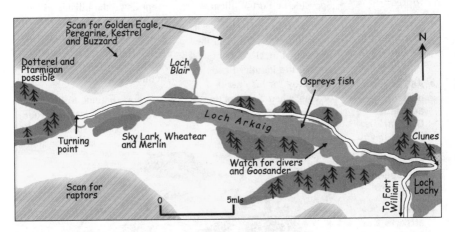

Likely bird species/other fauna

Summer	Osprey	Sky Lark
Red-throated Diver	Cuckoo	
Black-throated Diver	Stonechat	*Other wildlife*
Merlin	Whinchat	Red deer
Golden Eagle	Ring Ouzel	
Peregrine	Wheatear	

Key points

- **Full range of facilities (food, toilets and petrol) in Newtonmore and Spean Bridge,** otherwise no toilets or garages en route

- **Proper walking gear needed for Creag Meagaidh and the longer Strathmashie routes**

- **Chance of disruption if TV filming is taking place**

- **A86 is notorious for accidents. Use parking places if you want to get off road or let the speeding cars pass**

- **Glen Roy attracts the most visitors and is the busiest of the minor roads**

THIS DRIVE takes you through the landscape adopted as the mythical 'Glenbogle', as featured in the BBC drama series *Monarch of the Glen*. Many leaflets in the tourist offices delight in telling you exactly which building appeared in which shot.

When you tire of sightseeing, there is plenty of birding to be done with a remote valley, strenuous hill walk, woodland, rivers and a couple of lochs to explore. This drive can be approached equally well from either Speyside or Fort William.

According to Gaelic legend, the Celtic warrior Fingal the Giant (of Fingal's Cave fame) created the Parallel Roads in Glen Roy for his chariot driving when deer hunting. Somewhat more prosaically,

we now know that they are scars all down the valley marking the shores of a great glacial lake. The ice blocked Glen Roy in three main stages some 10,000 years ago. Whichever version you prefer, this is a geological sight not to miss.

It's a pretty good place for Golden Eagles, too. There is a small parking area here and you can walk further down the valley into the private estate. Typically on our last visit, as soon as we started pouring coffee from the flask, an eagle swept down the hillside in front of us. Scalding liquid went everywhere in a rush to get the scopes trained on this stunning bird as it gave once-in-a-lifetime views.

As you continue to head east, Loch Laggan appears on your right, stretching away for some

Snow Buntings breed on the highest parts of Creag Meagaidh.

ten miles or so. There are numerous parking areas where you can stop to scan, not least at the 'Big House' used in *Monarch of the Glen*, which dominates the opposite bank. The house and grounds are strictly private though.

Despite being a National Nature Reserve, it seems to be walkers and skiers who visit Creag Meagaidh, not birders. The dramatic cliffs and crags have been carved by ice and if you fancy the 3,700 foot climb and three-mile walk to the top, you are likely to be rewarded with the full range of breeding waders and montane species, not to mention some fantastic views of Ben Nevis to the west, the Grampians to the south and the Monadhliath mountains to the north.

Forest walks around Strathmashie Forest are still being developed as part of a local community enterprise, but there is something for everyone along the well-marked trails, ranging from a short stroll up to the waterfalls to an all-day hike around the tops of the woods, taking in a ruined Pictish fort. Felled conifers are being slowly replaced with a good selection of native trees.

Given that it is such a mighty Scottish river, and given some of the massive hydroelectric schemes you will encounter elsewhere, Spey Dam itself is something

Continues on page 52

How to get there

Nearest big town: Inverness is approximately 60 miles N of Newtonmore.

All the sites here are easily accessed off A86 Spean Bridge to Newtonmore road.

For Glen Roy, leave A86 N at Roybridge. The car park for the Parallel Roads is about half way along, just after a sharp left handed bend.

The large, well signed car park for Creag Meagaidh is about half way along Loch Laggan, ten miles W of Laggan village.

Strathmashie Forest is about half way between the east end of Loch Laggan and Laggan village. The car parks are well signposted.

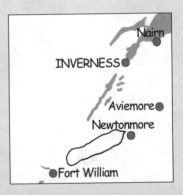

In Laggan, turn off towards Garva for the Spey Dam.

The Wildcat Trail starts in Newtonmore itself.

The distance from Spean Bridge to Newtonmore is 37 miles.

From page 51

Key points

- **Plenty of walking options from short strolls to full days out**

- **Glen Roy, Loch Laggan and Spey Dam can be watched from the car**

of an anticlimax, though the area features a nice mix of habitats and some excellent birding.

The eastern end of this route finishes in the small town of Newtonmore, where again, another community project has established a series of short, linked wildlife walks around the area.

Spring through to autumn is the best time to visit. If you are just visiting the western end of this tour, a morning trip to e.g. Glen Roy could easily be combined with an afternoon trip to Loch Arkaig (see page 48).

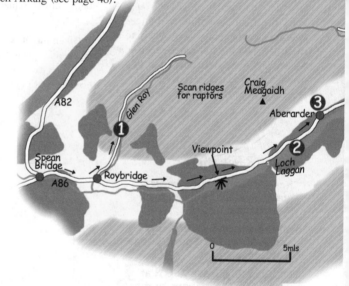

❶ Glen Roy
Background information

SHORTLY after entering the valley, the narrow road crosses a river at a sharp, right-handed turn. Park with care and watch for various woodland birds, including Wood and Willow Warblers, as well as Dippers and Grey Wagtails on the fast-flowing burn.

Look for Twite near the farm buildings, with Wheatears abundant as you get further into the valley. Buzzards, as ever, are common and you will probably hear the Ravens before you see them.

About half way down the valley, there is a large car park on the left. This is the best place to see the Parallel Roads and there are various interpretative panels, though several of these were missing on our last visit. Constant scanning of the ridges should produce a Golden Eagle sighting in time, either from here or the small car park at the end of the road.

There is relatively easy access to hills from Glen Roy and the whole area is popular with walkers, eschewing the made path at Creag Meagaidh. Most of the tops are over 2,000 feet so they will hold Ptarmigan and possibly Dotterel or Snow Buntings in summer.

If you do go walking, as ever, make sure that you have all the proper gear, food and water. Leave details of your intended route, either on your car wind-screen or with a third party. Hopefully you won't need their services, but it is a big help to the mountain rescue teams if they can narrow down the area to search.

From a birding point of view, if you do go climbing here, you are quite likely to be the first birder to do so! It would be really helpful if you could send in your records to the Highland recorder. Even the most basic sightings and counts will help to fill in a gap on the page.

Likely bird species

All year
Golden Eagle
Dipper
Grey Wagtail
Twite
Raven

Summer
Wheatear
Wood Warbler

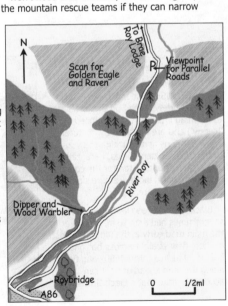

❷ Loch Laggan
Background information

THE BEST AREAS for birds are at either end of the loch, the middle being too deep to attract much wildlife. Both Goosanders and Red-breasted Mergansers are present and can often be seen at the dam end. There is an increasing flock of Greylag Geese.

Scan over the forestry at the western end for displaying raptors in spring,

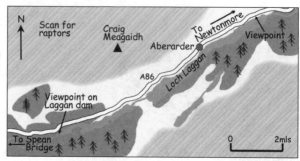

including Buzzard, Sparrowhawk and occasional Goshawk. Twite and Linnets often flit around the car parks. You might also see a Green Woodpecker anywhere along this area, a bird that is on the edge of its range here and one that you will struggle to see much further north than Newtonmore.

Likely bird species

All year	
Goosander	Goshawk (rare)
Red-breasted Merganser	Twite
	Green Woodpecker

❸ Creag Meagaidh
Background information

RED GROUSE, Golden Plovers, Dunlin and Curlews breed on the lower slopes of Creag Meagaidh (pronounced 'Meggy') and are replaced by Dotterel, Snow Buntings and Ptarmigan as you get to the tops. Golden Eagles, Peregrines and Kestrels hunt. Listen for the corvids going into alarm mode – a sure sign that a raptor is in the area.

Black Grouse breed locally. We have several times had a single male fly over the main road early in the morning. Most of them flew straight across but one individual turned through 90º and flew along the road ahead of us. I can accurately state that a Black Grouse can

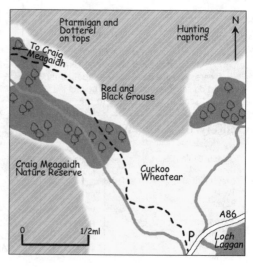

manage an impressive 40mph with a Ford Mondeo up its backside.

There are red, roe and sika deer present, plenty of wildflowers in spring, small pearl-bordered fritillaries and mountain ringlet butterflies in summer plus golden-ringed dragonflies.

Access is easy along a well-marked path from the large car park, complete with information boards. You could easily spend a full day here if you did the complete walk. Please take appropriate precautions before setting out for the tops. May and June are the best times to visit.

Likely bird species/other flora and fauna

All year	Stonechat	Golden Plover	*Other wildlife*
Red Grouse	Raven	Dunlin	Red, roe and sika deer
Black Grouse		Curlew	Wildflowers
Ptarmigan	*Summer*	Snow Bunting	Butterflies
Golden Eagle	Peregrine		Dragonflies
Meadow Pipit	Dotterel		

④ Strathmashie Forest

Background information

THERE ARE PICNIC sites on both sides of the road at Druim an Aird car park. A boardwalk on the south side leads up to a pretty waterfall where Grey Wagtails flash by. Various paths continue through the woods and you should get a good range of the commoner woodland species, including Crossbills of one sort or another. Summer migrants include Tree Pipit and Redstart.

As you explore some of the longer walks and climbs, so you come out above the treeline, even climbing so high as to make Ptarmigan a possibility. Black Grouse can be seen on the woodland fringes though, as ever, take care not to disturb them at their lek. Buzzards hunt over the woods with Merlins and Kestrels keeping an eye on the small moorland wildlife.

There are pine martens in the forest and other wildlife to look out for includes red, roe and sika deer, mountain hares and pearl-bordered fritillaries.

Likely bird species on page 56

Likely bird species/other fauna

All year		*Summer*	*Other wildlife*
Red Grouse	Tawny Owl	Merlin	Pine marten
Black Grouse	Long-eared Owl	Curlew	Mountain hare
Ptarmigan	Grey Wagtail	Tree Pipit	Butterflies
Buzzard	Stonechat	Whinchat	
Sparrowhawk	Crossbill	Redstart	
	Woodland species		

❺ Spey Dam
Background information

LEAVING THE MAIN road in Laggan, a minor road follows the River Spey and opens out with views of the dammed loch. There is a large breeding colony of Common Gulls on the islands in the river and the surrounding fields are full of hares in spring.

The far end of the loch is the best place to see the birds though it is not easy to find a great vantage point to park. Ospreys fish regularly in the loch throughout summer and Red-throated Divers often feed here. Look out too for Red-breasted Mergansers, Common Sandpipers, the occasional passage wader, Swifts, all three hirundines, Tree Pipits, Song and Mistle Thrushes, Tufted Ducks, Greylag Geese and Buzzards.

Continuing past the dam on the minor road takes you to a lovely stone bridge over the river, a good spot for Dippers and Grey Wagtails. Wheatears flash their white rumps at you and Sky Larks serenade you as you scan the surrounding mountain ridges for raptors.

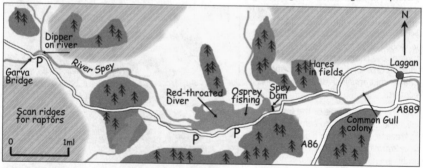

Likely bird species/other fauna

All year	*Summer*	
Golden Eagle	Red-throated Diver	Tree Pipit
Buzzard	Red-breasted Merganser	Wheatear
Common Gull	Osprey	
Dipper	Common Sandpiper	*Other wildlife*
Grey Wagtail		Hares

⑥ Newtonmore
Background information

IF YOU VISIT THE Wildcat Centre in Newtonmore, they will supply details of a six-mile circular walk around the town known as 'The Wildcat Trail.' Details are also available online at www.newtonmore.com

The complete walk takes about two and a half hours, but is also divided up into six parts if you just want to do a smaller section.

Though it is extremely unlikely that you will encounter one of these ferocious beasts, there is plenty of other wildlife to be seen, including salmon and trout, which in turn attract otters and Ospreys.

Other birds include Dipper, Buzzard, occasional Golden Eagle, Red Grouse, breeding waders, Buzzard, Kestrel, Sparrowhawk, Green and Great Spotted Woodpecker, Goosander, Red-breasted Merganser, Grey Wagtail and Ringed Plover. There are red squirrels in the woods, red deer, mountain hares and a variety of wildflowers and orchids.

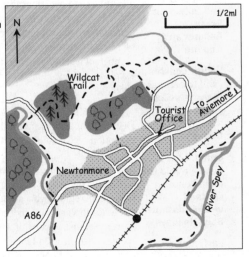

Likely bird species/other flora and fauna

All year	Dipper	*Other wildlife*
Red Grouse	Woodland birds	Otter
Golden Eagle		Salmon
Buzzard	*Summer*	Red squirrel
Sparrowhawk	Goosander	Wildflowers and orchids
Great Spotted Woodpecker	Red-breasted Merganser	
Green Woodpecker	Osprey	
Grey Wagtail	Ringed Plover	

Key points

- **Full amenities (food, petrol and toilets) in Braemar, Ballater and Aboyne**

- **Visitor centres (and toilets) at Glenshee, Glen Muick and Burn o'Vat (Muir of Dinnet)**

- **Can get very busy – avoid the main beauty spots at weekends and Bank Holidays**

- **Early mornings in spring and summer best for the woods**

- **First class roads – the only tricky bit to negotiate is the bridge at Glen Gairn**

- **Many of the areas here demand full exploration. Don't expect to do more than a couple of these sites in a day**

- **Programme of guided walks at Burn o'Vat**

EVER SINCE Queen Victoria and Prince Albert bought Balmoral 150 years ago, tourists have flocked to Deeside. As well as the royal connections, they found plenty of castles to explore, any number of beauty spots and excellent fishing along the river.

The birding around Upper Deeside is excellent. With the exception of Crested Tit, all the Speyside specialities are here. And, if you extend your birding to the whole of the Grampian region, you are likely to do very well indeed. A new Scottish record of 156 species seen in a 24-hour period was set in May 2004. This is a fantastic total and more than you are likely to see in a week on Speyside or the West Coast.

And yet for some reason, the birders just don't seem to visit the area. Apart from the occasional local, and one other birder heading to Speyside via Glenshee, I have yet to meet another birder on my travels here.

Even the local tourist industry, which is otherwise very active and efficient, seems to have a mental block when it comes to ecotourism. Look on the websites for various local hotels and the best you get is a general comment such as 'the whole area is very scenic and good for wildlife.' If you are really lucky, they might mention red squirrels and deer. And that's it. Royalty, history,

Summering Dotterel frequent the higher parts in Glenshee

golf and fishing, yes, birding no. It's all very strange.

I was in one of the local tourist offices trying to find some information when an American woman asked the assistant to identify the yellow flowers she was seeing on the moors. After hearing the proffered answer of winter jasmine (!), I felt that I had to interrupt. I told her the clean

Continues on page 60

How to get there

Nearest large town: Aberdeen is approximately 65 miles E of Ballater

The A93 between Braemar and Ballater is an excellent starting point to access all the sites.

For Dinnet Oakwood, head S through the village of Dinnet from the junction of A93 and A97. Immediately after crossing the river, you come to a T-junction with B976 and the entrance to the wood is immediately opposite you. To park, turn L and there is room for a couple of cars to pull off the road on R after about 50 yards.

For the Muir of Dinnet, head E out of Ballater on A93. After four miles, turn L onto B9119 and the Burn o'Vat visitor centre and car park are on L after a mile. The whole area is enclosed by the triangle of roads - A93, B9119 and A97. NB some older maps transpose A97 and B9119.

For Glen Muick, leave B976 on the southern edge of Ballater on a well-signed minor road heading SW. Follow this road to the car park and visitor centre at the end.

For the Linn of Quoich viewpoint, leave Braemar W on a minor road towards the well-signed Linn of Dee. The two lay-bys are on R after a couple of miles at NO 122903 and NO 118897. Continue W to the Linn of Dee. The road crosses the river and

hairpins back on itself. The car park, currently being totally renovated, is on L.

For Glenshee, continue on A93 S of Braemar for about ten miles. There is a massive car park on L and the visitor centre on R.

For the Glen Gairn area, either leave A93 onto A939, one mile W of Ballater or, if coming from Braemar, turn N onto B976 at Crathie. The hump-backed bridge is at the junction of these two roads, about five miles after leaving A93. Be very careful parking – see above.

To explore the surrounding moorland, continue N on A93 for the next six miles, stopping as appropriate. This is the way you would automatically come if coming over from Speyside/Tomintoul (see Glenlivet tour on page 142).

From page 59

Key points

- **Glenshee road often closed due to snow in winter**

- **Easy birding from the roadside in the Linn of Quoich, Glen Gairn and Glenshee sections. Limited access at Burn o'Vat and Glen Muick**

- **Disabled toilets at Glenshee, Glen Muick and Burn o'Vat**

version of the folklore that kissing is only in season when the gorse is in bloom, the joke being that gorse is always in bloom. The anecdote didn't go down well, however and I never did claim my free kiss.

The Dee is one of the most important salmon rivers and the surrounding grouse moors are actively shot over. This is immediately apparent in the plethora of country pursuit shops, nearly all of them by Royal Appointment. There is a lot of money in the area and it is reflected in the prices if you want to stay here or eat out. A rich man's Speyside, as someone rather cruelly put it.

The general feel of the countryside is that it is a lot prettier and less rugged than Speyside. There is a central wooded and wetland belt, with some prime moorland to the north and an excellent montane route to the south. Like the Speyside area, there is no set tour here, but rather a collection of sites that between them offer a diverse range of habitats.

The active promotion of a series of beauty spots means tourists tend to flock to a few well-defined places and nowhere else, so expect to find car parks full to overflowing. Weekends and Bank Holidays are probably best avoided at places like the Linn of Dee and Glen Muick.

Wherever you visit, early morning or evening visits are likely to be a lot quieter. Most visitors tend to stick to the obvious paths and routes and you shouldn't have to walk very far off the beaten track to get away from the crowds and increase your chances of finding the wildlife.

If you want to stay in the area, then Braemar, Ballater and Aboyne would make ideal bases. As ever, spring through to autumn are likely to be the pick of the times to visit, with the woodlands at their best in spring. Late autumn and winter is best for the geese at Muir of Dinnet and winter can produce very close views of Ptarmigan – if the road is open.

❶ Dinnet Oakwood
Background information

THIS IS A BEAUTIFUL WOOD to walk through, and an ideal antidote to all those conifers. The NNR at Dinnet Oakwood is a remnant of the deciduous forest (about 13 hectares) that once covered much of lowland Scotland. It is ideal for a dawn chorus, or at least an early morning visit.

Scottish Natural Heritage does nothing to promote the site though. There are no signs from the road. Even the entrance gate is very anonymous and you have no inkling whatsoever that you have come to the right place. About 50 yards down the path you will spot a discrete notice board telling you a bit about the place. While you stop to read this, listen out for Wood Warblers; there is a traditional territory on your right just about here.

My attention was first drawn to this place by a fellow birder telling me that this was a good spot for Pied Flycatchers. Sure enough, we found a female within ten minutes of our first visit. However, on a subsequent visit, we bumped into a local birder who told us that he had never seen one in 15 years of survey work in the wood, so don't let your hopes rise too high. Spotted Flycatchers on the other hand are supposedly at their highest density here, compared with other Deeside woods.

You will find an excellent selection of woodland birds, including Green and Great Spotted Woodpeckers, tits, finches, thrushes, Goldcrest, Treecreeper and a selection of summer migrants such as Willow Warbler, Tree Pipit and Redstart. As you return to the car, it is worth crossing the road and checking the River Dee for the likes of Grey Wagtail and Dipper.

There is plenty of interesting botany too, plus once mighty trees, now fallen and covered with a wonderful selection of mosses and lichens.

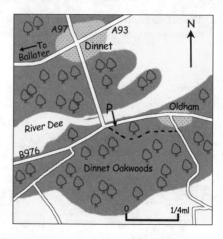

Mammals include badgers, roe deer and Daubenton's bats. If you love woods, you'll love it here.

Likely bird species/other flora and fauna

All year	Treecreeper	Redstart	*Other wildlife*
Green Woodpecker	Common woodland birds	Wood Warbler	Roe deer
Great Spotted Woodpecker		Willow Warbler	Lichen
Grey Wagtail	*Summer*	Pied Flycatcher (rare)	Wildflowers
Dipper	Tree Pipit	Spotted Flycatcher	

---

❷ Muir of Dinnet
Background information

LOCHS DAVAN and Kinnord are important wintering areas for Greylag Geese. Just under 30,000 birds use the lochs, nearly 30% of the British/Irish/Icelandic wintering population. Plenty of other wildfowl winters here too, including good numbers of Wigeon.

The main trail from the visitor centre leads you through woodland towards the Burn o'Vat. Common woodland birds might include the occasional Redpoll or Siskin. If you have come over from Speyside, you will notice plenty of Jays in the area, a decidedly scarce bird further west. Look for Woodcocks roding at dusk.

Just when you think that the path has petered out, a series of dodgy looking stepping stones lead you to the Vat, a huge, hidden cave rumoured to be the hideout of a notorious 17th Century outlaw, Gilderoy Macgregor. Grey Wagtails flit in and out. Expect to get slightly damp at least, or completely wet feet depending on levels of clumsiness!

Retracing your steps, the path climbs through the woods and offers several spectacular views over the surrounding countryside. As well as more woodland birds, use these viewpoints to scan for raptors, including Sparrowhawk and Buzzard. In spring and summer, migrants such as Tree Pipits and Willow Warblers will add to the number of species you see. Ospreys fish in the loch.

Though the information boards at the centre suggest places to stop as you drive round the lochs, you will find them very poorly signposted when you get onto the road and trial and error may be required to get the right place.

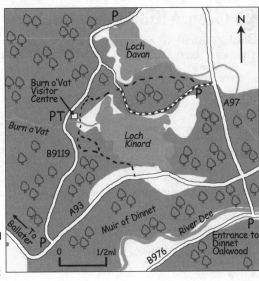

We found the north-western end of Loch Davan to be most productive, as we had fantastic views of a party of what appeared to be classic Scottish Crossbills, doing their best to drown out the other woodland birds and the chorus of Sedge Warblers calling from the reed bed on the other side of the road.

The centre is open from mid May to September (10am – 6pm) except Tuesdays and Wednesdays, though the trails are open at all times. As well as looking at the history, geology and natural history of the place, there is a hands-on box, ideal for kids, that lets you grope the likes of antlers, bird wings and so on. The car park is free and there is a picnic site.

There are toilets, including disabled toilets, at the centre and a wheelchair-friendly path leads through the trail for about a quarter of a mile. A full programme of guided walks is offered, phone 01339 881 667 for details.

Likely bird species/other fauna

All year		Summer	
Buzzard	Jay	Osprey	Greylag Goose
Sparrowhawk	Redpoll	Tree Pipit	Common wildfowl (big increase in numbers)
Woodcock	Siskin	Sedge Warbler	
Grey Wagtail	Common woodland birds		Other wildlife
Scottish Crossbill	Common wildfowl	Winter	Otter
		Wigeon	

❸ Glen Muick and Lochnagar

Background information

PRINCE CHARLES LOVES this area so much that he wrote a book – The Old Man of Lochnagar – for his younger brothers. Though you might not see the Little Green Men of Gorm or an underwater haggis on your visit, there is still plenty to keep you occupied.

A walk to the top and back is some 12-14 miles long, depending on the route chosen and shouldn't be attempted unless you are a serious hill walker. If you do venture up, you will find Ptarmigan replacing the Red Grouse as you get to the higher reaches and there is always the chance of a close encounter with a Peregrine or Golden Eagle. Snow Buntings also breed.

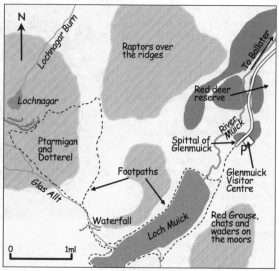

The star birds though are the Dotterel, which are at their greatest population density here, with more than 3% of the British breeding birds – some 28 pairs. Apart from that, you are likely to be alone, though that is what a friend thought until he was buzzed by a helicopter flying the Royal Standard, just checking to see if the man 'watering the heather' proved to be any great threat to security.

If you stay at ground level, you can walk round the loch itself – a circuit will take you about three hours – or just have a quick scan. One or two pairs of Red-throated Divers are often present and the occasional Black-throated Diver visits. Goosanders can usually be seen, though if you visit in late summer, you will only see females and young, the males having left for Norway where they moult. Common Sandpipers and Common Gulls patrol the loch edges. Ospreys are occasionally seen.

Red Grouse are common on the moors, though you will be lucky to come across the much shyer Black Grouse. Lapwings, Oystercatchers and Curlews all breed, but numbers of Dunlin, Golden Plovers and Redshanks have declined. Look for Meadow

Likely bird species/other fauna

All year	Dipper	Peregrine	Ring Ouzel
Ptarmigan	Common woodland	Curlew	Snow Bunting
Red Grouse	birds	Golden Plover	
Black Grouse		Redshank	*Other wildlife*
Golden Eagle	*Summer*	Dunlin	Red and roe deer
Buzzard	Goosander	Common Sandpiper	Stoat
Sparrowhawk	Red-throated Diver	Dotterel	Adder
Grey Wagtail	Merlin	Wheatear	

Pipits, Wheatears and Ring Ouzels in the heather. Merlins, Kestrels and Sparrowhawks hunt and Buzzards are common.

Arctic hares are the favourite meal for Golden Eagles. Red deer are easy to see and roe deer are present, though not as visible. Look for stoats hunting rabbits around the visitor centre. Adders bask in the sun and are particularly obvious in late summer when they give birth.

The visitor centre is at the Spittal of Muick (pronounced mick not muck). Spittal means place of shelter and this building was originally used by pig drovers as they were going to

market, though whisky smugglers are also thought to have made use of the shelter on occasion.

The centre has a large display covering the geology and wildlife of the area and the staff will happily pass on details of recent sightings. Leaflets are available for the various trails.

There is woodland around the centre and going back up the glen though one of the other sites in this chapter might serve you better for forest species. Many of the burns (small streams) in the area have Dippers and Grey Wagtails.

❹ Linn of Quoich viewpoint
Background information

A COUPLE OF MILES out of Braemar, two large lay-bys provide a good spot to scan not only the river, but also the cliffs and mountain ridges of the Linn of Quoich opposite.

Raptors are well represented here, with Buzzards and Kestrels almost guaranteed, Peregrines and Sparrowhawks likely and Golden Eagle a possibility. Finally, there is the outside chance of a Goshawk.

Look too for the likes of Common Sandpiper and Oystercatcher on the shingle banks in the river. Hirundines hawk for insects and there are usually a few loafing Common Gulls. Viewing is from the lay-by so there is no problem for wheelchair users.

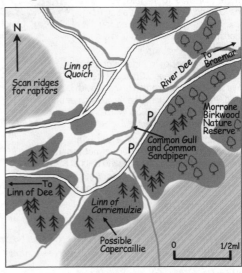

❺ Linn of Dee
Background information

THE WOODS SURROUNDING the Linn of Dee car park all hold Capercaillie and Scottish Crossbill. Early morning is your best chance of seeing one of the former as it takes grit from the road or flies over.

The Linn of Dee – the word 'linn' means waterfall or cascade pool - is yet another very popular beauty spot, where the River Dee hurtles through a narrow rock gorge. There is a chance you might see salmon leaping here in summer.

The woods contain all the usual species associated with pine forests and as most of the visitors do little more than walk to the falls, you don't have to go very far to get away from the crowds. The path leading roughly north-west towards Glen Lui is a good place to start.

Resident species include Goldcrest, Coal Tit, Treecreeper, Great Spotted Woodpecker and Scottish Crossbill with Dipper and Grey Wagtail along the river. Summer brings migrant Tree Pipits, Willow Warblers, Redstarts and Spotted Flycatchers.

If you do hear the popping calls of a Capercaillie or, as you get further out towards the moorland edge, the bubbling calls of Black Grouse, please think twice before getting any closer, especially if it is in the breeding season –

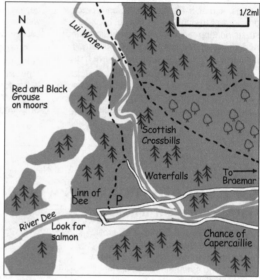

see the code of conduct for further details.

Watch the skies too for flyover birds. We hadn't got out of the car park on our last visit when a Peregrine flew low over our heads, something missed by the other 50 or so visitors.

This area isn't particularly suitable for wheelchair users.

Likely bird species

All year		Summer
Black Grouse	Grey Wagtail	Tree Pipit
Capercaillie	Dipper	Redstart
Great Spotted	Goldcrest	Willow Warbler
Woodpecker	Treecreeper	Spotted Flycatcher
	Scottish Crossbill	

❻ Glenshee
Background information

THE SKI-LIFT CENTRE at Glenshee, about ten miles south of Braemar, is famous for its Ptarmigan population, which is often forced down from the tops in winter. This means the birds can often be seen from the car park without having to leave the comfort of your own car. That's if you can get there in the first place – this stretch of road is often closed due to heavy snow.

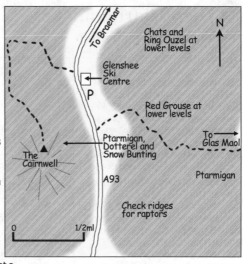

At other times of the year, there is still a chance of being able to see one from the car park, but you will need a lot of patience and a very good telescope. The occasional bird can be seen perched on a boulder near the skyline but beware, Red Grouse get up that high too, so don't automatically assume that you are looking at a Ptarmigan.

Failing that, your only other option is the hard slog of walking up well-marked paths to either The Cairnwell to the west (the usual choice) or Glas Maol to the east. Before you start though, it is well worth checking in the visitor centre. Staff can often pass on local knowledge as to which routes have been most productive recently.

If you do go climbing, the birds can still be difficult to find as they are superbly camouflaged and sit tight until you are right on top of them. Listen for the high-pitched cooing of the females and loud clicking of the males, together with a croaking, retching alarm call. If you have the time to explore the tops, look

out too for Dotterel and Snow Buntings and you might see a hunting Golden Eagle or Peregrine. As ever, the weather can change in an instant so make sure you are properly prepared.

The scenery as you travel through the glen is spectacular and other birds you could see include Osprey, Buzzard, Merlin, Short-eared Owl, Red Grouse, Raven, Ring Ouzel, Twite, Dipper, Pied and Grey Wagtails, Wigeon, Curlew, Oystercatcher, Common Gull, Stonechat, Whinchat and Wheatear. A nice scenic drive with a bit of birding en route or a full day's exploring for birds, the choice is yours in this beautiful area.

Likely bird species

All year		Summer	
Ptarmigan	Dipper	Osprey	Short-eared Owl
Red Grouse	Stonechat	Merlin	Whinchat
Golden Eagle	Raven	Peregrine	Wheatear
Grey Wagtail	Twite	Dotterel	Ring Ouzel
			Snow Bunting

❼ Glen Gairn and Area
Background information

ANYONE APPROACHING Ballater from the north will automatically pass through this area of prime moorland. There are plenty of places to pull in and scan and you should have no trouble finding Red Grouse, Wheatears and Meadow Pipits, with Stonechats or Whinchats perched on top of the gorse bushes. Listen out for calling Golden Plovers and Dunlin.

The area is good for Short-eared Owls and hunting Merlins, while Sparrowhawks operate out of some of the larger clumps of trees. You might suspect that this is a good site for Hen Harriers, but there is a lot of moorland to search and only the occasional pair is now known to be in the area.

One local birder reckoned he had 20 pairs of Hen Harriers on his local patch – reasonably near here – some 15 years ago. Now he doesn't have any, illustrating just what a decline there has been in the population of this beautiful raptor and not all of it, unfortunately, caused by natural changes to the habitat.

Where the B976 to Braemar splits off from the main A939, there is a sharp bend coupled with a narrow hump-backed bridge over the River Gairn. This area is good for Ring Ouzels and Black Grouse can sometimes be heard. Check the river for Grey Wagtails and Dippers.

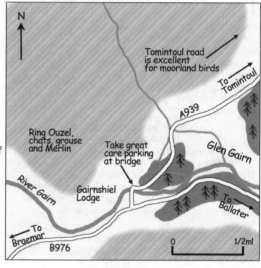

To avoid inconveniencing the many buses that use this road please don't park right by the bridge; go a couple of hundred yards away and park there, ideally in a space big enough for two cars at least. This really is a pig of a junction.

The road from the bridge towards Ballater passes through more cultivated land so expect to see Oystercatchers in the fields and hirundines hawking insects around the houses.

Likely bird species

All year		Merlin	Ring Ouzel
Red Grouse	Dipper	Golden Plover	Whinchat
Black Grouse	Stonechat	Dunlin	Wheatear
Meadow Pipit		Short-eared Owl	
Grey Wagtail	*Summer*	Cuckoo	
	Hen Harrier (rare)		

The Grampian Coast
Background information

THOUGH THEY ARE BEYOND the scope of this edition of the book, there are several coastal sites that are worth a day trip if you are staying in Deeside.

Kinnaird Head in Fraserburgh is the point where the North Sea meets the Moray Firth. It is an excellent seawatching spot in spring and autumn with waders, seaducks, skuas, Gannets, gulls, terns, auks etc. all passing. Huge numbers of gulls are attracted to the fishing fleet and the area has a good record for turning up rare species. Iceland and Glaucous Gulls can often be found in winter.

This is a horrible place to find. Though marked on all the maps, it isn't signposted. Aim for the Lighthouse Museum and look for a bit of waste ground beyond. This is actually a large car park with shelters, useful for bad weather. If you reach the docks, you have gone too far.

Loch of Strathbeg RSPB (signed from Crimond) attracts huge numbers of geese in winter (e.g. 30,000 Pinkfeet). Passage sees a good variety of waders move through and there is usually something out of the ordinary, such as Bittern, Spoonbill, Pectoral Sandpiper, Little Gull or Marsh Harrier, at different times of the year.

Immediately south of the loch, a minor road leads to Rattray Head. This road is good for Corn Buntings and the dunes at the Head can produce good numbers of migrants, including scarcities in spring and autumn.

Halfway between Peterhead and Aberdeen is the Ythan Estuary, one of the most studied ecosystems in the world. There are fantastic tern colonies in summer, huge numbers of Eiders and a good range of waders on the estuary itself.

Park at either end of the bridge over the river and explore the dune systems or head to the crossroads immediately north of the river. Here, a minor road to the west leads to the Waulkmill hide, the best place to watch waders either side of high tide. Alternatively

head east towards Collieston and park at the visitor centre on your right to again explore the dunes.

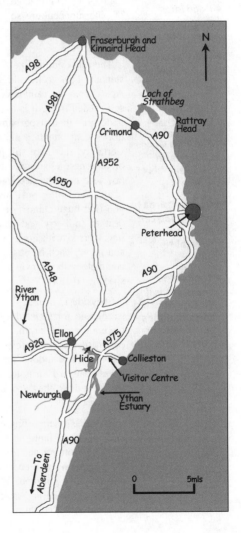

Key points

- **Full facilities (shops, toilets, petrol) at Aviemore and Grantown**

- **Good for all Scottish specialities**

- **Hides at Loch Garten, Boat of Garten, the Rothiemurchus fish farm and Uath Lochan**

- **The area contains an excellent mix of habitats**

- **Compact area to work – you can easily visit several sites in a day**

- **Take proper precautions if you are climbing the mountains – the weather is very changeable**

- **No access to the tops if you take the Cairngorms funicular railway**

THE ABUNDANCE of Crested Tits in Speyside is just one of the bonuses bestowed by the remnant Caledonian Forest, which bears no relation to the depressing, regimented blocks of pine monoculture so common elsewhere in upland areas.

The real thing is like stepping back to the old days. Apart from the randomness of self-seeded trees, it is the undergrowth that perhaps draws your attention the most. Certainly, there are still plenty of pine needles around, though nowhere near the deep sterile blanket you often see. Instead you find huge clumps of heather, bilberry and juniper, interspersed with areas of bog and moor, each habitat complete with its own specialised flora.

Speyside is Britain's stronghold for Crested Tits. Unlike the birds on the continent, our subspecies is sedentary and though the occasional bird turns up away from the area, they are few and far between.

The area's supporting cast of bird species is fantastic and includes Dotterel and Ptarmigan on the high tops, the unbelievably gorgeous Slavonian Grebe and Black-throated and Red-throated

Divers on the lochs. A full range of raptors, from the diminutive Merlin to the mighty Golden Eagle, compete with a superb range of woodland birds, including the huge, shy Capercaillie, and, what may or may not prove to be Britain's only endemic species – the Scottish Crossbill.

Then there are the mammals – otter, wildcat, pine marten, red squirrel, red and roe deer and mountain hare. You want flora, fungi, insects, lichen, dragonflies and butterflies as well? No problem. And all set in some of Britain's most amazing scenery.

If you are looking for somewhere to base yourself for a Scottish holiday, then Speyside is ideal. Look for somewhere in the Aviemore, Carrbridge, Grantown-on-Spey triangle, with Boat of Garten and Nethy Bridge being the birders' favourites. These give you easy access to all the sites listed on the following pages, as well as linking to the main roads if you want to explore further afield.

The area is slowly changing its character as Aviemore, the centre of the ski holiday industry, continues to spread. New housing developments are springing up, mostly going to second-home owners as the local people can't afford them.

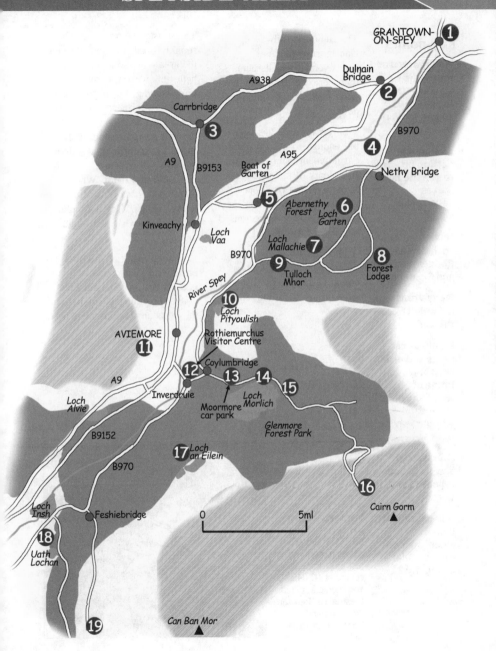

Key points

- **Many woods and footpaths to explore – OS Explorer 403 covers most of these sites**

- **Well worth getting up early to see the Loch Garten Capercaillie watch**

- **Guided walks at Loch Garten, Rothiemurchus and Glenmore**

- **Many areas can be birded from the car**

- **Plenty of car parks and picnic sites allow a range of woodland birds to be seen without leaving the car**

- **Full disabled access, including toilet at Loch Garten**

- **It is possible to take a wheelchair on the funicular at Cairngorm**

The funicular railway up Cairngorm remains controversial and it seems that there are applications for wind farms being submitted daily.

So far the area has been big enough to absorb these developments and there are still plenty of fantastic areas to explore, but one hopes it will be tightly controlled in future to ensure a precious landscape is protected.

This chapter of the book isn't presented as a tour, as it would be hard to do justice to so many great birding sites.

Those listed below – which run roughly north to south through the area – are some of the better-known ones for birdwatching, but if you want to explore further, a quick look at the latest large scale Ordnance Survey map will show any number of woods in the area, all with well-marked paths through them. Who goes there? The occasional dog walker maybe. Try a couple. Who knows what you might turn up?

Though many of the birds are present all year round, the area is at its best in May and June when everything is singing and the birds are looking their best.

❶ Grantown-on-Spey
Background information

THE WOODS east of the town hold Capercaillie, though a lot of luck is required to see them, with a dawn visit being best.

The best access point is from a track that leads east into the woods off the B9102. There are places to park the car just after the golf course at NJ 045283. You should also find Crested Tit, Redstart, Tree Pipit and Scottish Crossbill as well.

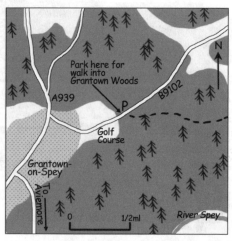

② Dulnain Bridge
Background information

JUST WEST of Dulnain Bridge on the A938, there is a large lay-by where the road lies next to the river. This is an excellent place to see Dippers and there are usually Grey Wagtails here, too.

Keep your eyes on the sky here. Buzzards are common and there is always the chance of an Osprey drifting over.

See main map on page 71 for location

③ Carrbridge
Background information

THE STRUCTURE that gives the village its name is a beautiful packhorse bridge, dating back to 1717, though the parapets were washed away in a great flood in 1829. It can be viewed from the B9153 and is a good spot for Dipper and Grey Wagtail.

If you continue along Station Road on the south side of the bridge, you head out under the A9 onto moorland. The fields at the end of the road often hold good numbers (up to 50) of feeding summer-plumaged Golden Plovers. The penultimate field on the right before the car park seems to be the favoured spot.

Curlews, Oystercatchers, Ringed Plovers and Lapwings also feed here and there is usually a pair or two of partridges – either Grey or Red-legged in the area. There is a chance of an Osprey fishing the River Dulnain. Look out for Merlin and Whinchat. Mountain hare, red and roe deer can also be seen.

Just south of the village lies the Carrbridge Landmark Centre - a sort of mini theme park. A path on the northern side of the centre can be good for both Crested Tit and Scottish Crossbill. Look out too for red squirrels.

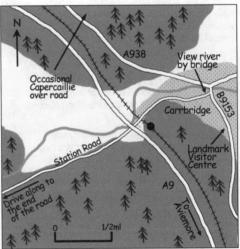

As you drive out of Carrbridge heading for the A9, take your time and keep an eye out for Capercaillies flying across the road. Over the years, this has proved to be our most successful spot for chance encounters.

④ Nethy Bridge
Background information

ALL THE WOODS here are worth exploring for the usual range of species. Check any garden feeders you see for Crested Tit, Siskin and red squirrel. A walk along the river should produce Dipper, Grey Wagtail and Common Sandpiper.

For a more or less guaranteed sighting of Dipper though, leave the village north-west on a minor road towards the A95. This is a nasty junction involving hump-backed bridges and blind corners, so take care.

Check the woods on your left as you leave the village; they have turned up the occasional Pied Flycatcher, right at the edge of its range.

Park carefully at Broomhill Bridge over the River Spey and scan the river both ways. As well as Dipper, you should see Goldeneye, and possibly Goosander and Red-breasted Merganser. There is a large Sand Martin colony here too.

Scan the skyline for Ospreys and Buzzards. This is a popular spot with anglers and you may get lucky and see a salmon being landed; the

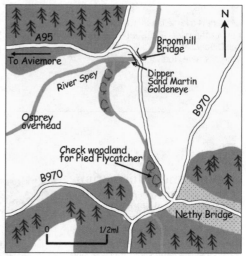

locals stand and watch, arguing about technique and laying bets as to whether the fish or the angler will eventually win.

In winter, Nethy Bridge regularly attracts Waxwings during irruption years.

⑤ Boat of Garten Area
Background information

THE VIEW of the Cairngorms from the bridge over the Spey at the east end of Boat of Garten is stunning, especially at dawn and dusk.

The river can produce sightings of Goldeneye, Goosander, Red-breasted Merganser, Dipper and Common Sandpiper. As well as a good range of common migrants and woodland birds in the surrounding trees, Daubenton's bats can

sometimes be seen taking insects from the river surface at dusk.

Walking back towards the village, you come to a T-junction. Turn right and you will see Milton Loch on your left after a couple of hundred yards. Though you can watch the loch from the road, better views are obtained from the hide – another excellent community effort. To reach it, turn left into Birch Grove just before you reach the loch. There is a car park at the bottom of the road where signs direct you into Milton Wood. The hide is off the path on the right.

There is a heronry here and birds are constantly moving in and out of the nests or hunting in front of you. Look for a selection of commoner wildfowl, including Little Grebes. Buzzards are present and Woodcocks rode at dusk. A selection of woodland birds and red squirrels come to the feeders in front of the hide.

Based on log book entries it appears few people visit the hide, but already, an impressive selection of birds have been recorded including Osprey, Peregrine, Sparrowhawk, Kestrel, Tawny Owl, Snipe, Jack Snipe, Green and Common Sandpipers, Siskins and Bramblings.

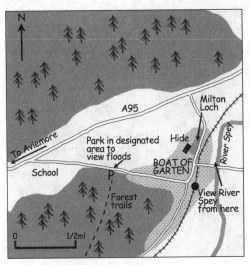

There are several paths leading through the pinewoods south of the village, which hold a typical range of species. These paths eventually reach the small Loch Vaa though you can also park a lot closer (see below). This loch has been designated a Special Protection Area by the Joint Nature Conservation Committee with up to five pairs of Slavonian Grebes breeding in recent years.

In practice though, the grebes have not shown very well here, if at all, for the last couple of years and if you want to watch them at length, Loch Ruthven remains the site of choice.

Just before you join the A95, west of the village, it is worth scanning the fields to your right. These are often flooded and hold the occasional Wigeon. Breeding waders such as Redshank and Lapwing often feed round the edge of the water and you may spot a passage wader. Recent visitors have included a large flock of Black-tailed Godwits and a Temminck's Stint.

You might see a Hooded Crow though it is more likely to be a Hooded Crow X Carrion Crow hybrid. Ospreys can drift over at any time and Buzzards are common.

Amazingly, these field floods have proved attractive to Slavonian Grebes. Indeed, so fed up did the locals get with cars pulling up and ruining their verges, that they created a special pull-in place, complete with viewing platform. Just look for the large picture of a Slavonian Grebe on your left as you drive out of the village.

A feeding station has recently been set up here in the car park and the feeders regularly attract Crested Tits as well as commoner woodland species. Note that the water levels are highly variable, In 2003 and 2004, there was barely a puddle.

Visitors to the area have the chance to watch at an active badger sett for an evening (contact Allan Bantick – see below). A hide operates from April to October inclusive. There is a fee payable, though accompanied children go free. The organisation is non-profit-making and all the fees go towards buying peanuts for the badgers and other expenses.

Book as early as you can, though it might be possible to squeeze you in at short notice if there is space. Allan will arrange to meet you in Boat of Garten before the drive down to the hide.

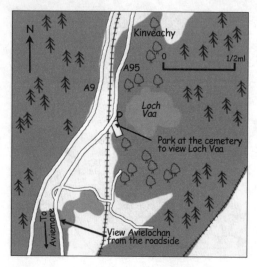

N

Kinveachy

A95

A9

0   1/2ml

Loch Vaa

P

Park at the cemetery to view Loch Vaa

To Aviemore

View Avielochan from the roadside

Full details of all the recent activity can be seen by visiting www.allanbantick.net and then clicking on 'Wildlife Diary'. Contact Allan on 01479 831768 or email allanbantick@hotmail.com

Heading south towards Aviemore on the A95, you can park at the cemetery if you just want a quick scan of Loch Vaa. About half a mile further south, there is space by the side of the road to pull in and check Avielochan.

❻ Loch Garten Area
Background information

AFTER MANY years of waiting, this most famous of RSPB reserves now has a full set of visitor facilities, complete with a large shop and self-composting toilets, a boon for the hundreds of coach party visitors that arrive every year.

For anyone new to the area, the first surprise is that the famous Osprey nest isn't actually by the loch side, but on the opposite side of the road. The walk down to the hide (fee payable for non-members) is suitable for

wheelchairs and the feeders should provide views of Crested Tit, Siskin and red squirrel. You might also see a flock of Scottish Crossbills.

Creasted Tits can be seen on the woodland walk next to Loch Garten and at bird tables in Nethy Bridge

The welcome inside the hide is always warm, as the volunteers make sure that you don't miss a thing - very useful for the casual birder. A video shows highlights of last year's breeding season to help pass the time during quiet periods, though this reverts to a live video feed if the birds show any sign of activity. Two notice boards give details of what the Ospreys have been doing that day and other birds seen locally. There are plenty of telescopes available.

The nest site is a pretty ugly affair, held together with iron girders after vandals tried to cut down the tree a few years ago. Distant views of the Ospreys are restricted to the occasional glimpse of the top of a head until the other parent returns with a fish and the birds change over. The camera has a more elevated position and looks right down into the nest.

It should be noted that though birds turn up every spring, they don't always know what to do and in 2002 and 2003, the male in particular was very backward in coming forward. The result of this was that the female got fed up and disappeared, leaving no birds to breed. Things were back to normal in 2004 when the male finally got his act together.

Other birds that you should see include Redstarts, which often nest right in front of the hide, Coal Tit, Tree Pipit, Great Spotted Woodpecker, Cuckoo, Buzzard, Mistle Thrush and Spotted Flycatcher.

Capercaillies do occasionally turn up in front of the hide. However, in the last couple of years, visitors have been able to watch a lek where up to six male birds have been displaying.

This is a fantastic opportunity to watch 'the horse of the forest', probably the most sought-after of all the Scottish specialities. It also takes the pressure off other birds and all visitors are encouraged to come here in April and early May rather than trying to find your own birds. The RSPB is to be heartily congratulated for the success of this scheme.

The birds show at first light and you can judge the success of the scheme from the fact that up to 80 birders a day are prepared to get up in the wee small hours to see the show. As only a few people can watch at any given time, depending on how and where the birds are showing, you might be given a raffle ticket to ensure a fair queuing system. Full, up-to-date details of the lek are available from the visitor centre. In 2003, birds were seen on about 90% of the days when the scheme was running.

The centre operates a full programme of guided walks throughout the summer and

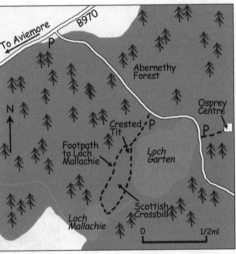

there is usually an illustrated lecture in Boat of Garten village hall every week. Phone the Osprey Centre on 01479 831 476 for full details or pick up a leaflet when you visit.

You can follow the fortunes of the Loch Garten Ospreys on the Internet by visiting www.rspb.org.uk/features and clicking on 'webcam'.

During the summer months, pictures from the nest are updated every 15 minutes. Away from the breeding seasons, you can see highlights from previous years, as well as pictures of the Capercaillie lek and inside nestboxes of Goldeneyes and Redstarts.

77

❼ Towards Loch Mallachie

Background information

HALF A MILE north-west of the Loch Garten reserve car park, a car park is the start of a well-marked path that leads along the edge of Loch Garten towards Loch Mallachie. This is an excellent walk and should add a variety of water birds to your list, as well as more of the species already mentioned.

Look for Common Sandpipers along the loch margins. The loch itself holds Goldeneye, Teal and Wigeon with the occasional diver or sawbill seen – usually early in the morning. Otters are increasingly seen.

The woods hold Crested Tits, Scottish Crossbills, Redstarts, Siskins, Tree Pipits, Willow Warblers, Goldcrests and Treecreepers. Curlews breed in the boggy area behind Loch Mallachie. Woodcocks rode at dusk. If you are really lucky, a pine marten might cross your path.

The woods around the loch can appear empty in winter if you don't catch up with the roving flocks. Depending on weather conditions, Greylag Geese, Goosanders and large numbers of Black-headed Gulls can roost, including the occasional white-winged gull.

There has been a spate of cars being broken into recently, so don't leave any valuables in the car.

Loch Mallachie is shown on the Loch Garten map on page 77.

❽ Abernethy Forest

Background information

LOCH GARTEN forms just a small part of the Abernethy Forest reserve. With most of the visitors straying no further than the area around the hide, you will probably have huge chunks of ancient Caledonian forest to yourself, ideal if you prefer finding your own birds.

By far the most popular starting point, if you can find it, is Forest Lodge. Head south-west on a path towards Rynettin (marked on OS maps) before looping back to the car park.

This is one of the best walks through this sort of habitat and you would be unlucky not to see Crested Tits and crossbills of some persuasion as well as a full range of typical supporting species.

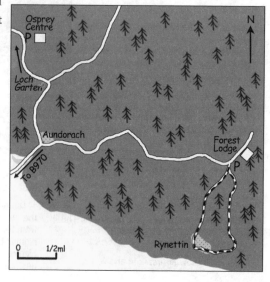

Capercaillie, as ever, prove more elusive (see the section on Code of Conduct to ensure your behaviour does not in any way threaten an endangered species).

The RSPB has just bought a large area of land around the Revack Estate, north of Nethy Bridge. There are no visiting facilities at the time of writing, but check at Loch Garten for details.

⑨ Tulloch Mhor
Background information

A LONG the minor road to the south of Loch Garten, you may see Black Grouse in the more open areas and spring and summer sees plenty of chats, Tree Pipits and Cuckoos. Small lochans hold the ocassional Teal, Wigeon, Goldeneye and Little Grebe.

Towards dusk, you can often get very good views of the Loch Garten Osprey bringing in his last fish of the day. Woodcocks rode over the area and you might hear a Long-eared Owl or Tawny Owl calling.

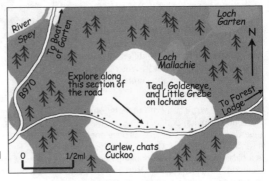

⑩ Loch Pityoulish
Background information

A BOUT halfway between Boat of Garten and Coylumbridge on the B970, this loch is always worth a quick scan for wildfowl, including Goosanders on the loch itself and Buzzards and Ospreys on the skyline.

On our last visit, we watched a Buzzard pluck a Mallard duckling from the surface of the loch, almost Osprey-like in its technique. It then flew to the reeds on the edge of the loch and deliberately drowned its prey.

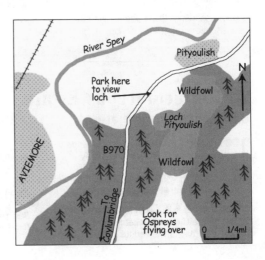

79

11 Aviemore
Background information

JUST WEST of Aviemore lies Craigellachie NNR, home to a well-known Peregrine nest. Park at the Tourist Information Centre at the south end of town, walk a bit further south and take a footpath through the Youth Hostel grounds, under the A9 until you reach the reserve which is well signed.

There are a series of trails through the birch wood, which should produce sightings of Redpoll, Redstart, Tree Pipit, Spotted Flycatcher and possibly Wood Warbler. The location of the Peregrine nest on the cliff can be identified by the white splash marks below it. Watch only from the path. Spring and summer are the best times to visit.

On the town's southern outskirts, off the road to Coylumbridge, is the Inverdruie Fish Farm, which has developed a terrific reputation for Osprey sightings. There is a hide (fee payable) overlooking one of the fishponds regularly used by Ospreys, especially juvenile birds in late summer. You can get some spectacular close-up views, and photo opportunities of fishing birds.

Understandably, this is popular with the

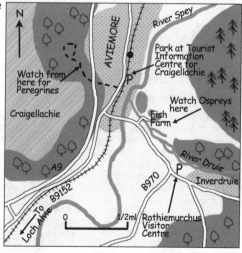

tourists so early mornings and evenings should be quieter. Check the surrounding trees and bushes for warblers and flycatchers.

A couple of miles south of Aviemore on the B9152 is Loch Alvie, always worth a quick scan for waterfowl including Goldeneye.

12 Rothiemurchus Estate
Background information

THIS HUGE ESTATE offers a whole range of activities from off-road driving to clay pigeon shooting. There are regular guided walks, though these are aimed more at general wildlife viewers rather than birdwatchers.

Your best bet is to call in to the shop/visitor centre, where there are toilet facilities. After picking up a map of the various footpaths, ask

to speak to one of the rangers. They are really helpful and will suggest the best areas to explore, or tell you where, for example, crossbills have been seen recently.
Check activities on www.rothiemurchus.net

See the Aviemore map above for the location of the Visitor Centre.

13 Moormore car park
Background information

B ETWEEN the Rothiemurchus visitor
centre and Loch Morlich lies this delightful
little picnic site that is good for Crested Tits.
If you don't get them in the trees
immediately around the area where you park,
walk down the path to the River Luineag and
check the trees on either bank.

Moormore is how my latest map spells it,
but I've seen various combinations of 'Mhor',
'Mor', 'Moor' and 'More' on other maps.
Whatever, this site also seems to be used as
a staging area for Ospreys waiting their turn
at the fish farm (see above) and I have seen
a 'flock' of four circling over the car park.

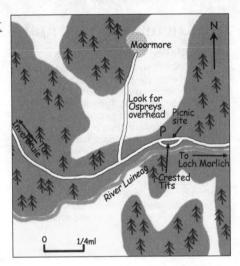

14 Loch Morlich
Background information

T HIS LOCH often holds
a Red-throated or
Black-throated Diver, as
well as Red-breasted
Mergansers and
Goldeneyes. If the birds
are present, they are
often fairly distant so you
will probably need a
telescope.

The area is very popular
with water sports
enthusiasts, so there is a
considerable amount of
disturbance. Early
mornings and late
evenings are the best for
birding. There are three
car parks (fees payable)
along the edge of the
loch.

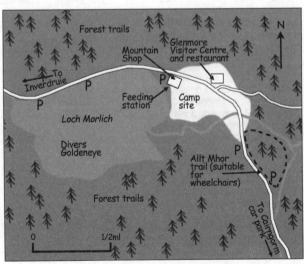

⑮ Glenmore Mountain Shop and Forest Park

Background information

THE SHOP IS on the right hand side of the road before you reach the Glenmore Forest Visitor Centre and there are plenty of signs to the large campsite here. There is a small café in the shop, with plenty of bird feeders outside to entertain you while drinking your coffee. Most of the visitors are Chaffinches, but you might pick out the occasional Siskin, Crested Tit, Great Spotted Woodpecker or red squirrel.

The excellent visitor centre (fee payable for all their car parks) has a multimedia display about local wildlife. There are several waymarked paths to explore, ranging from 30 minute strolls to six hour treks. A leaflet is available giving full details and trail descriptions. The Allt Mhor Interpretative Trail is suitable for wheelchairs. Facilities at the centre include a café and toilets.

Pine martens visit the rubbish skips here. Other mammals in the area include red and roe deer, badgers, foxes, wildcats and mountain hares. Birds include all the typical Caledonian forest species.

The Forestry Commission also arranges a series of nature-related walks every year. Phone 01479 861 220 for more details.

⑯ Cairngorm

Background information

FAMOUS for its montane species – Dotterel, Snow Bunting and Ptarmigan – the Cairngorms have long acted as a magnet for birders. Traditionally, birders would take the chairlift up to the top and start exploring from there, but things have changed recently with the introduction of the funicular railway.

To prevent huge numbers of visitors causing damage to this precious habitat, it was decided that anyone taking the railway to the tops, would not be allowed outside the immediate area round the café/shop/exhibition.

I have spoken to several disgruntled birders who, having made the expensive trip (£8 per person in 2004), hadn't realised that they couldn't go past the viewing platform. Having said that, a quick visit in typically mixed weather in 2004 produced sightings of two Ptarmigan, Snow Bunting, Ring Ouzel and Wheatear from the viewing platform and there is the occasional report of Dotterel.

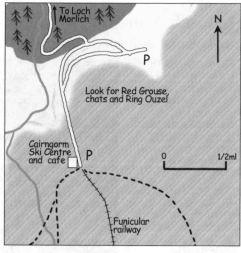

If you do want to explore the tops, it is perfectly possible, but you will have to start from the visitor centre and walk up from there – it takes about an hour before you reach the main birding areas. Go to the visitor centre first and ask about which routes have been most productive.

If you do decide to walk up, most birders follow the well-marked path to the summit of Ben Macdui. Other birds you might encounter include Meadow Pipits, Ring Ouzels, Peregrines and Golden Eagles, which hunt the plentiful mountain hares.

Snowy Owls are reported on rare occasions and you might encounter the occasional passing skua or wader. If Dotterel is your target species, mid-May to July is the optimum period to visit, most birds having moved away by the first week in August.

Despite the lack of access from the funicular, there are still disturbance problems from both walkers and birders. The situation is being monitored and there is a fair chance that you will be watched, so please behave responsibly and don't give birders a bad name. Keep to the paths. Don't fan out trying to flush birds if you are in a group and remember it is an offence to disturb a Schedule 1 bird at the nest.

Be prepared for weather that can change dramatically in an instant. You could easily find yourself engulfed in low cloud or caught up in a serious snowstorm, so wear appropriate clothing and make sure you have food, drink, good maps and a compass if you intend to stray far from the main paths. If you can't see the tops, it is not worth a visit. Go somewhere else and come back another day.

As you drive up to the large car park and visitor centre, look out for Wheatears and Red Grouse, as well as Britain's only herd of reindeer on the surrounding slopes.

Ptarmigan and Snow Buntings come down to the car park in winter, but the area is usually so busy that birds keep a low profile apart from the occasional Raven croaking as it flies over.

Check www.cairngormmountain.com for the latest details. There are toilet and café facilities at the visitor centre and at the Ptarmigan restaurant at the top.

⑰ Loch an Eilein
Background information

PLACE a ruined castle, once the haunt of the notorious outlaw, the Wolf of Badenoch, on an island in a loch and surround it with beautiful woodland and the entire world goes 'aaaaah'. This site, lying south of Aviemore off the B970, is one of the most attractive walks in Speyside and justifiably popular. It was recently voted the third most romantic location in Scotland.

From the car park (fee payable), head towards the visitor centre (toilet facilities) where displays show you, among others, the differences between pine cones chewed by squirrels and those that have had their seeds extracted by crossbills.

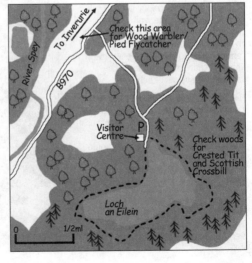

The walk round the loch takes a couple of hours and should provide you with views of all the main forest species including Crested Tit and Scottish Crossbill, Redstarts and Tree Pipits. The castle was the site of the last pair of Ospreys to nest in Speyside before they became extinct. While they no longer breed here, they do occasionally drift over.

As you leave the loch and drive back to the B970, the trees on the opposite side of the road often hold Wood Warblers and the occasional Pied Flycatcher.

---

⑱ Uath Lochans
Background information

L EAVING the B970 at Loch Insh, a minor road drops south to Glenfeshie Lodge, following the course of the River Feshie. Uath Lochans (Vath on some maps) are tucked away in a Forestry Commission picnic site on the western side of the river.

Apart from a few dog-walkers, I have never met another soul there, strange, because it is a delightful little spot to pass an hour or so and can easily be combined with further exploration of Glen Feshie or the nearby Insh Marshes.

There are three colour-coded trails to follow, though the white trail is likely to be the most profitable, taking in a full range of habitats in its short length. The red and green trails climb through the woods and afford stunning views over Loch Insh.

Look for Crested Tits and Scottish Crossbills around the car park area and along the way to the first of the four small lochans. A small hide overlooks the largest body of water and should produce sightings of Goldeneye and Wigeon, usually at the back edge of the lochan.

There is a good selection of raptors in the area with Buzzards, Osprey and Sparrowhawk over the woods, Peregrine and Merlin hunting – the

open area on the boardwalks is a good place to scan – and Golden Eagle, Hen Harrier and Short-eared Owl further down the glen.

If you drive on, you soon come to a car park on your left overlooking the river. This is a good place to look for Dippers, Grey Wagtails, Oystercatchers and Common Sandpipers as well as scanning the mountain ridges for raptors.

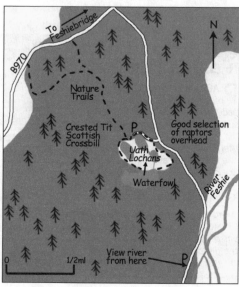

⑲ Carn Ban More
Background information

THE ROAD down the eastern side of Glen Feshie, reached via Feshiebridge, is nowhere near as pretty as its western counterpart but it does lead to the car park at Achlean (Auchlean on some maps), the starting point for the walk up Carn Ban More.

This is the other main route used by birders to explore the mountain tops of the Cairngorms. The advantage of this route is that it is a lot quieter, so your chances of seeing your target species are that much greater. The disadvantage is that you have to start from ground level, so expect a two-hour climb to the tops as opposed to a one-hour trek if you start from the visitor centre by the funicular railway.

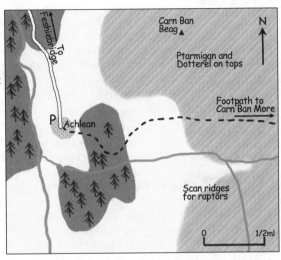

Likely bird species/other fauna and flora for the area

All year	Mistle Thrush	Hen Harrier	Pied Flycatcher (occasional)
Teal	Goldcrest	Merlin	
Wigeon	Crested Tit	Peregrine	*Winter*
Goldeneye	Treecreeper	Oystercatcher	Greylag Goose
Little Grebe	Raven	Dotterel	Waxwing
Red Grouse	Siskin	Golden Plover	Fieldfare
Ptarmigan	Lesser Redpoll	Lapwing	Redwing
Black Grouse	Common Crossbill (in	Dunlin	Great Grey Shrike
Capercaillie	irruption years)	Snipe	(more or less annual)
Grey Partridge	Scottish/Parrot Crossbill	Redshank	
Red-legged Partridge	Snow Bunting	Curlew	*Other wildlife*
Buzzard		Common Sandpiper	Pine marten
Golden Eagle	*Summer*	Cuckoo	Badger
Sparrowhawk	Goosander	Short-eared Owl	Otter
Woodcock	Red-breasted	Tree Pipit	Red squirrel
Tawny Owl	Merganser	Ring Ouzel	Mountain hare
Long-eared Owl	Red-throated Diver	Whinchat	Red and roe deer
Great Spotted	(occasional)	Wheatear	Reindeer
Woodpecker	Black-throated Divers	Willow Warbler	Daubenton's bat
Grey Wagtail	(occasional)	Wood Warbler	Wildflowers
Dipper	Slavonian Grebe	Redstart	Butterflies
Stonechat	Osprey	Spotted Flycatcher	Dragonflies

Key points

- **Facilities (food, petrol and toilets) in Kingussie**

- **Fantastic all-round wildlife**

- **Take your time**

- **Evening guided walks particularly recommended**

- **Free access at all times**

- **Three hides including the visitor centre**

- **No disabled access to trails**

- **Loch Insh can be viewed from car at a couple of points**

INSH MARSHES has always been one of my favourite RSPB reserves. To start with, it is massive, covering some 2,300 acres. A drive all round the reserve covers a distance of about 15 miles and you could easily spend a whole day in the area, or combine a visit with one or more of the Speyside sites.

Not everyone agrees with me though: the sightings book gets a few comments about how writers spent a 'whole half hour' here and only saw half a dozen birds. This is not a 'quick' reserve, but like a glass of Speyside malt whisky, it needs to be sipped slowly and savoured, not gulped in one.

The main reason to visit is simple; this is one of the most important wetland areas in Europe, with about 1,000 breeding pairs of waders – some 25% of Strathspey's wader population – together with about 50% of the UK's breeding Goldeneyes. There are significant breeding populations of Ospreys, Wood Sandpipers, Spotted Crakes and Wigeon, with important wintering counts of Hen Harriers and Whooper Swans. It has recently been afforded National Nature Reserve status.

More than 200 bird species have been recorded with about 120 seen each year. However, this is a good all-round reserve with records of 27 mammals, 500 invertebrates, 63 fungi, 100 lichen and 147 mosses. We were talking to an expert on lichens from Aberdeen University who was having a great time. She had recorded nearly 30 species of lichen already and was still on her first tree!

I suggest visiting some of the more obscure sections of the reserve. You'll be the only person around and who knows what you might find. A passing Wryneck perhaps, or even something a bit more exotic? Bluethroats once bred here and Icterine Warblers have been heard singing.

If you do only have a limited

Summer visitors are likely to see family parties of Goldeneye once the chicks have left the nest holes.

amount of time available, then I strongly recommend one of the regular guided walks from April through to August where the warden can focus your attention on some of the key spots. Leaflets detailing all the walks are available from the Visitor Centre, Loch Garten or one of the tourist offices. Details are also printed in the local newspapers.

Particularly recommended are the Night Noises walks. Not only is this your best chance of hearing the elusive Spotted Crake, but you get excellent views of displaying waders, a bit of bat watching, some moth trapping and, if you are lucky, sightings of a badger. Exploring the reserve at 2am is an experience not easily forgotten.

Dawn can be a magical time too, as the mist lifts to reveal maybe a family of fox cubs frolicking in front of the hide, accompanied by the dawn chorus. This is a fairly noisy reserve, with the calls of the various gulls and waders just about managing to drown out the rumble of the lorries thundering past on the A9.

This tour starts from Kingussie (pronounced King-you-see) and works its way anti-clockwise around the reserve and Loch Insh. If you see any sports being played on the local fields, stop to watch for a bit. Kingussie is the centre of excellence for shinty, a game that seems to involve hitting your opponent with a big stick, the little white ball being almost incidental.

The reserve is of interest throughout the year though, as usual, spring and early summer are the most dynamic times. Partial flooding in winter brings excellent numbers of wildfowl as well as the harrier roost.

The trails are not suitable for disabled access. There are no toilet facilities on the reserve, the nearest are in Kingussie. If you enjoy longer walks, the newly created Badenoch Way takes in the whole eastern side of the reserve. Leaflets are available from the usual sources and these include fuller descriptions of the various trails.

For more information about the reserve, including an old systematic report, visit www.kincraig.com/rspb

How to get there

Nearest large town: Aviemore is 15 miles N of Kingussie, which is well signed off A9.

From Kingussie, head E on B970, stopping off as indicated on the map overleaf. Three miles after passing through Insh, turn L on minor road to Kincraig. After crossing the Spey, turn L on B9152 back to Kingussie.

The distance of this tour is 15 miles

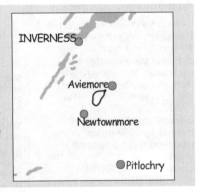

❶ RSPB Visitor Centre

Background information

THE ENTRANCE TO the main RSPB reserve (free admission, open all hours) is on your left, about three-quarters of a mile past the barracks, SE of Kingussie. The information centre has good views over the reserve but a better vantage point is probably from the Gordonhall hide. Breeding waders are the star birds here in spring and summer with Snipe, Redshanks, Lapwings and Curlews all strutting their stuff, while simultaneously trying to repel birds from the large Black-headed Gull colony. Roe deer can usually be seen and this is a good spot to scan for raptors.

Marsh Harriers are seen most years, while Hen Harrier numbers build up from late summer with the winter roost sometimes reaching 15 birds. The views over the Monadhliath Mountains to your left produce the occasional distant Peregrine. Sparrowhawks often use the fence posts just to the right of the hide as a lookout.

Buzzards are ever-present and you sometimes glimpse a distant Osprey, though you will probably get better views at the other end of the loch. There are at least four pairs of Ospreys, in the general area, so you should catch up with one in the course of a day's birding.

Breeding waterfowl include Wigeon, Teal and Goldeneyes, which are doing particularly well here. Pintails are suspected of breeding. Numbers of wildfowl increase dramatically in winter when the reserve floods and there are usually a hundred or so Whooper Swans present as well as a roosting flock of Greylag goose.

Wood Sandpipers no longer breed on the reserve itself but are still in the general area. Your only real chance to see one is high above the reserve. They display higher than any other breeding waders and this is a useful distinguishing feature. Having said that, I have only ever seen birds once and that was against a background of total cloud cover. Despite my graphic attempts at describing the shapes of the clouds I failed to get anyone else to see the birds.

Ruthven Barracks, were built after the 1715 rebellion on the site of yet another of the Wolf of Badenoch's castles. It dominates the local landscape and the extra height gives you a good view of the reserve spreading out in front of you.

The barracks are floodlit at night and it is worth a walk up to the top towards dusk where you can watch Snipe drumming at eye level.

On still spring and summer nights, listen for the *'quip, quip'* of Spotted Crakes, the squeal of Water Rails, metallic chunnering of a Sedge Warbler or the non-stop reeling of a Grasshopper Warbler. There is usually a pipistrelle bat or two flying round your head.

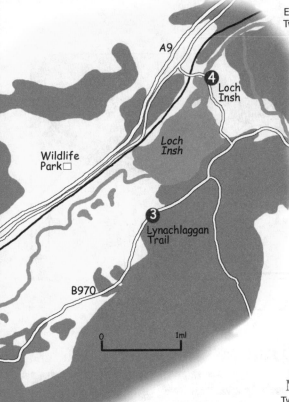

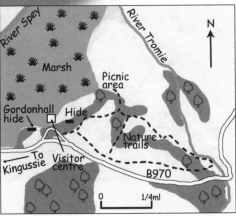

Equally elusive are the Spotted Crakes. Two or three birds are heard calling most years, though not always from the same areas. Talking to the warden, he reckoned that only one bird had actually been seen in getting on for 20 years. That was when one of the assistant wardens almost trod on it. The bird flew ten yards down the path, disappeared into the vegetation and that was that. Still nights in May and June are the best times to listen. If you get the chance though, go on one of the night walks (see above) as the warden will know where that year's birds are calling from.

There is always the chance of an otter sighting too. Look out for a change in bird behaviour. Normally, there is a running battle between the waders and wildfowl on one side against the marauding gulls and corvids. If all the birds suddenly start fighting on the same side, and mobbing something, it's a pretty sure bet that an otter is out looking for eggs or chicks.

Nature trails

Two trails starting from the car park offer walks of about one and a half and three hours. These lead through woods to another hide and a picnic area with the longer trail taking in a stretch of the River Tromie. In spring and summer you should pick up Willow Warbler, Spotted Flycatcher, Great Spotted Woodpecker, Redstart and Tree Pipit here, with the outside chance of a Wood Warbler or a Pied Flycatcher. The river should produce Grey Wagtail and Dipper.

This is a very good spot for wild flowers and orchids. Butterflies include Scotch argus and there are red squirrels in the woods.

For likely bird species see page 91

② River Tromie
Background information

A MILE OUT of the reserve, the road crosses the fast-flowing River Tromie. Parking is limited here so take care not to block anyone in. The bridge is a good spot to look for Dippers. You can often see the birds in flight as well as walking under water. For such a dumpy bird, they zoom along on whirring wings, so keep your eyes peeled.

If you are looking for a longer walk, a path leads along Glen Tromie on the east side of the river. After passing through woodland, the path opens out onto moorland. Merlin, Peregrine and Hen Harrier are all present in the area.

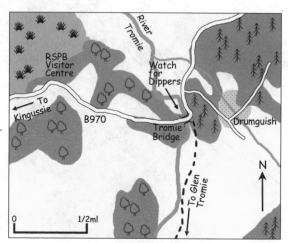

③ Lynachlaggan Trail
Background information

JUST AFTER DRIVING through the village of Insh, look for an RSPB sign on the gate on your left and park in a lay-by on the opposite side of the road. This is very poorly signed and easy to miss. This is the start of the Lynachlaggan trail, leading through a mixture of birch wood and large juniper bushes to overlook one of the wettest areas of the reserve.

This trail is good for waterfowl with more Redstarts and Wood Warblers in the wood, plus Scotch argus butterflies in the clearings on warm summer days. Winter brings good numbers of Redwings and Fieldfares, together with mixed flocks of Siskins and Redpolls in the birches.

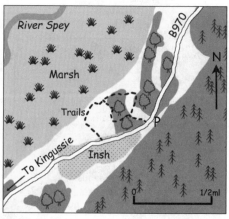

As ever, expect the unexpected. We have had a Corn Crake fly over the bonnet of the car near here.

④ Loch Insh

Background information

FOR VIEWS OVER the loch, continue on the B970 from Lynachlaggan and take the next turn on the left by the water sports centre on a minor road to Kincraig and park by the church, famous for its ancient Celtic bell. The trees and bushes from here to the loch are usually alive with tits, warblers and Goldcrests and it is hard to miss the large rookery. Ospreys regularly fish in the loch.

Goldeneyes are always present among a good selection of wildfowl. Walk down to the bridge over the River Spey for another good vantage point where Goosanders and Red-breasted Mergansers are often seen.

After driving over the bridge, turn left towards Kingussie on the B9152 and park after a mile for one of the best views over the loch. A mile further on, you come to the entrance to the Highland Wildlife Park (fee payable,

check www.highlandwildlifepark.org for details). The theme here is creatures that roamed the Highlands, past and present, with everything from wolves to eagles.

Even if zoos are not your cup of tea, it is still worth stopping here after dark in spring and summer to listen for possible Spotted Crake and Grasshopper Warbler. Dusk visits might also produce Tawny Owl and Woodcock.

Continue back to Kingussie to finish the loop.

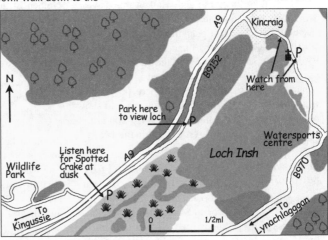

Likely bird species/other flora and fauna

Spring to autumn	Spotted Crake (chance	Sedge Warbler	Fieldfare
Teal	of hearing)	Wood Warbler	Redwing
Pintail	Water Rail	Willow Warbler	Siskin
Wigeon	Redshank	Goldcrest	Redpoll
Goldeneye	Snipe	Spotted Flycatcher	
Goosander	Lapwing	Pied Flycatcher	*Other wildlife*
Red-breasted	Curlew	(occasional)	Bats
Merganser	Wood Sandpiper (rare)		Roe deer
Marsh Harrier	Woodcock	*Winter*	Otter
Osprey	Tree Pipit	Greylag Goose	Badger
Sparrowhawk	Grey Wagtail	Whooper Swan	Red squirrel
Buzzard	Dipper	Common wildfowl	Wildflowers
Golden Eagle (rare)	Redstart	(large numbers)	Orchids
Peregrine (possible)	Grasshopper Warbler	Hen Harrier	Scotch argus butterfly

Key points

- **Both routes very remote — no facilities apart from a teashop or two around Glenelg**

- **Nearest garage in Shiel Bridge, also a Tourist Information office there**

- **Northern leg popular with tourists — can be busy**

- **Some difficult driving towards the end of southern leg**

- **Choose a fine day if you are going over the northern leg**

- **Wheelchair friendly throughout — bird from or by the car except walk from Kinloch Hourn and area round the brochs**

THE TWO legs of this west coast tour couldn't be more different as it visits both ends of Loch Hourn, reputed to be one of the prettiest sea-lochs on the west coast and not in the least bit justifying its name – The Loch of Hell.

Though separated by just six miles as the Hooded Crow flies, the journey by road covers more than 70 miles, end to end. Half of this drive came about by accident. I was just planning to include the area around the Five Sisters of Kintail, but the lure of a long, unclassified road into the middle of nowhere proved irresistible. It just goes to show what you can find if you are prepared to get off the beaten track.

Both legs are accessed from a main road that leads to Kyle of Lochalsh and the bridge over to Skye. Taking the minor road westwards from the A87, the first leg starts off gently, following the wooded shoreline of Loch Garry before opening out as you follow the River Garry through a dark, brooding, at times almost malevolent, valley.

Skirting Loch Quoich as you approach the coast, the already meagre road narrows even further and its twists and turns mean several bends and

humps in the road are taken totally blind. Even though you are unlikely to meet anyone else, there is still a feeling of driving into the unknown.

The birds too seem to add to a feeling of remoteness. A Cuckoo might call without being seen, or a Greenshank stalk the river shallows near the dam. If you are really lucky, you might come across a Golden Eagle in hot pursuit of a mountain hare, only to lose sight of it seconds later as it disappears down a gully you hadn't noticed.

Even when you get to the coast, you can't sit back and enjoy the views. You have to get out and walk round the headland before many more species offer themselves up. The whole feeling is that you have to work for your birds here. It really is mean, moody and magnificent.

What a contrast with the second leg, which approaches Loch Hourn from the north. This is how everyone imagines the west coast to be. Chocolate-box perfect views of more mountains than you can shake a stick at. There are about 30 Munros here (mountains over 3,000 feet) and impressive vistas whichever way you look.

This route takes you over the tops, giving you a totally

different view of the local topography. Being on high gives you a better chance to look for raptors, but it is not as easy as it seems. There are far more mountain ridges to scan, leading to the inevitable feeling that while you are looking one way, a Peregrine or whatever is flying behind you.

As you descend to Glenelg (apparently the only palindromic place name in Scotland), check for Twite around the farm buildings. There are great views over to southern Skye and a ferry at the bottom of the road takes you straight over to the Kylerhea otter reserve (see page 108).

So, which Hourn of the dilemma to choose? The second Hourn is undoubtedly more scenically stunning, and you will probably see a few more species. However, it is a very popular tourist drive so avoid weekends and Bank Holidays if possible.

The first route only reaches the end of the loch, so gives poor views if you want to birdwatch from or near your car. But it comes into its own if you want to explore the valley and that wilderness and solitude is fantastic. Heads or tails?

The best times to visit are spring, summer and autumn. You wouldn't want to attempt either drive in winter.

How to get there

Nearest large town: Fort William lies about 25 miles S of the A82-A87 junction at Invergarry.

The A87 runs to Kyle of Lochalsh and the bridge over to Skye.
For the southern Hourn route, leave A87 on minor road about six miles W of Invergarry, travelling 22 miles to Kinloch Hourn along N edge of Loch Garry. There is only one road so you can't get lost. Retrace your steps to the main road.

For the northern route, continue along A87 and take the minor road W from Shiel Bridge to Glenelg, Turn L in Glenelg and follow the coast road round to the

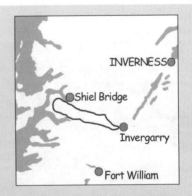

end, again about 22 miles. The road to the Pictish brochs is well signposted.

From Fort William, southern leg is 100 miles, northern leg is 156 miles.

Loch Hourn southern approach
Background information

SHORTLY after leaving Invergarry, a minor road follows the north shore of Loch Garry. The road starts off wide and is lined with birch trees, alive in summer with the ubiquitous song of Willow Warblers and common woodland birds. The scenery is pleasant but nothing out of the ordinary – yet.

After passing the loch, you enter the wilderness proper. This is a road that looks, and drives, a lot better going in than coming out, so take your time and stop frequently en route to Kinloch Hourn and then return at a faster pace.

There is a massive hydro-electric dam on Loch Quoich and you won't see much on the loch itself – the River Garry which joins the two lochs is much more productive. Look out for Snipe displaying. Tree and Meadow Pipits need careful separation.

Halfway along Loch Quoich, there is a

360° panorama, an excellent place to stop for a coffee and scan the mountain ridges for raptors. With some serious watching, you would be very disappointed if you didn't see Golden Eagle, Merlin and Peregrine somewhere along this route.

The last stretch of road is challenging as it twists, turns and drops away from you in a roller coaster ride of extremely narrow blind bends. Park sensibly here and don't wander too far from the car in case you need to move it quickly. As well as more raptors, you should see Stonechat, Whinchat and Wheatear. Mammals include red deer and wild goats.

Kinloch Hourn is such a romantic

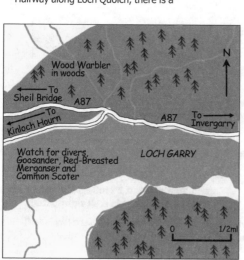

sounding place yet it is little more than a few houses at the end of the road. There's not a great deal to be seen from the village itself, though this depends on the state of the tide. Avoid driving past the car park (small fee payable); the narrow road just ends and you will find yourself having to attempt a 27-point turn.

For the best views of the loch, continue walking past the car park. The scenic path beside Loch Hourn towards Barrisdale Bay, about seven miles away, is well maintained with a few short ascents, but it can be quite dangerous when wet. The full walk takes about three hours, but everyone reckons on about four hours coming back. There is a bothy there for serious walkers intending to stay overnight.

As you explore the sea loch, look out for more divers, both Red-throated and Black-throated feeding on the sea, along with Shags and Black Guillemots. Along the shore, typical species will include Rock Pipits, Oystercatchers and Ringed Plovers. One of the offshore islands has a small heronry and birds can often be seen fishing the shallows. A few Arctic and Common Terns breed and can be seen fishing offshore. Otters and seals can be seen.

Continues on page 96

Likely bird species/other fauna

All year	Common woodland birds	Peregrine	Ring Ouzel
Shag	Common wildfowl	Merlin	Wood Warbler
Grey Heron		Snipe	Willow Warbler
Golden Eagle	*Summer*	Ringed Plover	
Black Guillemot	Goosander	Greenshank	*Other wildlife*
Rock Pipit	Red-breasted Merganser	Arctic Tern	Red deer
Grey Wagtail	Common Scoter	Common Tern	Feral goats
Stonechat	Red-throated Diver	Wheatear	Pine marten
Raven	Black-throated Diver	Whinchat	Otter

From page 95

If you have time on the return leg, it might be worth driving along the A87 to look at the three large lochs in the area – Garry, Loyne and Cluanie – which hold small numbers of Common Scoters. Rarely will you get a better chance to study at close range, a duck normally only seen distantly on the sea. Very attractive they are too, with the bright yellow bill contrasting well with the jet-black body of the males.

Look out for divers too with Red-breasted Mergansers and Teal also on the loch. Typical birds of the loch edge are Pied and Grey Wagtails and Common Sandpipers.

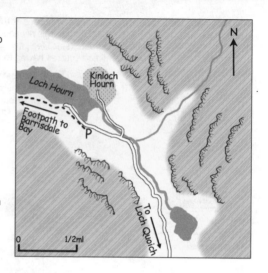

Loch Hourn northern approach
Background information

SHIEL BRIDGE, which lies at the southern point of Loch Duich, is a good starting point for this leg of the tour. As well as filling up with petrol, check out the Kintail Outdoor Centre, which can offer advice on the best places to walk as well as pass on any information on recent bird sightings. The rangers here run

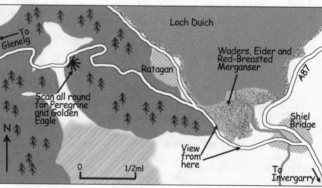

a full range of guided walks. As always, if you intend to do some serious walking, perhaps in search of Ptarmigan on the tops, make sure that you are properly prepared.

As you leave Shiel Bridge, there is a good place to scan the sea loch just after you cross

the cattle grid. The tide line and various channels should produce a good range of feeding and scavenging birds. Look out for the five common gull species, Goosanders, Eiders, Grey Wagtails, Grey Herons, Common Sandpipers and Hooded Crows.

The trees where you park hold Wood and Willow Warblers. The whole area is great for mammals, though your chances of seeing them during daylight hours are remote. The list includes wildcat, pine marten, fox, badger, otter, seals and porpoises.

This is the last birding you will do at ground level for a while, as the road climbs rapidly in a fantastic switchback drive through the Mam Ratagan Pass to Glenelg. This is one of those rare roads where the drive is just as good in either direction.

Immediately at the end of the first long climb, there is a large car park. This is a great place to scan for raptors, but as it is a very popular tourist spot, you can guarantee a never-ending series of questions if you set up your telescope.

The road eventually drops down into Glenelg from where you can scan the Sound of Sleat. Look out for Red-throated Divers, Cormorants, Shags and Black Guillemots on the sea and Ringed Plovers and Rock Pipits along the shore. Curlews and Whimbrel move through in spring. There is an outside chance of a White-tailed Eagle from Skye moving through. Look for every bird for miles around mobbing it.

Seals are usually present and this is the area where Gavin Maxwell lived when he wrote *Ring of Bright Water*, so otters are always a possibility anywhere along the shore here. Turn left in Glenelg and head towards Arnisdale. Again, there are plenty of places to stop and scan and

you should find the occasional auk and Eider for your list if you have not seen them already. Ravens are easy to find here though you will probably hear their deep bass '*kronk*' before you see them.

To complete your trip, retrace your steps from Arnisdale and take a minor road inland at Eilanreach towards two Iron Age brochs. These fortified dwelling places are well over 2000 years old and remarkably well preserved. There are Whinchats and Stonechats in the surrounding fields, Wood Warblers in the woods and Dippers on the stream. There is a large Sand Martin colony here too.

Likely bird species/other fauna

All year	Dipper	Black-throated Diver	Curlew
Eider	Stonechat	Peregrine	
Grey Heron	Hooded Crow	Common Sandpiper	*Other wildlife*
Shag	Raven	Ringed Plover	Grey and common seals
Cormorant	Twite	Sand Martin	Otter
Golden Eagle		Whinchat	Porpoise
White-tailed Eagle (rare)	*Summer*	Wood Warbler	Wildcat
Black Guillemot	Goosander		Pine marten
Rock Pipit	Red-breasted Merganser	*Spring/autumn*	
Grey Wagtail	Red-throated Diver	Whimbrel	

Key points

- Plenty of facilities (food, toilets, petrol) on the island

- Many places now open on a Sunday, though don't take it for granted

- No toll charges to drive onto the island

- Though the island is very popular with tourists, they tend not to go to the places mentioned in the text

- One of the best places in Britain to see Golden Eagles and White-tailed Eagles

- Genuine Rock Doves

- Weather can be very changeable. Mountain ranges can disappear into low cloud in an instant. Be prepared if you go hill-walking

- The whole island is very good for coastal wildlife

IT IS DIFFICULT to find anywhere on Skye where the views are anything less than sensational. Golden Eagles are present here in a higher density than anywhere else in Europe. There are White-tailed Eagles and Corn Crakes too, as well as plenty of places to seawatch. The supporting cast of otters, whales and dolphins is pretty good too. Yet for some reason, birders just don't come here, preferring either Mull to the south, the Western Isles or staying on the mainland. Access to Skye, since the road bridge has opened, is easy, with no ferries involved for those with a tendency towards seasickness. Now that the much-hated toll road charges have been scrapped, there isn't a single remaining reason why you shouldn't visit this amazing island.

Having said that the views are great, you might have to take my word for it. It has been known to rain here and combinations of an abundance of the wet stuff, low cloud and seemingly permanent mist can serve to obscure a lot of the island. As one friend put it, 'I've been to Skye three times now and haven't seen it once!'

But when the weather does clear, you can be left with many memorable images. Hooded Crows have learned how to drop shellfish onto rocks on the beach as an easy way to open them. On the sea behind them, seals and porpoises play while maybe a Black-throated Diver arrives for the winter. Get the weather right and seabirds can stream past your chosen headland, where a sudden feeding frenzy might attract the attention of a passing minke whale.

Raptors can be spectacular too. We have eyeballed Peregrines and Merlins, perched on fence posts right

The 'flying barn door' nickname makes sense once you've seen your first giant-sized White-tailed Eagle.

How to get there

Nearest large town: Kyle of Lochalsh is on E side of the bridge.

From the bridge, follow A87 to Portree. This road passes through Broadford and also goes past the Aros centre (well signed), just before you get into Portree itself.

Leave Portree N on A855 towards Staffin. As you continue N, scan the lochs on your R and continue until you see Loch Mealt on your L. A large car park on your R gives you access to the cliffs and waterfall of Kilt Rock.

Continue N through Staffin for a couple of miles, then turn L onto a minor road in Brogaig, signposted to the Quiraing. Park in second car park (the first one is by a cemetery).

Turn L at bottom of road into Uig unless you are particularly looking for Corn Crakes, in which case, turn R and explore the road between here and the Flora Macdonald monument.

After exploring Uig, head towards Portree on A87 but turn off R towards Dunvegan on B8036/A850 after about nine miles. Continue into Dunvegan and follow signs to castle.

Keep straight on past the castle for 3/4 mile and park on your L in one of the larger passing places.

For Neist Point, continue on A850 to A863 Sligachan-Dunvegan road. Just S of Dunvegan turn onto B884 towards Glendale, and then follow signs along a minor road on your L towards Neist Point.

Retrace your steps along A850/A87 to Portree. If you are heading for the bridge, take A863 E towards

Sligachan, Broadford and Kyleakin.

The Kylerhea Otter Haven is well signposted from the Kyleakin-Broadford stretch of A87. Follow the road towards Kylerhea and the Glenelg Ferry and the car park is on your L just before you get to Klyerhea itself.

For the Sleat peninsula, take A851 off the Kyleakin-Broadford stretch of A87 and head down to Armadale. On your return, turn L on a minor road to Tarskavaig and follow the minor road around until it rejoins the A851.

Glen Brittle is well signposted off B8009. Take A863 Sligachan to Dunvegan road and turn L onto B8009 towards Carbost and the Talisker distillery. Glen Brittle is on your L after a couple of miles. Simply follow the minor road down to the car park. There is a small shop and toilets in the seasonal campsite. The mileage for the northern loop is approximately 110 miles. The southern loop is approximately 120 miles taking in Kylrhea, Broadford and Glen Brittle but not including the Sleat peninsula.

Key points

- Plenty of wildlife cruises available

- All the sites mentioned except Kylerhea can be birded from, or no more than a few yards from the car

next to the car. Having just watched a massive White-tailed Eagle fly in front of us, a quick scan of the sky produced five Golden Eagles and nine Buzzards riding the same thermal of hot air. If you see nothing else on your stay, sights like that become indelibly etched into the memory banks.

The bridge has certainly opened up the island to tourism and there has been a marked shift

Ferries to Western Isles

Loch Snizort

B886

B884

6

Neist Point

5 Dunvegan

0   5mls

A863

To Sligachan

from God towards Mammon with many visitor facilities now opening on Sundays, something unheard of, even a few years ago. Every other house on the island now seems to double up as a craft shop.

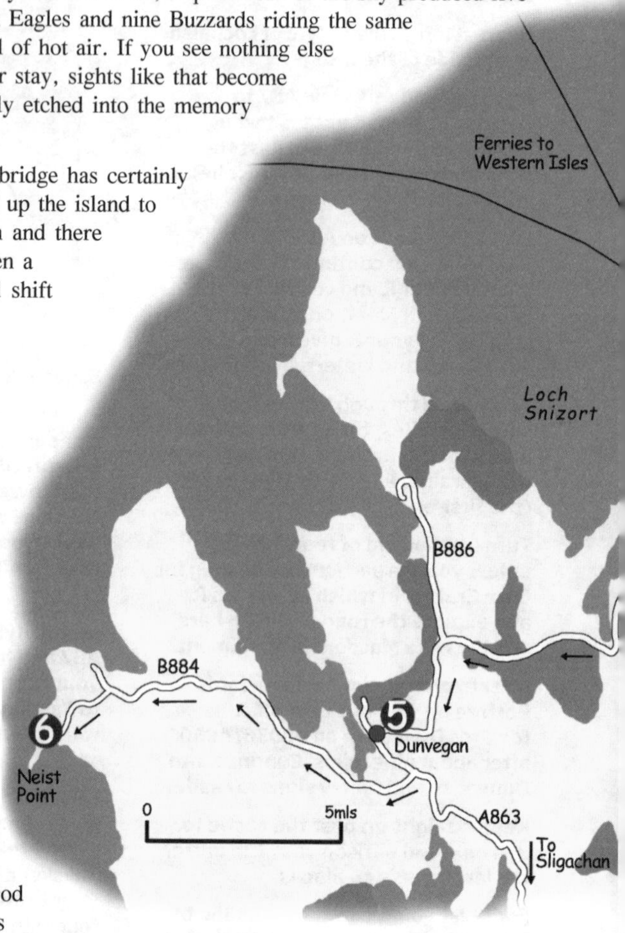

There shouldn't be any trouble finding food, petrol or accommodation. Not every one has moved with the times though. One of the biggest – and poshest – hotels on the island looked at us as though we were Martians when someone in our

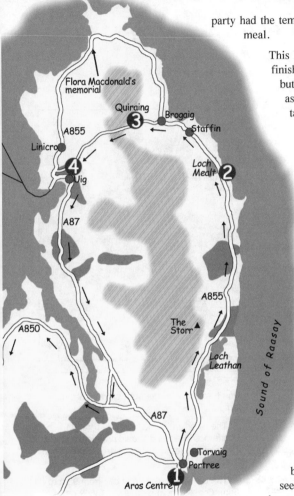

party had the temerity to ask for a vegetarian meal.

This Northern loop tour starts and finishes at Portree, the island's capital but it is perfectly possible to do this as a day trip from the mainland – it takes about an hour from the bridge to Portree, plus any time for additional stops. There are plenty of other places to visit on the island and you could easily spend your entire holiday here and not get bored. Several of these extra sites are included in the Southern loop tour.

Skye is an excellent centre if you want to combine your birding with a walking holiday. The Cuillins – both Red and Black – attract walkers and climbers from all round the world and anyone managing to reach the tops can expect to get close-up views of Ptarmigan as well as eagles.

If you want a large bird list, then spring and summer are the best times to visit – the island can seem very quiet once all the migrants have gone. Having said that, seawatching, and the mini-pelagic – see page 107 – are at their best in autumn. This would be my pick if you wanted to find something out of the ordinary. Eagles will still be showing very well with plenty of young birds on the wing and there is always the chance of the unexpected turning up – a rare shearwater perhaps, or an American wader, as well as the first returning winter migrants such as geese and thrushes. With so few birders around, simply enjoy finding your own birds.

The Northern Loop

❶ The Aros Centre
Background information

A MILE OR SO south of Portree you see a big sign for the Aros Centre, which acts as the cultural centre on Skye, together with a smaller one for woodland walks. It is the third sign that is most likely to attract your attention though – the Sea Eagle Exhibition.

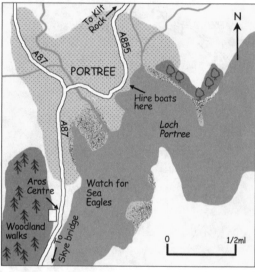

The Aros Centre has a cinema and theatre as well as shops and a restaurant. If you go in to the eagle exhibition (free for RSPB members), you will see live CCTV footage of a White-tailed Eagle's nest. Or not, as the case may be; the nest failed in 2002 and there were recorded highlights on display. A warden will answer your questions throughout the summer, with the centre staff on hand at other times.

There are currently four pairs of White-tailed Eagles (Sea Eagles is their old name) on Skye. For obvious reasons, no-one is going to tell you exactly where they are nesting, though the centre did suggest a couple of spots where you have a good chance of seeing them.

A good place is round Portree itself. Purely by chance, the Aros Centre has a fantastic view down Portree Bay and into Loch Portree so you can sit outside the café and watch from there.

Birds are sometimes seen from the impromptu wildlife cruises offered by some of the fishermen in the harbour. There are no organised boat trips as such, you just have to see if anyone is willing to take you out.

The eagles – you won't miss them, they've been likened to a flying solar eclipse – can be seen anywhere around here though as usual,

you have to be in the right place at the right time.

The woodland walks here are through coniferous forest and should produce a typical range of species including Siskin, Goldcrest and Treecreeper.

The centre is open every day from 9am to 6pm. Contact them on 01478 613649 or email aros@demon.co.uk

Likely bird species

All year
White-tailed Eagle
Common woodland birds

② Loch Mealt and Kilt Rock
Background information

A S YOU HEAD north along the eastern edge of the Trotternish peninsula, your view will be dominated on your left by the Old Man of Storr, a magnificent natural 165-foot obelisk perched on top of the ridge. To your right, there are views over the Sound of Raasay. Parties of Ravens and Hooded Crows squabble overhead, usually in pursuit of a Buzzard or two.

The fresh water lochs by the side of the road sometimes hold Red-throated Divers; a couple of pairs breed on the smaller mountain lochans. Black-throated Divers used to breed but are now only occasional visitors. Greenshanks and Dunlin breed on the peatlands and can sometimes be seen feeding along loch edges or in any of the tidal bays around the island.

Check out the pigeons round here. They are likely to be Rock Doves, the ancestors of the feral pigeons found in every town and city. This is one of the best places to see pure birds – look for the white rump and two complete black wingbars.

Stonechats greet you as you pull in to the viewing spot at Kilt Rock. It is the seabirds though that take centre stage, with colonies of various gulls, Fulmars and Kittiwakes on the impressive black basalt columns and assorted horizontal strata. The tartan colours give the rock its name.

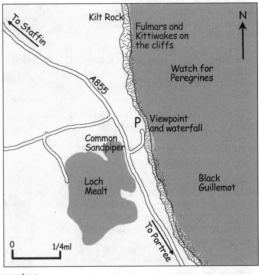

If you don't get vertigo, look for Rock Pipits on the shore with Black Guillemots in the bay. Razorbills and Guillemots are occasionally seen on the sea with Gannets, dolphins and porpoises as the summer progresses. Peregrines patrol the cliff.

Explore the edges of Mealt Loch – on both sides of the road - for Greylag Geese and Common Sandpipers.

Likely bird species/other fauna

All year	Spring/summer		Other wildlife
Rock Dove	Red-throated Diver	Dunlin	Grey and common seals
Rock Pipit	Peregrine	Greenshank	Dolphins
Stonechat	Fulmar	Guillemot	Porpoises
Hooded Crow	Kittiwake	Razorbill	
Raven		Black Guillemot	

❸ The Quiraing
Background information

ENERGETIC BIRDERS who enjoy upland walks will enjoy the challenge of walking up to the Quiraing, a geological fault caused by land slipping. Quiraing means 'round fold or pen', though the translation doesn't do any sort of justice to these amazing rock formations, all entirely natural and dating back some 150 million years.

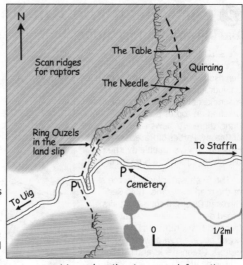

The Needle is a 120ft high pinnacle, while the Table is a flat summit which makes a good spot for scanning for raptors and, on clear days, enjoying the views back to Wester Ross and Torridon.

As you climb into the mountains, to the Quiraing, Wheatears become common and Ring Ouzels thrive in the areas of landslip. But it is the raptors that are the stars, with Golden Eagle, Hen Harrier, Merlin, Peregrine and Kestrel present.

The views from the road are fine but if you want to explore the strange rock formations further, and increase your field of view, then park in the second car park and follow the well-marked path. The path is good to begin with but the narrow tracks higher up are steep and gravelly, so care is needed.

The return trip takes about 90 minutes without stopping for birding, so allow at least double that as you scan the ridges. Wandering Red Kites from the Black Isle reintroduction programme are also seen occasionally.

Likely bird species	
All year	Red Kite
Golden Eagle	Peregrine
	Merlin
Spring/summer	Wheatear
Hen Harrier	Ring Ouzel

---

❹ Uig area
Background information

THE ROAD BETWEEN Uig and the Flora Macdonald monument can be very good for Corn Crakes. Listen for their rasping '*crex crex*' calls on warm summer nights, particularly where you

Likely bird species		
All year	Rock Dove	***Autumn/spring***
Eider	Twite	Turnstone
Shag		Ringed Plover
Gulls	***Summer***	Oystercatcher
Black Guillemot	Corn Crake (more likely to hear than see)	Curlew

come across iris beds. The villages of Linicro and Uig itself have been productive in the past. You would be very lucky to actually see one of these elusive birds though. Look out too for Twite around the crofts on this stretch of road.

The bay at Uig attracts large numbers of gulls and the occasional passage wader to supplement the usual Curlews and Oystercatchers. Late summer sees numbers of Turnstones and Ringed Plovers building up.

There is usually a Black Guillemot or two around the ferry terminal, with a few Eiders scattered among the Shags. It is from here that you catch the ferry to the Western Isles (see below).

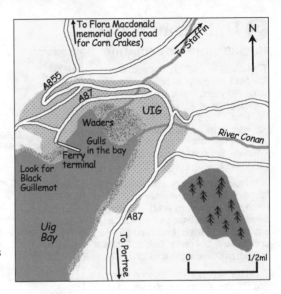

Ferry from Uig to the Western Isles

THIS ISN'T AN organised wildlife cruise as such, but a trip that will appeal more to the hardened seawatcher, though don't let that put you off. Anyone will enjoy the sheer spectacle on offer here.

It is hugely expensive to take your car over and not really practical unless you are planning a long stay. What you can do instead is to travel as a foot passenger. You have two options. The cheapest way is to go on a non-landing cruise; the ferry sails out, turns round and comes back with you birding all the way, something like a three and a half hour trip.

Alternatively, during the summer months, there are various tours on offer whereby you sail across to eg. Harris, take a coach across the island, ferry across the Sound of Harris to North Uist, coach across that island and then the final ferry back to Skye. These are superb tours if you get the chance and give you a chance to see the wildlife around some of the remotest parts of Britain.

The main ferry is huge, complete with restaurants, bars and television lounges though we sampled none of those as we were too busy watching the birds. The Minch was like a millpond when we crossed in September, so many of the birds were on the sea rather than moving through.

Consequently we *only* saw about 20,000 auks, 50,000 Kittiwakes and several thousand Gannets and gulls together with a few porpoises, divers, skuas etc. And that was only the stuff flying next to the boat. Who knows what we missed.

With different weather conditions or at different times of the year, you can expect to see whales, dolphins, shearwaters and petrels. This is a fantastic wildlife experience and one that is strongly recommended.

For ferry and tour information, contact Caledonian MacBrayne Ltd in their Uig office on 01470 542219 or visit www.calmac.co.uk

⑤ Dunvegan Castle
Background information

DUNVEGAN CASTLE, home to the MacLeod clan, has been lived in for some 700 years. This is supposedly the longest continuously occupied castle in the UK. What's the secret of this longevity? As you wander round the various artefacts, you can't help but notice a decided 'fairy influence'. Belief in folklore culture is very strong here.

No-one could ever describe this bird as fairy-like, but this is the other recommended spot to watch for White-tailed Eagles. Continue past the castle entrance for about 3/4 mile and then look back towards the castle. Golden Eagles and Buzzards are in the area too.

On the islands in the sea loch, there is a large colony of seals and you should see

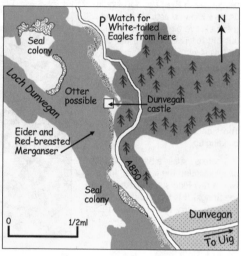

Likely bird species/ other fauna	
All year	White-tailed Eagle
Eider	Stonechat
Red-breasted	
Merganser	**_Other wildlife_**
Grey Heron	Grey and common seals
Golden Eagle	Otter

good numbers of Grey Herons, Eiders and Red-breasted Mergansers around the shorelines with, as ever, the chance of an otter. Stonechats are in the scrub.

Grey and common seals are particularly easy to see here and there are regular boat trips if you want really close-up views.

---

⑥ Neist Point
Background information

AS THE WESTERNMOST tip of Skye, this makes an excellent seawatching point and there is an outside chance of both eagle species. Seabirds are ever-present in good numbers from April through to October though the site is at its most dynamic in September and October when northerly gales are blowing. If

you can find a sheltered spot, you should see birds such as Gannets and Kittiwakes streaming past in their tens of thousands.

Arctic and Great Skuas are the most likely skuas to be seen, with Pomarine and Long-tailed only rarely recorded. Similarly, Manx Shearwaters will be the predominant species, with reasonable numbers of Sooty Shearwaters in suitable conditions. Scarcer shearwaters undoubtedly pass but there are so few people looking ...

Though a car park is marked on the map, there is currently a dispute going on with the landowner, so you may have to park on the roadside instead. You can get perfectly good views from here without going to the lighthouse itself. There are Twite by the crofts on the approach road to the Point.

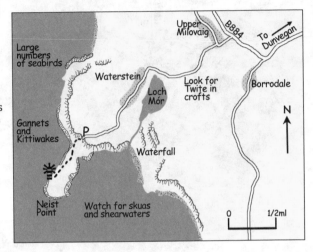

Likely bird species/other fauna

All year	*Spring/autumn*	Gannet	Great and Arctic Skua
Shag	Sooty Shearwater	Fulmar	
Rock Dove	Storm Petrel (autumn)	Gulls	*Other wildlife*
Twite	Leach's Petrel (autumn)	Kittiwake	Whales
Raven	Manx Shearwater	Auks	Dolphins

Wildlife Cruises

THERE ARE ANY number of boats around Skye offering wildlife trips of one sort or another. Most of them concentrate on the large mammals – otters, seals and cetaceans – but all of them should give you close-up views of some of the seabirds. Here are a couple to give you an idea of the range of what's on offer.

The Seaprobe Atlantis actually operates out of the Kyle of Lochalsh, but explores the area around the Skye Bridge. The unusual feature here is a large underwater gallery, an extension of the glass-bottomed boat idea, which means that as well as sitting up on deck, you can climb down to explore the different seabed habitats.

Typical underwater wildlife includes pollock, sandeels, jellyfish, crabs, starfish and sea urchins while on top, you should get close up views of otter, grey and common seals, Eiders, Guillemots, Black Guillemots, Shags, Grey Herons, Red-breasted Mergansers etc.

Visit www.seaprobe.freeserve.co.uk or email seaprobe@email.msn.com

The Sea-fari operates out of Armadale in the south of the island and uses a high speed rigid inflatable boat similar to those used by the Navy and Royal National Lifeboat Institution. These trips – often towards the islands of Eigg, Rhum and Canna – work the open oceans more than some of the others and have a higher success rate for finding whales and dolphins, June to September. Contact www.seafari.co.uk or email skyeseafari@aol.com Tel 01471 833 316

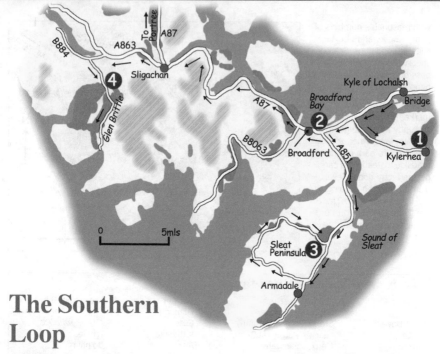

The Southern Loop

❶ Kylerhea Otter Haven
Background information

FROM THE FORESTRY Commission car park, a walk of about half a mile takes you through a small visitor centre (toilet facilities) down to a large hide. Though ostensibly for otter watching, look for Peregrines tangling with Ravens on the hills opposite, Golden Eagles, White-tailed Eagle (outside chance), Buzzard, Wheatear, Stonechat, Cuckoo, coniferous woodland birds, Black Guillemot, Red-breasted Merganser, Shag, Grey Heron and seals.

The otter haven is open from 9am until one hour before dusk. Though the path is supposed to be wheelchair friendly, it is somewhat bumpy in parts.

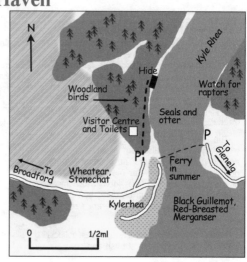

It might be possible though, to get permission to take your car closer to the hide. Contact Donnah Murray, the Recreation Ranger on 01320 366322 or email donnah.murray@forestry.gsi.gov.uk for further details.

Likely bird species/other fauna

All year		*Summer*	*Other wildlife*
Red-breasted Merganser	White-tailed Eagle (rare)	Cuckoo	Otter
Shag	Peregrine	Wheatear	Grey and common seals
Golden Eagle	Common woodland birds	Willow Warbler	

❷ Broadford Bay

Background information

AS YOU ENTER Broadford from the direction of the bridge, look for a Co-op store and garage on your right. There is a large car park immediately after the garage, which gives you good views of the Bay. Great Northern Divers linger into May. You should also see a few common waders such as Curlews, Redshanks and Ringed Plovers.

Look for Rock Pipits and Hooded Crow, along the beach, with the likes of Red-Breasted Mergansers and Black Guillemots offshore. Shags far outnumber Cormorants, as they do all round the island. Seals are the commonest mammals but otters, porpoises and various dolphins are regularly seen.

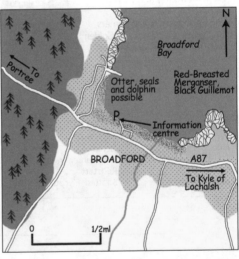

Also in the car park, you will see a Tourist Information Centre which doubles up as an office for the International Otter Survival Fund. Inside, you will find a notice board complete with the latest wildlife sightings. Though these are mostly mammalian, they are happy to receive and pass on any bird sightings, so please let them know of anything you have seen, especially if you come across any wing-tagged White-tailed Eagles. Contact them on 01471 822 487 or visit http://www.otter.org/sightings.html for recent sightings.

Likely bird species/other fauna

All year	*Autumn to spring*	*Other wildlife*
Eider	Great Northern Diver	Otter
Red-breasted Merganser	Ringed Plover	Grey and common seals
Rock Pipit	Turnstone	Dolphin
Hooded Crow	Curlew	Porpoise
	Redshank	

❸ Sleat peninsula
Background information

THE SOUTHERN CHUNK of Skye, the Sleat (pronounced 'slate') peninsula has most of the island's deciduous woodland and is the best place on the island to find the likes of Redstarts and flycatchers in spring and summer. Try the woods round Armadale Castle.

The minor coast road to Tarskavaig off on your left as you head north from Armadale is the best drive on Skye. Look for Merlins, and possibly Hen Harriers, hunting over the moors and Golden Eagles over the Cuillins as well as the usual array of seabirds and mammals in the bay.

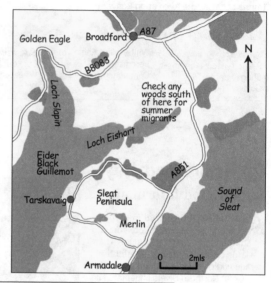

Likely bird species/other fauna

All year	Summer	Other wildlife
Eider	Merlin	Grey and common seals
Red-breasted Merganser	Hen Harrier (rare)	Otter
Golden Eagle	Redstart	
Black Guillemot	Spotted Flycatcher	

❹ Glen Brittle
Background information

THIS IS AN EXCELLENT area for Golden Eagles and Peregrines. The bay at the end of the road usually produces a few passage waders such as Dunlin, Turnstone, Greenshank and Curlew. These are susceptible to disturbance by dog walkers but usually relocate within a couple of hundred yards when flushed. Check the bay

Likely bird species

All year	Ringed Plover
Golden Eagle	Dunlin
Peregrine	Curlew
Black Guillemot	Redshank
Dipper	Greenshank
	Turnstone
Spring/autumn	
Oystercatcher	

for auks, Shags and Red-breasted Merganser. Autumn to late spring should produce a diver or two.

The campsite here is very popular with walkers – you are in the shadow of the Black Cuillin Mountains, the most dramatic mountain range in Britain – so it can get very busy.

A signposted picnic site half way along the glen is a good place to scan for raptors though birds can turn up anywhere along this road. We have seen both Peregrine and Merlin perch on roadside fence posts. Dippers are likely anywhere along the river.

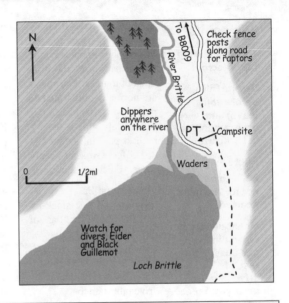

GOLDEN EAGLES

IT'S NOT for nothing that Buzzards are known as 'tourist eagles'. There are two rules of thumb that are usually quoted – 'if you have to think about it, then it's a Buzzard', and 'you'll know when you see an eagle'. When you see an eagle being mobbed by a Buzzard, then the size difference really becomes apparent. When you see a single bird soaring over a distant mountain ridge, it's not always as easy.

A recent poll suggests that the Scots see the Golden Eagle as their national bird though votes for the Red Grouse were disqualified after a concerted campaign by a well-known whisky manufacturer. You can easily understand the popularity of the bird of prey. I've never had an encounter with a Goldie yet that was anything less than memorable.

There are currently about 400 pairs in Scotland but despite that, birds are not necessarily easy to see. Unlike the Osprey, which can be more or less guaranteed at certain sites, Golden Eagles have huge territories – approximately 400 square miles.

That's an awful lot of land to scan. It doesn't take a lot of imagination to see yourself scanning

a mountain ridge while a Goldie pops up over the ridge behind you and disappears again behind the mountains. Patience is a definite virtue when mountain watching.

Juvenile birds show a lot of white in the wings and inner tail. This white disappears as the birds reach adulthood (it takes about six years) but it does so variably and cannot be used as a reliable ageing technique.

Golden Eagles have a powerful flight, often with half a dozen flaps, followed by a short glide. You are just as likely to see a bird soaring on a thermal though and not flapping at all as it uses the air currents coming off the mountains to gain height. Surprise is another hunting technique with birds flying very low and very fast as the swoop majestically a few feet over the ground in pursuit of a grouse or hare.

In Speyside the best place to see Goldies is the Findhorn Valley, not least because there will probably be several other birders already there. If you want to find your own birds, then northern Skye or the Ardnamurchan peninsula around Strontian hold particularly high densities of eagles

Key points

- **Toilets and shop in Applecross**

- **Garage (fill up before you leave) and other amenities in Lochcarron**

- **Route over Bealach na Bà not for the faint hearted**

- **Mountain top viewpoint can get busy – the rest of the drive is quiet – until you meet someone coming the other way**

- **Choose a fine day for best views**

- **Wheelchair-friendly sites apart from Rassal Ashwood – all other birding can be done from the car**

SPECTACULAR views and the chance to see Ptarmigan without leaving the car park make this drive one not to miss. Ptarmigan are normally only found on peaks over 2,000 feet. Fortunately, this is the highest pass in Scotland at 2,053 feet, so scan keenly when you reach the top.

Bealach na Bà (pronounced bee-alack-na-ba), the Gaelic for 'Pass of the cattle' is one of the ancient Scottish drove roads. Records from 1794 show some 3,000 cattle being driven through the mountains before being herded through the glens towards the market at Muir of Ord. Despite the wonderfully romantic-sounding name, this is a definite white-knuckle ride for those afraid of heights and is for confident drivers only. A sign at the bottom of the Pass of the Cattle warns that the road is unsuitable for learner drivers, caravans and anyone of a nervous disposition. How right they are. This is supposed to be the steepest road in Scotland.

Though it starts off fairly gently, it is not long before you are ignoring Meadow Pipits and Wheatears as your grip tightens on the steering wheel. Passengers might see a Ring Ouzel, but note that under no circumstances should you stop and get out; wait until you get to the top. The steepest drops are now fenced off, but the ever-increasing gradients, sharp hairpin bends and tightest of passing places all lead to the feeling in the pit of your stomach that you are going to meet someone coming

Buzzards are the most common birds of prey in the area.

towards you who is twice as scared as you are.

The views over to Raasay and the Cuillins of Skye are sensational and you will definitely want to stop here and scan the mountain ridges for raptors, all the time persuading yourself that the road wasn't too difficult at all. Actually, it's not as bad as it once was, as the local council has put in extra passing places, widened the road in parts and increased the numbers of protective barriers.

You now descend relatively gently into the village of Applecross, one of the early centres of Christianity in Britain. The Irish monk Maelrubha established a monastery here in 673AD. It is worth stopping here to scan the sea, before

taking the road round the edge of the peninsula, until it ends up at Shieldaig. This is another of those villages with a good claim to be called the 'prettiest in the Highlands.' The seafront here is an excellent vantage spot and your last chance to scan the water before returning back to Lochcarron.

A lot of the woodland on the west coast consists of block after block of conifer plantations, so Rassal Ashwood stands out like an oasis in a desert, it is such a beautiful place. The most northerly ashwood in Britain, Rassal has been a National Nature Reserve since 1956, though its status is currently under review. A spring visit here is sure to send your spirits soaring.

How to get there

Nearest large town: Inverness lies 60 miles E of Lochcarron.

Coming from Inverness, take A835 to Garve. Turn L onto A832 and then L again after 16 miles onto A890. Loch Gowan is the first loch on L and there is a large lay-by there. Continue on A890/A896 to Lochcarron.

From Lochcarron, head W on A896 past the Applecross turn-off for about a mile. Look for a car park on R at entrance to Rassal Ashwood. After your walk, head W towards Applecross. In village, turn L at T-junction and immediately R into a car park. When you leave, turn R for detour to Toscaig. Alternatively, turn L to follow the peninsula until reaching A896 again. Turn L and L almost

immediately into Shieldaig. Continue through the village and rejoin A896, turning R back to Lochcarron.

Approximate length of tour from Lochcarron is 60 miles.

① Lochcarron
Background information

LOCHCARRON, the start of this drive, is a pretty little lochside village, about 22 miles north east of Kyle of Lochalsh and 60 miles west of Inverness. There are shops, a tourist information centre and a garage. A nearby hide and the waterfront are good places to kick-start your birding day. Likely birds include Red-breasted Mergansers and Eiders though there is the chance of the occasional auk fishing in the loch. Scan the foreshore for otters.

Two miles east of Lochcarron, at the head of the loch, lies the Smithy Heritage Centre. As well as displays of local history and a pottery, there is also a short walk to a hide overlooking a burn. Grey Wagtails breed and can be seen feeding young in summer. Otters are regularly seen and feeders attract a range of woodland birds including Siskins. There are Stonechats and Sedge Warblers along the trail. Grey Grey Herons stalk the area and Cuckoos call in summer.

The occasional Golden Eagle is seen over the ridges, though most of the sightings in the logbook, from local school kids, refer to Buzzards. The hide has plenty of display material on the local wildlife as well as identification guides for plants, insects and birds.

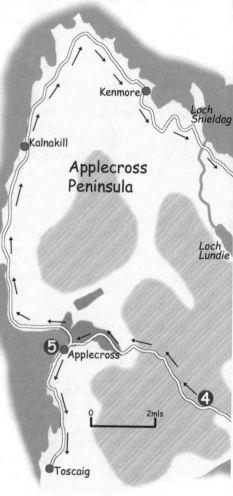

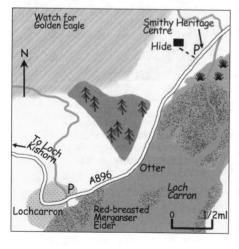

Likely bird species

Resident	
Eider	Grey Wagtail
Red-breasted	Stonechat
Merganser	Siskin
Grey Heron	
Buzzard	*Summer Migrants*
Golden Eagle	Cuckoo
Auks	Sedge Warbler
	Willow Warbler

② Loch Kishorn

Background information

LOCH KISHORN first comes into view just after the hamlet of Ardarroch. Pull up immediately on your left as soon as you see the loch. There are Wood Warblers in the trees on your right. Scan the mud, seaweed clumps and channels for wildfowl and waders. This is a pretty reliable spot for Goosanders and you might pick out a Greenshank among the Oystercatchers, Redshanks, Curlews and Ringed Plovers.

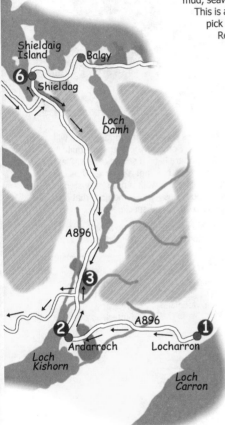

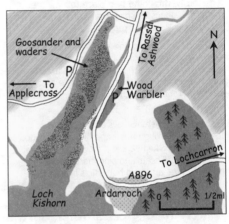

Depending on the state of the tide, you may get better views from the other side of the loch. There is a large pulling-in spot just after you start the Applecross climb.

Likely bird species

All year	Passage
Goosander	Whimbrel
Common wildfowl	Greenshank
Oystercatcher	
Ringed Plover	Spring/summer
Dunlin	Wood Warbler
Curlew	

❸ Rassal Ashwood
Background information

THE WOOD will take you an hour or so to walk round. As well as a typical range of woodland birds, including both Pied (occasional) and Spotted Flycatchers, the whole area is carpeted with a wonderful array of wildflowers in spring.

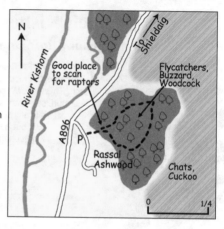

The path climbs steeply at the start, though fortuitously, this is the best place to view the mountains opposite, so you can catch your breath as you scan for raptors.

Though one of the first areas where Redwings were recorded breeding, there is no guarantee of seeing them today, but Buzzards and Woodcocks nest in the wood. The area seems surrounded by Cuckoos in spring, often affording good views.

Check the drystone walls and barbed wire fences on the rough moorland behind the wood for chats and Wheatears and maybe a Merlin will zip through. Wildcats and pine martens are present in the area and butterflies include speckled woods and pearl-bordered fritillaries.

The whole area is fairly boggy so you will need boots. Some of the paths are quite steep and there is no disabled access. Please keep to the paths – not always easy as the second half of the walk is not signposted and less than obvious – and remember that it is illegal to collect plant specimens.

This is a special place; the best time to visit is early morning in spring or early summer.

Likely bird species/other flora and fauna

Spring/summer	Cuckoo	Wheatear	*Other wildlife*
Buzzard	Flycatchers	Warblers	Pine marten
Merlin	Whinchat	Common woodland	Wildcat
Woodcock	Stonechat	species	Butterflies
			Wildflowers

❹ The Pass of the Cattle
Background information

AT THE MOUNTAIN top, there is a large car park on both sides of the road to Applecross and this is where you can explore for Ptarmigan. Scan the ridges on either side of the radio mast (telescope necessary) or take a 15-minute or so stroll up a well-defined and obvious track to the mast itself. There are Red Grouse in the area, so don't assume that every grouse you see is automatically the one you want.

Of course, you might be really unlucky like we were on our first visit; we managed the road reasonably well only to find the top of the mountain encased in low cloud with the 'sensational view' amounting to little more than ten feet in front of our faces. This is definitely a trip for fine days and the road is almost certainly going to be closed in winter.

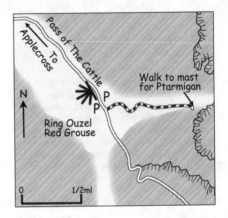

Likely bird species

All year	Peregrine
Red Grouse	Meadow Pipit
Ptarmigan	
Buzzard	**Spring/summer**
Golden Eagle	Wheatear
Kestrel	Ring Ouzel

❺ Applecross and the peninsula

Background information

ONCE YOU HAVE reached Applecross, continue to a T-junction and turn left. Immediately on your right, there is a car park with toilet facilities plus a shop on the other side of the road.

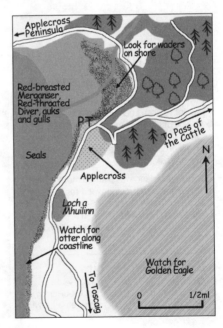

The car park makes a good place to scan the bay and the Inner Sound, looking for Red-breasted Mergansers, Red-throated Divers, auks and gulls. Whales, dolphins and porpoises can sometimes be seen and seals are usually present in the bay. Otters, wildcats and pine martens are all in the area.

The shore should produce the likes of Ringed Plover, Rock Pipit and wagtails, though you could pick up something a little more unusual such as a late Whimbrel still moving north. There is an outside chance of one of the Skye White-tailed Eagles putting in an appearance and the ridges are always worth scanning for other raptors.

If Applecross is busy – and it frequently is these days, then a worthwhile detour is to turn right out of the car park in the village and head south along the minor coast road towards Toscaig. Apart from a few locals, the only other people you are likely to meet are other owners of this book!

There are several bays on your right to explore where, as well as a similar range of coastal species to Applecross itself, the abundance of seaweed and rocks makes ideal otter habitat. The hills on your left can be good for Golden Eagle. As you drive through the assorted hamlets, check the telegraph wires which provide lookouts for an assortment of pipits, chats and finches.

The road ends at a small picnic site in Toscaig (common woodland birds). A stone jetty here acts as an excellent place to scan the small sea loch for divers, auks, Shags, Grey Herons and Red-breasted Mergansers etc. Retrace your steps to Applecross and continue round the peninsula.

There are plenty of places to stop and look for birds – at sea or over the land. Ravens are quite common and you can often watch family parties tumbling in the air, flying seemingly for fun. Wheatears and Meadow Pipits are plentiful and you might see a hunting Merlin flash by.

Likely bird species/other fauna

All year		*Passage*	*Spring/summer*
Red-breasted	White-tailed Eagle	Whimbrel	Wheatear
Merganser	(rare)		
Red-throated Diver	Common waders		
Black-throated Diver	Occasional auks	*Autumn to spring*	*Other Wildlife*
Golden Eagle	Rock Pipit	Great Northern Diver	Otter
	Raven	Waders (increase in winter)	Seals

➏ Shieldaig

Background information

THE SEA FRONT is an excellent vantage point to scan Loch Shieldaig for any birds you might have missed earlier. This is another very good place for otters though you will probably need to be here at either dawn or dusk.

The small island was planted more than 100 years ago to provide wood for the local fishermen. Today, it is an SSSI and holds Long-eared Owls, Red-breasted Mergansers, Grey Herons, Kestrels and Black Guillemots.

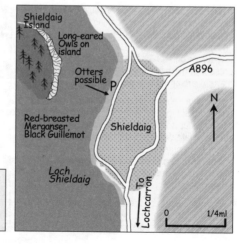

Likely bird species

All year	
Red-breasted	Grey Heron
Merganser	Black Guillemot
	Long-eared Owl

Loch Gowan
Background information

THOUGH SLIGHTLY off the set route, the loch makes an excellent spot to stop for a coffee break if you are approaching Applecross from Inverness.

Over the years, we have seen Red and Black-throated Divers, Common Scoters, Wigeon, Greenshanks and Green Sandpipers moving through or feeding.

The woods opposite the lay-by are very good for Redpolls and you may get lucky and see a Golden Eagle along the ridges, something guaranteed to annoy the breeding Buzzards which will immediately fly out to try to see off the intruder.

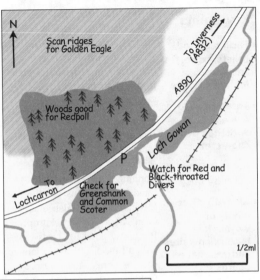

Likely bird species

All year	Spring/summer	Passage
Buzzard	Wigeon	Common Scoter
Golden Eagle	Greenshank	Red-throated Diver
Grey Wagtail	Common Sandpiper	Black-throated Diver
Redpoll	Cuckoo	Green Sandpiper

COPING WITH MIDGES

THE VIEWS might be breathtaking and the birds spectacular, but there is one creature in Scotland you will be unhappy to encounter. Its scientific name is *Culicoides impuntatus*. To the rest of the world, these tiny, biting insects are called midges and, if you get badly bitten, you are sure to have a few choice names for them yourself.

Midges are most prevalent in the west of Scotland. They are at their worst in July and August though there is some overspill into June and September. Dawn and dusk are times of peak activity.

It has now been demonstrated that they are attracted by the smell of sweat. Only a particular extract though, which is present in variable amounts from person to person.

Midge bites don't carry disease, but do cause massive itching and annoyance, especially the next day when the itching becomes worse.

You can try different chemical insect repellents though there is no guarantee of success. Even then, people report back that what worked for them one year didn't work the next. The latest theory is to eat some Marmite before you go out. Apparently, the odour of this foodstuff emanates from the skin and repels the mozzies.

So what's to be done? Well, start by keeping as much of your skin as possible covered up. Avoid tee shirts and shorts in the early morning and evening and keep away from areas of still water at those times. At least the birds love midges, and you will see all sorts of species, not renowned for their flycatching skills launching themselves at the massive insect clouds.

Key points

SPEND ANY TIME near Loch Ness and you are sure to hear about Glen Affric. It has a reputation for being one of the most beautiful glens in the Highlands.

It's got the lot; woods, mountains, waterfalls, lochs, rivers, moorland, short walks, long walks, Munros aplenty (hills over 3000 feet) and stunning views all round. Landseer's famous painting 'Monarch of the Glen' has Glen Affric for a backdrop. It's pretty good for birds too with all the Scottish specialities here or hereabouts – Osprey, Golden Eagle, Crested Tit, Capercaillie and Scottish Crossbill.

But, and it is a big but, every single guidebook and tourist office can't wait to tell you how wonderful it is and how you really must visit. This results in the world and his wife heading there. The last time we visited, the place was full to capacity and that was midweek and away from the main tourist season. I would hate to be there at weekends and Bank Holidays. Birding among all those day-trippers was no fun at all.

What the guidebooks don't tell you though is that there are two other glens in the immediate vicinity – Cannich and Strathfarrar - holding a similar range of birds and which have never entered the consciousness of the average tourist. If you prefer your own space, head for one of these instead.

All these glens are easily accessed off Strathglass, itself well worth exploring. Try the minor road running east of the river, which is fished by Ospreys.

The trees here were much prized for their timber, which was used for shipbuilding and the iron industry. Today, no more than 1% of the original forest remains in Glen Affric. Nevertheless, it is still the third largest remnant of Caledonian pine forest.

Hydroelectricity is the modern industry, and all three glens end at dammed lochs, the one in Glen Cannich being the largest dam in Scotland, a massive half-mile long concrete edifice.

Just round the corner from Glen Affric lies Corrimony, one of the RSPB's newest reserves. This is being specially managed for Black Grouse, another species in heavy decline. Preferred habitat is a combination of open moorland and mixed woodland. As a result, non-native trees are being uprooted and replanted with the likes of birch, Scots pine, juniper and rowan. One other advantage of this habitat management is that the area is becoming more attractive to Crested Tits and a couple of pairs have now moved into the area.

Occasionally you come across something that seems totally out of the ordinary. The local community of Abriachan, a small village along the edge of Loch Ness, has put an enormous amount of time and energy into developing their local woodland.

The result is a wonderful wheelchair-friendly boardwalk through the woods, leading to a hide overlooking the pretty Loch Laide (pronounced 'latch') where local legend has it that kelpies – malevolent, horse-shaped water spirits –

Continues on page 122

How to get there

Nearest town: Inverness is 12 miles E of Beauly.

Head west from Inverness on A862 towards Beauly. There are several lay-bys along this stretch of road from which to scan the firth. Continue until you come to the junction with A831 signposted towards Cannich and continue towards the hamlet of Struy. The road to Glen Strathfarrar is on R just before Struy. Look for a sign to Leishmore. It is not an easy road to find with the lack of signposting almost designed to keep you away.

Continue along A831 to Cannich. Cross the bridge, then turn R up a steep hill signposted to Glen Cannich and Mullardoch.

The road to Glen Affric is immediately after the entrance to Glen Cannich and you can't miss it, as there are brown tourist signs everywhere. All the glens are single tracked roads and you will need to retrace your steps back to A831.

Continuing along A831, you will see signs off on R to Corrimony and the Chambered Cairns. The RSPB reserve wasn't signposted at the time of writing. There is a large lay-by on L just before the Cairns. Park here and continue down road for half a mile or so to the reserve entrance.

Retrace your steps back to A831 and turn R. Continue E for about eight miles and turn L onto A833 towards Beauly. After about six miles, turn R onto the first minor road you come to (unsigned). Turn R at the crossroads towards Abriachan and continue for about three miles. The entrance to the car park (signed) is on R. If you see the loch on R, you have gone too far.

Turn R out of the car park, past the loch and turn L at the junction. Follow this minor road for about eight miles (birding en route) until it joins A82. Turn L and continue back in to Inverness.

Total mileage of the tour is 44 miles plus the length of any of the glens.

From page 121

inhabit the crystal clear, reed-fringed water. There are reconstructions of Bronze Age dwellings, tree houses for the kids, picnic sites, eco-friendly toilets and plenty of leaflets to pick up, describing the area. All in all, this is a fantastic effort by the Abriachan Forest Trust and well worth an hour or two of your time.

There is no way you will be able to visit all the sites mentioned below in just one visit. You can probably do two of the glens in a full day out but don't be surprised if you find yourself spending all day exploring just one of the major areas.

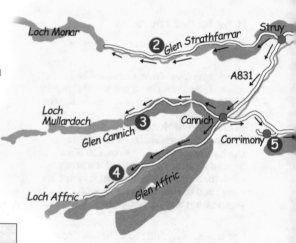

❶ Beauly Firth

Background information

AS YOU LEAVE Inverness westwards towards Beauly, there are several lay-bys where you can stop and scan the south side of the Beauly Firth for wildfowl and waders, depending on the state of the tide. With luck, you might also pick up a bottle-nosed dolphin.

Look for Ospreys and Buzzards overhead as you head towards the glens.

Likely bird species/ other fauna

All year	Other wildlife
Buzzard	Bottle-nosed dolphin
Common wildfowl	
Common waders	

❷ Glen Strathfarrar

Background information

AS YOU ENTER the glen, you will find that the road is gated. Stop at the gatekeeper's house to collect a permit for your car. Permits are available from 9am, April to October, excluding Tuesdays and Sunday mornings. The road is unsuitable for coaches

and caravans. Telephone the gatekeeper on 01463 761260 for further details.

Only 25 cars at any given time are allowed into the glen. If you are number 26, it is just tough luck. You will have to wait for someone to come out. There is unrestricted access though for cyclists and walkers.

Glen Strathfarrar is a National Nature Reserve managed by Scottish Natural Heritage. The name is something of a contradiction in terms – glen refers to a narrow, steep-sided valley, whereas a strath is a wider, flat-bottomed valley. The best way to work the area is to take your time and stop frequently.

As if to celebrate the fact that you have actually managed to make your way into this hidden glen, the first section of woodland produces an absolute cacophony of sound in spring. Wood and Willow Warblers compete, like supporters of two opposing football teams, to produce a blanket of noise in glorious stereo, either side of the road. Redstarts and Tree Pipits can also be seen.

As the wood thins out, look for Cuckoos flying over, their silhouettes not dissimilar to that of a Sparrowhawk. An unusual sight here was a Great Spotted Woodpecker, feeding on the ground in a manner recalling its Green cousin.

Spotted Flycatchers are one of the last summer migrants to arrive and even the end of May can produce small falls of birds. We have seen flocks of up to ten birds feeding in the one clump of trees. The pinewoods hold good numbers of Siskins, Redpolls and Goldcrests and you should find Crested Tits and Scottish Crossbills if you look hard enough.

The streams hold that typical trio of birds - Grey Wagtail, Common Sandpiper and Dipper. The open areas should produce Curlew, Oystercatcher, Wheatear, Whinchat and Stonechat with Meadow Pipits everywhere. Golden Eagle, Peregrine and Buzzard patrol the skies, with a chance of Merlin or Osprey.

The loch at the end of the road beyond the dam might produce divers, Goosanders or Red-

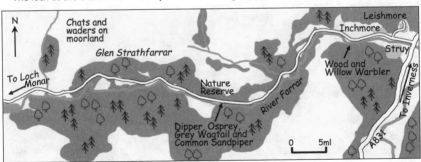

breasted Mergansers. There is an outside chance of Common Scoters on any of the lochs in the three glens. The tops of the higher hills could produce Dotterel, Snow Buntings and Ptarmigan. Mammals include red, sika and roe deer, red squirrels and, if you are very lucky, pine marten. All the species

mentioned here can also be seen in Glens Cannich and Affric.

There are no facilities in this glen and the area is unsuitable for wheelchairs away from the road. However, many of the birds can be seen and heard from the car and parking spaces.

Likely bird species/other fauna and flora (all three glens)

All year	Siskin	Red-throated Diver	Redstart
Ptarmigan	Lesser Redpoll	Osprey	Spotted Flycatcher
Capercaillie	(Scottish) Crossbill	Peregrine	Snow Bunting
Buzzard	Yellowhammer	Merlin	
Golden Eagle	Common woodland	Dotterel	*Other wildlife*
Great Spotted	birds	Curlew	The whole area is very
Woodpecker		Oystercatcher	good for: -
Grey Wagtail	*Summer*	Common Sandpiper	Mammals
Dipper	Wigeon	Cuckoo	Butterflies
Meadow Pipit	Goosander	Tree Pipit	Dragonflies
Stonechat	Red-breasted	Whinchat	Plants
Goldcrest	Merganser	Wheatear	Insects
Crested Tit	Common Scoter (rare)	Willow Warbler	Lizards
Treecreeper	Black throated Diver	Wood Warbler	

❸ Glen Cannich

Background information

THIS IS PROBABLY the least beautiful of the glens. Huge amounts of tree felling have left ugly scars across the landscape in the initial stretches. Where the area opens out, the land is rugged and lacks the 'chocolate box' quality of the other two glens.

All this means that you are unlikely to be

disturbed as you scan the mountain ridges. This glen produced the most inquisitive Golden Eagle we have seen in Scotland, flying low over our heads, backwards and forwards, as it gave us a good going over. Other wildlife too seems unfazed by human presence and red deer often feed close to the edge of the road.

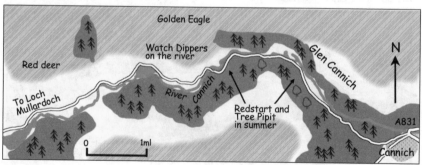

❹ Glen Affric
Background information

THE STRETCH OF the river immediately on your left as you enter the glen, is a good spot for Dipper. As you move further into the valley, you will find large tracts of ancient Caledonian forest which still hold Capercaillie, Crested Tit and Scottish Crossbill, though you will need to walk well away from other visitors and have a lot of luck if you want to see Capers here. Please refer to the Capercaillie code of conduct on page 20.

The first main car park is at Dog Falls and you should get a good range of woodland birds as you walk to the falls. You can also follow the way-marked paths here and climb above canopy level as you head towards a small lochan giving fine all round views.

As usual, scan all the lochs for waterbirds such as Wigeon, Red-breasted Mergansers, Goosanders and Black- and Red-throated Divers. Yellowhammers can often be found around the farms.

The road opens out into moorland as you move further down the valley and there are better views of the mountain ridges allowing you to scan for raptors. There is always the chance of the unusual here. We picked out a Honey Buzzard moving through on one occasion, riding a thermal with half a dozen Buzzards The road ends at a large car park where a short climb takes you to a spectacular viewpoint well worth the effort of lugging your picnic and telescope with you as you sit and watch for Peregrines and Golden Eagles to appear.

The glen is full of other wildlife too. Pine marten is the main predator but look out for stoat, weasel, fox, badger, three species of deer and red squirrel among the mammals. Spring sees plenty of primroses and rare plants include lesser twayblade, creeping ladies tresses and twinflowers. In summer, pearl-bordered fritillaries and Scotch argus butterflies and

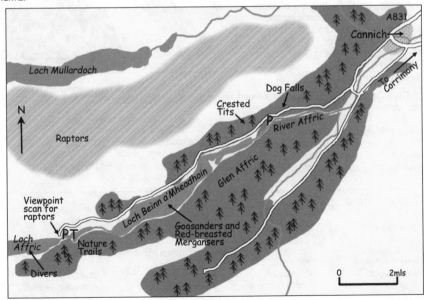

golden-ringed dragonflies are on the wing. Adders, slow worms and common lizards are probably best seen as they sun themselves.

Spring and summer are the best times to visit

though despite the plethora of wildlife on view at those times, the glen is supposed to be at its best scenically in autumn. Winter can be bleak. Try an early morning or evening visit to avoid the crowds. The main car parking areas have toilet facilities.

❺ RSPB Corrimony

Background information

IF YOU PREFER a long walk to the drive and stop, drive and stop approach, then the RSPB's new reserve at Corrimony is probably your best bet. From the car park walk along the road past the ancient chambered cairns for about half a mile until you come to a signed track on your left, just before you cross the river. This is the start of the reserve.

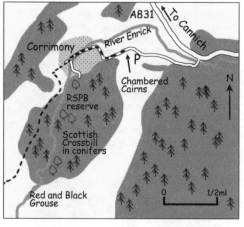

Non-native trees are being replaced with Scots pine seedlings from Glen Affric and these, coupled with a mix of native deciduous trees hold, among others, Capercaillie, Scottish Crossbill, Wood Warbler, Redstart, Tree Pipit, Spotted Flycatcher, Goldcrest and Great Spotted Woodpecker. Crested Tits have just started to colonise.

The river holds Dippers, Grey Wagtails and Goosanders. Loch Comhnard attracts the occasional diver, fishing Osprey and feeding waders including Greenshanks, Common Sandpipers and Lapwings. Winter attracts a small flock of Whooper Swans. Beyond the loch, the area opens out into open moorland,

which is being managed especially for the benefit of Black Grouse.

This is a beautiful reserve, well off the beaten track and therefore relatively undisturbed. As the trail passes through a working farm, please make sure that you leave all the gates as you find them. There are no facilities.

Likely bird species

All year	Crested Tit	Black-throated Diver	Redstart
Capercaillie	Treecreeper	(occasional)	Willow Warbler
Black Grouse	(Scottish) Crossbill	Osprey	Wood Warbler
Great Spotted		Common Sandpiper	Spotted Flycatcher
Woodpecker	*Summer*	Lapwing	
Grey Wagtail	Goosander	Greenshank	*Winter*
Dipper	Red-throated Diver	Tree Pipit	Whooper Swan

⑥ Abriachan

Background information

A LONG THE PATHS, there are various stopping points where you can play the recorded calls of different species you might encounter in that bit of the wood, such as Woodcock and Tawny Owl. A platform overlooking a pool is ideal for watching assorted dragonflies in late summer.

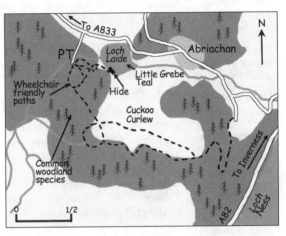

A hide overlooks Loch Laide. On the side of the hide, there are more buttons to press, playing the calls of the likes of Whooper Swans (winter visitors) and Slavonian Grebes. If the latter is your target species though, you will be better off looking elsewhere (Loch Ruthven); we have never yet seen them here and you are far more likely to hear the whinnying calls of one of the several Little Grebes instead.

Meadow Pipits breed in the heather in front of the hide. The male will drop in to a point several yards away from the nest and have a good look round to make sure that the coast is clear before taking his food back to the nest.

Wildfowl on the loch includes Teal and Tufted Ducks. There are mountain ridges to scan for raptors. Cuckoos look for nests to parasitise while Hooded Crows are on the lookout for nestlings. The woods hold Willow Warblers in summer, Goldcrests and Coal Tits.

The drive back to Inverness along minor roads affords fantastic elevated views of the area, including the Beauly Firth, and offers more chances for roadside birding.

Likely bird species/other fauna

All year		Summer	Winter
Little Grebe	Treecreeper	Curlew	Whooper Swan
Common wildfowl	Hooded Crow	Woodcock	
Meadow Pipit	Raven	Cuckoo	Other wildlife
Goldcrest	Common woodland birds	Willow Warbler	Dragonflies

Key points

- No facilities — nearest towns are Inverness and Aviemore

- Ten species of raptor in a day possible

- Limited off-road parking — don't block passing places

- Leave all gates on Farr Road open or shut as you find them

- Driving along the Farr Road can be daunting

- Hide at Loch Ruthven

- Some views of Loch Ruthven from car park but no disabled access to hide

- Rest of the trip can be birded from the car

FINDHORN VALLEY is a place to avoid if you happen to be a mountain hare, Meadow Pipit, Red Grouse, small rodent, Woodpigeon, brown trout or small woodland bird. This drive takes you straight into the heart of some of the best predator country in the Highlands.

A drive that gives you the possibility of seeing ten or more species of raptor in a day has got to be pretty special. Birds you might realistically expect to see along the Findhorn Valley – known locally as Strathdearn – and surrounding area are Golden and White-tailed Eagles, Osprey, Hen Harrier, Peregrine, Merlin, Kestrel, Buzzard, Red Kite, Sparrowhawk and Goshawk. There is a fine supporting cast of mountain and moorland birds too.

Sightings are often a matter of luck. I know of birders who have visited several times before they saw an eagle. Others connect within five minutes of parking. On our last visit, two Cockney lads gave up in disgust having failed to see a bird. Just after their car was out of view, we had four birds in the same field of view.

There are no facilities in the valley though there is plenty of privacy away from the car park area if you need to answer a call of nature. Beware though. I know of someone who thought that no-one was looking and ended up mooning at an RAF pilot as he screamed through the valley in his Tornado jet on a low level training mission.

After driving along the bottom of a valley, there is the opportunity to go over the tops on the Farr road, which climbs steeply over some prime moorland. On some occasions, it can seem the most desolate, bird-free zone on earth and you get to the other end feeling lucky to have seen so much as a Meadow Pipit, but when it is good, it is very good indeed. You will either love or hate this area. There is no middle ground.

A few years ago, we stopped for a coffee and enjoyed watching a young Golden Eagle being mobbed by a couple of Buzzards. We had just packed the 'scopes and tripods away when there was an unfamiliar sound nearby.

A male Hen Harrier appeared and started his display flight, climbing and falling through the sky with a total nonchalance, calling all the time until he persuaded his mate to join him, whereupon they started a series of food passes. We watched for an hour or so before heading on to Loch Ruthven. The birds were still displaying when we returned several hours later. Sadly, the harriers no longer breed in the immediate area, though you still see the occasional hunting bird.

On the other side of the moor, you drop down to Loch Ruthven with amazing close up views of summer-plumaged Slavonian Grebes complete with their yellow fright wigs. There is a hide here and as well as the grebes, you can scan the mountain ridge at the back for more raptors.

Most fly across from side to side, but on one occasion, I spotted a Red Kite from the Black Isle reintroduction programme and it started flying towards us. It got closer and closer until the only way we could track it was to lie on the benches looking up through the viewing slots. That was when the door opened and that, M'lud, is the explanation as to what six of us were doing in the hide that day. Honest.

This trip to the Findhorn Valley and Loch Ruthven is probably my favourite drive in the whole of the Highlands. And that's saying something.

How to get there

Nearest big town: Inverness is 16 miles N of Findhorn Bridge.

The starting point is Findhorn Bridge. Head up A9 towards Inverness. Just after you reach Slochd Summit (signed on A9, about 12 miles N of Aviemore), take a minor road on L signed Raibeg and Balvraid (note - do not follow signs for these places once you have left A9).

If you are coming S from Inverness, leave A9 at Tomatin (15 miles S of Inverness) and continue through the village. In either case, stop at the bridge where it crosses the River Findhorn.

A minor road at N end of the bridge and signposted Coignafearn follows the river as it heads SW into the Monadhliath Mountains. Take this single-track road and follow it for some 11 miles to a car park at the bottom.

Coming out of the valley, turn L on the only road there is, signed to Farr. At

the end of the road, turn L along B851 then R on a minor road in East Croachy. Loch Ruthven is signed from here. Car park is on L after a mile.

Heading S down A9, all lay-bys are numbered so you can prepare well in advance for number 151.

Total distance from Findorn Bridge to the end of the valley, over to Loch Ruthven then back to Findhorn Bridge is about 60 miles.

❶ Findhorn Bridge

Background information

AFTER YOU LEAVE the A9 at Tomatin, south east of Inverness, you come to a massive stone bridge, built by Thomas Telford, spanning the River Findhorn. Looking to the east, the shingle islands in the river hold a colony of Common Terns in summer, whereas views to the west give you your first chance to see Dipper, though these can turn up anywhere along the river. Common Gulls and Oystercatchers are easy to find.

Likely bird species

All year
Common Gull
Dipper

Summer
Common Tern

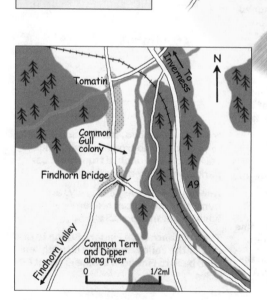

② Findhorn Valley

Background information

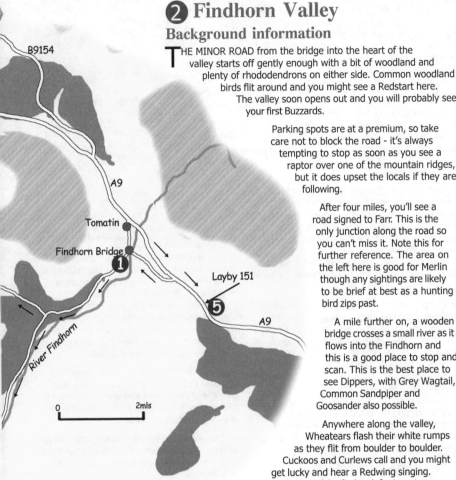

THE MINOR ROAD from the bridge into the heart of the valley starts off gently enough with a bit of woodland and plenty of rhododendrons on either side. Common woodland birds flit around and you might see a Redstart here. The valley soon opens out and you will probably see your first Buzzards.

Parking spots are at a premium, so take care not to block the road - it's always tempting to stop as soon as you see a raptor over one of the mountain ridges, but it does upset the locals if they are following.

After four miles, you'll see a road signed to Farr. This is the only junction along the road so you can't miss it. Note this for further reference. The area on the left here is good for Merlin though any sightings are likely to be brief at best as a hunting bird zips past.

A mile further on, a wooden bridge crosses a small river as it flows into the Findhorn and this is a good place to stop and scan. This is the best place to see Dippers, with Grey Wagtail, Common Sandpiper and Goosander also possible.

Anywhere along the valley, Wheatears flash their white rumps as they flit from boulder to boulder. Cuckoos and Curlews call and you might get lucky and hear a Redwing singing. Hirundines and Swifts hawk for insects over the river. Listen out for the deep '*kronk*' of a Raven; they often come out to tussle with Peregrines. Scan the ridges for Golden Eagles though you probably stand a better chance further along the valley.

As the road enters a private estate, use the car park on your left. You now have the choice between being what that fine old Scottish ornithologist Desmond Nethersole-Thompson described as being either 'an arser or a legger'. In other words, you can stay put and let the birds come to you or carry on walking. You can't drive any further but you can walk as far as you want along the valley.

Continues on page 132

From page 131

It's not just being bone-idle that makes me prefer watching from the car park. Raptor watching can be a social activity like seawatching. You have a 360° panorama and the more pairs of eyes scanning the ridges, the more you are likely to find. I also enjoy the banter. You might have long periods to fill in before birds show.

There is a cliff immediately in front of you on the far side of the river. In recent years, the area to the left of this cliff, about half way between the cliff and the road, has been the most productive area for Golden Eagles.

Most of the eagles you see are likely to be immature birds - there are no adult territories locally. The last few years have also seen a juvenile White-tailed Eagle present as well and one of my most memorable views was of a Goldie and White-tailed Eagle coming over a ridge together, dipping down again only to be replaced by a Buzzard and Osprey together.

The car park area is also good for Peregrines and you often see them hunting Red Grouse. Kestrels and Sparrowhawks fly across the valley and there are usually good numbers of aerial dogfights and mobbing among the various raptors and corvids. Recent battles I have witnessed include Osprey v Peregrine, Merlin v Peregrine (fascinating to see the huge size difference between a tiny male Merlin and huge female Peregrine), Kestrel v Buzzard and everything v eagle. I've seen three Buzzards, five Ravens, Peregrine and Kestrel all mobbing one unfortunate Golden Eagle.

If you stand in the car park with the river

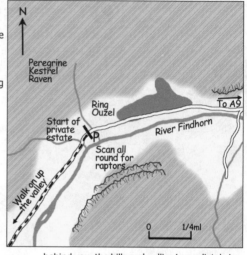

behind you, the hills and gullies immediately in front of you are very good for Ring Ouzels and there are usually a couple of pairs knocking about. Whisper it quietly, but I have met birders here who were more pleased to see this 'Blackbird with a white bib' than they were to see an eagle soaring over. Strange people. If you choose to walk down the valley, then Ring Ouzels are pretty easy to find.

Mammals are plentiful, with huge herds of red deer to be seen, along with feral goats, brown and mountain hares and, if you leave in the late evening, the usual near misses with the suicide rabbit squadrons.

The valley is at its best in spring through to autumn. By winter, only the Golden Eagles and Red Grouse remain and the road can be very treacherous.

Likely bird species/other fauna

All year	*Spring/Summer/ autumn*		*Other wildlife*
Red Grouse	Goosander	Peregrine	Red deer
Golden Eagle	White-tailed Eagle	Merlin	Feral goats
Buzzard	(outside chance)	Kestrel	
Grey Wagtail	Osprey	Common Sandpiper	
Dipper	Sparrowhawk	Cuckoo	
Stonechat		Wheatear	
Raven		Redstart	
		Ring Ouzel	

❸ The Farr Road

Background information

IF YOU THOUGHT that the Findhorn Valley road was minor, wait until you try this one! There is the added fun of it being gated, so please remember to shut any gates that you pass through.

The road starts off sedately enough, passing through an area of coniferous woodland where you stop by a pleasant stream to look for more Common Sandpipers with the likes of Siskin, Redpoll, Treecreeper, Goldcrest, Crossbill and Coal Tit in the woods.

The road climbs steeply out of the wood and it is worth stopping when it starts to plateau out and look back on where you have just come from. If you are lucky, you might see a Goshawk displaying over the vast plantation, though it is much more likely to be a Sparrowhawk.

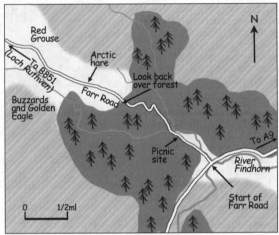

The road continues over the moor and if it is a clear day, you get excellent views of the distant peaks on the north-west coast. If the thermals are good, Buzzards are seemingly over every ridge - we have had more than 20 in the air at once.

Chats and Wheatears often perch on the fence wires. Meadow Pipits appear everywhere and Red Grouse and Golden Plovers breed on the moors. Migrants seem to use this route and you might see parties of Redwings and Fieldfares in early spring replaced by small flocks of Swallows, House Martins and Swifts as spring progresses. This is a good spot for close-up views of mountain hares, which often retain some of their white winter plumage well into May.

If there are Hen Harriers and Short-eared Owls in the area, they tend to be seen along the second half of the road though the area you need to scan is huge, so be patient. Red Kites are increasingly seen hunting in this area too.

Likely bird species/other fauna

All year	Common Crossbill	Goshawk (rare)	*Other wildlife*
Red Grouse	Common woodland	Red Kite (rare)	Mountain hare
Golden Eagle	birds	Hen Harrier (rare)	
Buzzard		Short-eared Owl	
Meadow Pipit	*Summer*		
	Sparrowhawk		

❹ RSPB Loch Ruthven

Background information

LOCH RUTHVEN, one of the prettiest of all the RSPB reserves around, lies south of Farr off the B851. Star birds are the breeding Slavonian Grebes that are present in spring and summer. This is the best place in the country bar none to see them.

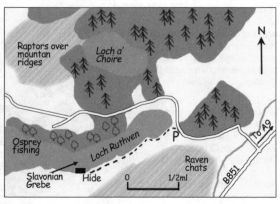

The grebes can usually be seen from the car park at the east end of the loch and this is the best place to find Wheatears, Whinchats and Stonechats. Tree Pipits are usually in the plantation just over the road and Ravens, Peregrines, Merlins and Hen Harriers are all possible, with an outside chance of a Goshawk.

A rough path, not suitable for wheelchairs, leads to a hide about a mile away. Check the birch wood for occasional Wood Warblers and Redstarts among the commoner species such as the ubiquitous Willow Warblers and Chaffinches.

Slavonian Grebes can usually be seen at extremely close quarters in the reed bed right in front of the hide, though there are often pairs out on the open water too. Look out for Reed Buntings here and the Ospreys that regularly fish in the loch.

The loch margins should produce Common Sandpiper, Oystercatcher and maybe Curlew with Teal, Goosander and Red-breasted Merganser all possible. Red-throated Divers are seen fairly regularly but Black-throated Divers are only occasional.

Scanning the mountain ridges opposite the hide regularly turns up raptors, though they are distant and you will need a good telescope to sort them out. Golden Eagle, Peregrine, Kestrel and Buzzard are the most likely.

Looking from the hide, you'll see a farm on the right hand side of the opposite shore. Check the top left hand field of the farm, next to the wood, as this often produces views of Black Grouse though numbers seem to have declined in recent years. We once saw a large cat heading into this wood, but it was impossible to decide if it was a genuine wildcat, or a hybrid. The reserve is very quiet in winter though the occasional Smew has been recorded.

Likely bird species/other fauna

Spring and summer	Osprey	Whinchat	*Other wildlife*
Goosander	Golden Eagle	Stonechat	Brown trout – usually
Red-breasted	Buzzard	Wheatear	only seen being carried
Merganser	Goshawk (rare)	Raven	by an Osprey!
Slavonian Grebe	Hen Harrier (rare)	Reed Bunting	
Red-throated Diver	Merlin		
Black Grouse	Peregrine		

❺ The A9 and lay-by 151

Background information

TRAVELLING ALONG the stretch of the A9 between Inverness and Aviemore regularly produces sightings of Osprey and Peregrine with a chance of Short-eared Owls if it is a good year for them. Early in the morning there are often Ring Ouzels feeding by the side of the road as you pass the Slochd summit.

A much better bet for Ring Ouzels is to stop at lay-by 151 as you head south on the A9. It is known locally as the German's Head because of a rock formation that looks like, well, a helmeted head certainly, but you would be struggling to pin it down as German. Depending on how you squint at it, anything from a Roman soldier onwards is possible!

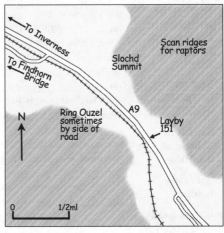

Likely bird species

Summer	
Osprey (over A9)	Short-eared Owl (over A9)
Peregrine (over A9)	Ring Ouzel

Whatever you call it, there are usually a couple of pairs of Ring Ouzels flitting round the bushes on the side of the slope and you should be able to get some pretty good views. The birds are one of the earliest migrants to arrive and last to leave.

Other Sites

IF YOU HAVE the time, the B862 south from Loch Ruthven towards Fort Augustus is worth exploring. Look for Hen Harriers and Short-eared Owls along the first stretch of the road, farmland and hedgerow birds as you pass through some of the hamlets and then Golden Eagles further on.

There is a fantastic panoramic viewpoint just north of Loch Tarff and this makes a good place to scan.

Alternatively, turn left out of Loch Ruthven and have a drive round Lochs Ashie and, particularly, Duntelchaig. This area is good for Peregrine and Merlin. Any of the lochs could turn up a Red- or Black-throated Diver. Loch Ness is too deep for much bird life and can safely be ignored.

Likely bird species

All year	Summer
Golden Eagle	Black-throated Diver
Yellowhammer	Hen Harrier
	Short-eared Owl

Key points

- **Food, petrol and toilets in Grantown-on-Spey and Forres**

- **Best moorland in Speyside area**

- **Easy Red Grouse on the moors**

- **Breeding waders**

- **Whole area excellent for raptors**

- **Lochindorb area good for Short-eared Owl and divers**

- **Excellent at dawn and, especially, dusk**

- **Location makes Lochindorb easy to combine with a trip to the coast**

- **Lochindorb and Dulsie area suitable for watching from roadside**

TAKE A RUINED castle, once the haunt of the notorious 14th Century outlaw, the Wolf of Badenoch. Set it on an island in the middle of a cold, black loch and surround it with mile after mile of bleak, unyielding moorland. It sounds like the setting for a bad romantic novel. All that's missing is a ghost or two. Those I can't promise, though you might come across a pale, grey wraith-like apparition looming out of the twilight.

Lochindorb – the name comes from the Gaelic for 'loch of trouble' - is a great place to visit for a whole range of moorland species, raptors, breeding waders and waterbirds. It doesn't matter if you just give it a quick drive past as you head off for somewhere else, or spend some considerable time in the area exploring here and the nearby River Findhorn: you are sure of some first class birding.

Because of its proximity to Speyside, this is a popular spot with visiting birders and you can usually find someone else to swap the latest news and gossip with. Not all conversations turn out quite as you anticipate though.

This is a good place to find Merlins, especially in the area of moorland near the lodge. I was talking to one birder who was excited by this, as it was a bird he had always wanted to see.

'Keep your eyes open just round here,' I said, 'it's a good spot.' Half an hour or so later, we pulled into another lay-by just as a bird hurtled over the bonnet of the other driver's car in pursuit of a hapless Meadow Pipit. I went to talk to him again, flushed with a sense of omniscience.

'There you are,' I gloated. 'I told you that you would see one here.'

'What?' he replied.

Large tracts of moorland are attractive to Hen Harriers

'A Merlin. A male's just flown straight over your bonnet.'

'You're joking.' His head was thrown back in a sort of stunned disbelief. 'I was just showing my wife a Common Sandpiper on the loch edge.'

We left just as the marital row was starting to develop, accompanied by the sound of a fieldguide being slammed against the dashboard.

Though it is not a great area for mammals, the largest wildcat recorded in Scotland in recent times was trapped near here in the 1940s. It measured 48 inches from nose to tail.

The rest of this tour allows you to explore two different areas of the River Findhorn, once as it meanders through an open valley, the other in a heavily wooded area as it rushes through a narrow gorge en route to the sea at Findhorn Bay (see page 157).

The whole area is fairly remote and devoid of services. You are not too far though from Nairn and Forres to the north, an area good for castles, houses and archaeological sites if you want a bit of culture. Grantown-on-Spey to the south is the start of malt whisky country, which may appeal slightly more, depending on whether you feel the need to drown your sorrows (see above).

How to get there

Nearest large town: The tour begins at Grantown-on-Spey.

From Grantown-on-Spey, either head N on A939 or head W along A938 for five miles then turn R onto B9007. In each case, a minor road leads to Lochindorb after seven miles. Continue along the length of the minor road, following the shore of Lochindorb.

Either complete the loop back to Grantown or, for Dulsie Bridge, continue N along B9007 for another three miles then turn L onto a minor road to Dulsie. After crossing the bridge, turn L in the village and follow the river. Take a sharp R turn at Drynachan Lodge to Highland Boath. Turn R at the T-junction and follow the minor road back to Dulsie.

Turn L onto B9007 and continue N until it joins A940. Turn L towards Forres

and after two miles, you come to a picnic site on L, about four and a half miles south of Forres, signed Sluie Forest Walks (NJ 021 540). Park here and explore the area to the west of the road, leading down to the river. NB This is a very easy car park to miss.

The total mileage of the tour is approximately 80 miles.

❶ Lochindorb

Background information

THE LOCH IS situated north of Grantown-on-Spey. Main roads leading north, flank either side of the loch and the loch itself is accessed from a minor road that runs along the southern shore. This makes for a nice circular route though I would recommend going in an anticlockwise direction first thing in the morning and clockwise if you visit at dusk, so that the sun is behind you.

As you head up the B9007, check out some of the little lay-bys and quarries, which inevitably hold Wheatears and might produce the occasional pair of Twite. As you turn off the main road, you immediately find yourself in prime moorland. The moor is one of the easiest places around to see Red Grouse - listen for their 'get back, get back' calls. Listen out too for the plaintive cry of Golden Plovers and the bubbling call of Curlews. Other waders in the area are Lapwings, Dunlin and Snipe. Redshanks, Oystercatchers and Common Sandpipers are obvious along the loch edge.

At the risk of stating the obvious, stick to the paths when you walk over the heather. The ground is nowhere near as solid as it looks and the water and mud that makes this such a wonderful habitat can be surprisingly deep. Memories of a non-birding friend doing an impromptu

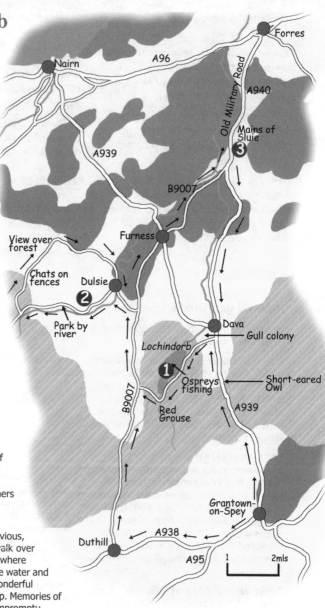

Highland Fling as he tried to avoid ruining his expensive shoes will linger for a long time.

The commonest small birds are Meadow Pipits and in spring, you should hear Cuckoos on the lookout for a convenient nest to parasitise. Clumps of gorse hold Stonechat and Whinchat. The trees round the lodge hold the ubiquitous Willow Warbler and Chaffinch. You might even come across something unusual such as a singing Redwing.

Both Black-throated and Red-throated Divers turn up. Black-throated Divers tend to prefer the southern end of the loch as far as the island, whereas Red-throated Divers favour the other end. There are usually one or two pairs of Wigeon knocking about too.

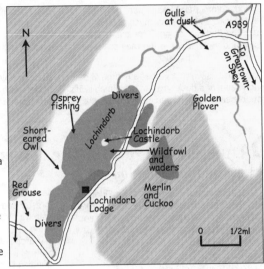

The whole area is good for raptors. Peregrines are occasional, Merlins regular and Ospreys increasingly seen fishing, sometimes two or three at the same time. Buzzards and Kestrels are easy to spot. At the eastern end of the road there is a large gathering of pre-roost gulls – mainly Common Gulls and Black-headed Gulls - towards dusk and these are often the best indicator that something is hunting; beware though, the gulls also go up for, and mob, the likes of Grey Herons.

Hen Harriers hunt in the area and can turn up anywhere over the heather though there is an awful lot of moorland to search and your chances of seeing a bird are at best slim. Even though they are relatively easy to see in

Southern England over the winter months, there really is something special about seeing one hunt over moorland - its 'proper' habitat - especially if you catch up with a pale grey male.

As everywhere, Short-eared Owl numbers fluctuate considerably depending on the abundance or otherwise of the local rodent population. Though we have seen them at both ends of the loch and along the far bank, the best area seems to be at the eastern end, on either side of the A939.

If you drive back along the A939 towards Grantown at dusk, there is a good chance of a Woodcock roding over the woods just outside the town.

Continues on page 140

Likely bird species

All year	Black-throated Diver	Dunlin	Whinchat
Red Grouse	Red-throated Diver	Redshank	Wheatear
Stonechat	Osprey	Curlew	Twite
	Hen Harrier	Common Gull	
Summer	Merlin	Black-headed Gull	
Wigeon	Golden Plover	Short-eared Owl	

Spring, summer and autumn are the best times to visit. Winter is very much quieter, though the Red Grouse and Stonechats are ever present and you might turn up the occasional Whooper Swan on the loch.

Lochindorb is worth a visit at any time of day, though dawn and dusk have an extra magic. Its location means that you can easily combine a

drive past the loch with other sites in the area, e.g. driving past first thing in the morning en route to the coast, then again on the way back at night.

The road hugs the edge of the loch and there are plenty of parking places so that any birders with mobility problems shouldn't have any trouble watching from the car.

❷ Dulsie Bridge and the River Findhorn
Background information

IN DULSIE, the bridge over the River Findhorn provides spectacular views of a steep gorge. Dippers and Grey Wagtails fly through and you can look down on a colony of Swallows, a view you don't often get.

Just through the village, turn left on a minor road, which follows the edge of the River Findhorn. There is ample parking by the side of the river and from here, you can scan for raptors over the mountain ridges. Look out for the likes of Golden Eagle, Peregrine and Osprey. The river itself holds Goosanders, and there are more Dippers and Common Sandpipers as well as the ubiquitous Oystercatchers to look for.

The area here is part of a massive game estate and in 2002, the place was crawling with Pheasants of various strains and Red-legged Partridges. The woods hold good numbers of Woodcocks and birds can often be seen flying over, well before dusk.

Again, be prepared for the unexpected. I once found a female Pied Flycatcher here, well north of its usual range.

The road then climbs steeply through moorland. Whinchats, Stonechats and Meadow Pipits often use the wire fences as lookout posts. As you reach the top, you

get excellent views out over the surrounding forestry and this makes another good place to scan for birds of prey, maybe another Osprey flying out either to the coast or to Lochindorb in search of a fish or a pair of Buzzards riding a thermal and displaying high over their woodland nest.

This part of the tour offers a good range of habitats to explore and the drive can be easily coupled with a trip to Lochindorb. Best times to visit are spring through to autumn. Timing during the day is not critical. Much of the birding can be done from the car for disabled birders though there are no other facilities nearby.

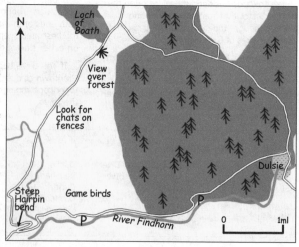

Likely bird species

All year		Stonechat	Osprey
Buzzard	Dipper		Peregrine
Golden Eagle	Red-legged Partridge	*Summer*	Common Sandpiper
Grey Wagtail	Grey Partridge	Goosander	Whinchat
	Woodcock		

❸ Sluie walk
Background information

THE PICNIC SITE here is set up to allow access to the dramatic gorge but there are great views over the forest canopy looking west and north and this is a good spot for raptors including the occasional Goshawk, Osprey and Peregrine. Fine days in February and March are probably your best bet if you want to see Goshawks displaying.

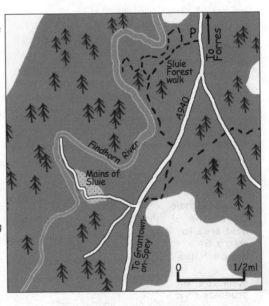

The Scots pine and beech woods contain a typical range of species including Crested Tit and spring brings plenty of migrants such as Redstart and Tree Pipit. The river here cuts through a series of gorges and is fast flowing and spectacular. Nevertheless, you should still see Dippers here, using boulders as stopping off points before embarking on another underwater feeding trip. Look for rocks covered with birdlime, a good sign that they are being used regularly. The way-marked trail is about three miles long.

The walks here contain some fairly steep terrain and are not suitable for wheelchairs. Stout boots are recommended and you should take extra care near the river as the rocks often get wet and slippery.

Likely bird species

All year		*Summer*	Redstart
Buzzard	Dipper	Osprey	Willow Warbler
Goshawk (rare)	Crested Tit	Peregrine	Spotted Flycatcher
Sparrowhawk	Common woodland birds	Tree Pipit	

Key points

- **Limited facilities in Tomintoul. Use Grantown and Dufftown. Toilets also at Visitor Centre**

- **Pick up trail leaflet from the Estate office**

- **Fantastic display in visitor centre**

- **More than 100 miles of paths to explore**

- **Hide at Glenmulliach Forest**

- **Main road often closed after snow**

- **Poor access for wheelchair users - the best area to watch from the car is the A939 Tomintoul to Braemar road which passes through some spectacular moorland**

- **Proper walking gear needed for trips into the Ladder Hills and Hills of Cromdale**

STRANGE as it may seem, not everybody immediately thinks of birds when you mention the word 'Speyside'. This is prime malt whisky country and the many distilleries in the area, including Glenlivet, are happy to show you how *uisgebeatha* – water of life – is made, and let you sample their produce.

Bordered by the River Livet and Ladder Hills (internationally important for Hen Harriers) to the east and the River Avon (pronounced A'an) and Hills of Cromdale to the west, this huge estate (c 58,000 acres or 90 square miles) was acquired by the Crown Estate in 1937.

The Crown Estate is a UK-wide property organisation. It is part of the Hereditary possessions of the monarchy, but the land doesn't belong to the Queen or the Government, so all revenues are handed over to the Treasury for the benefit of the public. Though it is very much a working estate, with farms, forestry, shooting and fishing businesses, visitors are welcome to explore the area.

The area's biggest village is Tomintoul (pronounced Tom-in-towel), which claims to be the highest village in the Highlands. It isn't; Dalwhinnie has that honour

and curiously, two villages in the Scottish Lowlands are also higher. The village hit the news a few years ago when a conman stole several million pounds from Scotland Yard and started buying up the village and effectively acting as Laird before the police got hold of their man. Not surprisingly, this little escapade doesn't sit well and it is best not to bring it up with the locals.

The village has always had something of an unpopular reputation. Built, along with several of the local bridges and nearby Corgarff Castle (good for Merlin), by English soldiers in hot pursuit of, first, local Jacobites and then, even more importantly, whisky smugglers, it is easy to see why.

Even Queen Victoria, who loved the Highlands, hated it, describing it as 'the most tumble-down, poor-looking place I ever saw.' Don't be put off; it's not that bad. Today it is promoted as the centre of the 'Three W's' – whisky, walking and wildlife.

At the south-eastern end of Tomintoul, the Glenlivet Visitor Centre is open from 9am to 6pm throughout the year, though the toilet facilities and leaflets are available at all times.

Staffed by some of the friendliest and most helpful

people in the Highlands, there are various multimedia and hands-on exhibits to explain the management of the Estate and its wildlife. Rangers will help you decide where to go and tell you what's around. Make sure that you pick up the free map of the area, which details all the various trails. The centre is an excellent resource and anyone looking for a role model, would do well to visit. Contact the centre on 01807 580 319.

This tour will appeal to those birdwatchers who enjoy a good walk. Within the estate there are more than 100 miles of way-marked walks taking in a variety of different habitats. These range from a couple of miles to huge stretches of long-range footpaths, so there is something to suit all abilities. I've picked out a couple of spots on the edge of, or just outside, the estate together with some general birding notes.

The A939 that crosses this area is always one of the first to be closed when it snows, so winter is probably best avoided.

How to get there

Nearest large town: Grantown-on-Spey is approximately 16 miles NW from Tomintoul.

The Estate lies to the N of Tomintoul and is roughly bounded by B9008 to the E and B9136 to W. Start at the visitor centre in Tomintoul, which is at the S end of Main Street.

Head E from Tomintoul on A939 towards Braemar. After about three miles, you will see a car park/picnic site signed on L. This is the start of the Glenmulliach trail. Four miles further along A839, you reach the Well of the Lecht picnic site on L and three miles further brings you to the Lecht ski centre.

For Ben Rinnes, leave B9008 at

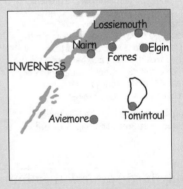

Auchbreck on B9009 towards Dufftown. This road skirts the eastern edge of the mountain and a minor road on L takes you along the northern edge. Return on A95 and B9008 to Glenlivet.

Total mileage for the tour is approximately 50 miles

❶ Glenmulliach Forest

Background information

THIS IS WALK ONE on the estate map and takes you up to a woodland hide. The path is steep and slippery after rain so wear boots. It is not suitable for wheelchairs.

Birds here are typical of coniferous forests and include Common Crossbill, Redpoll, Siskin, Coal Tit, Bullfinch, Great Spotted Woodpecker, Treecreeper and Goldcrest. Sparrowhawks, Kestrels and Buzzards nest. They are always easy to see, unlike the Tawny and Long-eared Owls; you are only likely to come across these if you encounter lots of small birds mobbing a roosting bird and so betraying its presence.

In spring and summer, you are likely to hear, if not see, Cuckoos on the forest edge looking for suitable nests to parasitise. Tree Pipits also breed. Willow Warblers are common though Chiffchaffs and Blackcaps only occasional. Spotted Flycatchers are the last of the summer migrants to arrive.

Good numbers of mammals are present though, as ever, extremely shy and/or nocturnal so sightings are few and far between. Red squirrels and roe deer are the most likely sightings with pine martens, wildcats, foxes, badgers and bats are all in the area. Pick a still day to get the best out of this area; the birds tend not to leave the dense cover if it is windy or raining.

If you continue up into the hills towards the viewpoint at Breac Leathad, look out for

Likely bird species/other fauna

All year	Cuckoo
Red Grouse	Tree Pipit
Black Grouse	Whinchat
Stonechat	Wheatear
Redpoll	Ring Ouzel
Common Crossbill	Spotted Flycatcher
Summer	
Golden Plover	*Other wildlife*
Dunlin	Red squirrel
Short-eared Owl	Roe deer

Black and Red Grouse as well as breeding waders such as Snipe, Curlew, Dunlin and Golden Plover. Wheatears, Whinchats, Stonechats and Ring Ouzels are all present. This area, together with the other side of the main road from the car park, is good for Short-eared Owls.

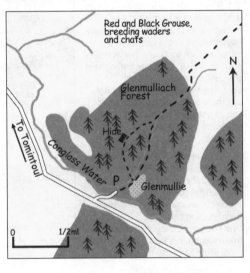

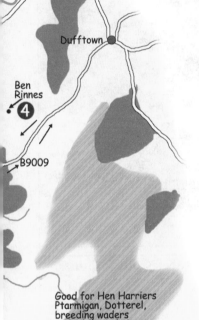

②Well of the Lecht
Background information

A FEW MILES east of the forest, the next car park is the start of yet another long distance footpath and a good place to explore the local moorland habitat. If you don't fancy the whole walk, it is worth doing the first mile or so as far as the Lecht mines where they used to extract manganese ore.

Small birds in the heather include Stonechat, Whinchat, Wheatear, Sky Lark and Meadow Pipit with breeding waders and grouse, as you get further into the moor. Dipper and Grey Wagtail flit along the burn. Merlin and Kestrels are the most likely raptors.

See map on page 146

Likely bird species

All year	Summer
Red Grouse	Merlin
Dipper	Curlew
Grey Wagtail	Golden Plover
Meadow Pipit	Wheatear
Stonechat	Whinchat
	Ring Ouzel

❸ Lecht ski centre

Background information

RECENT WINTERS have not been kind to the Scottish skiing industry and in an effort to diversify, management at the Lecht have introduced all sorts of other activities such as go-karts as they try to make the centre viable all through the year. The whole area is pretty ugly, but there is a large car park where you can stop and scan, and a café if whatever snow is present chills you too much.

The main reason for stopping here is to try for Ptarmigan. I've lost count of the number of times people have told me that the area is too low for them, but we have seen and heard their retching calls here a few times over the years, though they are far from guaranteed. Red Grouse are far more likely and easy to see here.

Wheatears, chats and Ring Ouzels are all in, or around, the gullies though what you see is likely to depend on how far away from the crowds you get. Dunlin often fly around the car park area and there is a chance of a hunting Peregrine or Merlin, or an Osprey drifting over.

This map covers both Well of the Lecht and the Lecht ski centre

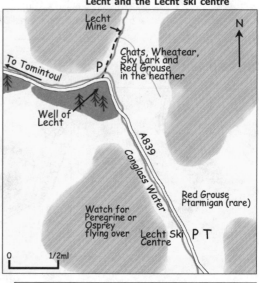

Likely bird species/other fauna

All year	Dunlin
Ptarmigan (outside chance)	Ring Ouzel
	Wheatear
Red Grouse	
	Other wildlife
Summer	Arctic hare
Osprey	
Peregrine	

---

❹ Ben Rinnes

Background information

SITUATED JUST NORTH-EAST of the Estate, at 2,759 feet, this is the highest peak in the area. Red Grouse give way to Ptarmigan on the top, where Snow Bunting and Dotterel are occasionally seen; spring is the best time to look for the latter. Raven, Peregrine, Hen Harrier and Golden Eagle are all in the area (see main map for location).

Likely bird species

All year	*Spring*
Ptarmigan	Dotterel (outside chance)
Golden Eagle	
Raven	

5 General area

Background information

MORE THAN 100 SPECIES have been recorded on the Estate, with most of them seen annually. Of these, about 60 species breed. Goosanders are present on both the Rivers Avon and Livet, especially where the banks are wooded. A few pairs of Teal and Wigeon are present in summer. Look for Dippers and Grey Wagtails on fast-flowing stretches of river and stream. Capercaillies are in some of the woods though elusive. Check farmland for both Grey and Red-legged Partridges.

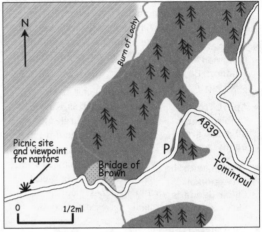

Hen Harriers are present in both the Ladder Hills to the south-east and the Cromdale Hills to the north-west though you are likely to have to do some serious walking to find them. The Bridge of Brown, right on the western edge of the Estate is good for Peregrine. Golden Eagles are seen only occasionally (try the Ladder Hills) but you have a much better chance of connecting with a flyover Osprey.

Dotterel move through some of the higher peaks in spring, with the occasional pair staying to breed in the Ladder Hills. Similarly, there are Ptarmigan on the tops. All the peaks are well off the beaten track though and require some serious walking.

Breeding waders include Woodcock, Redshank, Snipe, Oystercatcher, Lapwing, Golden Plover, Dunlin and Common Sandpiper. Barn, Tawny and Long-eared Owls all breed,

with Short-eared Owls on the moors.

Summer visitors include Redstart and Spotted Flycatcher. Willow Warblers are common, Sedge Warblers regular but Blackcaps and Chiffchaffs only occasional. Bramblings, Fieldfares and Redwings are common winter visitors but Twite, Linnets, Yellowhammers and Reed Buntings are resident.

Mountain hares are common on the tops, one of an impressive 27 species of mammal recorded. Common lizard, adder, slow worm and palmate newt are among the reptiles seen. The flora is, as you might expect, impressive. Butterflies include northern brown argus and Scotch argus.

Likely bird species/other flora and fauna

All year	Tawny Owl	Hen Harrier	Spotted Flycatcher
Goosander	Long-eared Owl	Peregrine	
Red Grouse	Twite	Merlin	*Other wildlife*
Black Grouse	Yellowhammer	Golden Plover	Mammals
Ptarmigan		Dunlin	Butterflies
Grey Partridge	*Spring*	Short-eared Owl	Reptiles
Red-legged Partridge	Dotterel	Common Sandpiper	Wildflowers
Woodcock		Redstart	
Barn Owl	*Summer*	Sedge Warbler	
	Osprey		

Key points

- Food, petrol and toilets in all major towns

- Hides at Longman Point, Findhorn Bay and Loch Spynie

- Apart from Culbin Sands, all sites are easily accessed

- Terrain, with the exception of Culbin Sands, is very easy going

- Most places can be birded from the immediate vicinity of the car

- Use car to view Nairn and Burghead harbours and Lossiemouth and Spey Bay river mouths if it is wet

- Telescope useful for scanning sea and roosting wader flocks

- Car parks at Wellhill in Culbin Forest and Roseisle Forest good for Crested Tits

THE SOUTHERN EDGE of the Moray Firth holds internationally important numbers of waders and wildfowl and is at its best from late autumn to early spring, away from the main holiday season.

It stretches east from Inverness as far as Kinnaird Head in Fraserburgh (see page 69 in Deeside) where it joins the North Sea and this tour, which is easily accessed from the main A96 heading east from Inverness, concentrates mainly on assorted coastal sites as it passes through the towns of Nairn, Forres and Elgin.

It features an eclectic collection of viewpoints, starting with the back of an industrial estate, before passing a football stadium, military fort, a massive forest planted to stop the coast blowing away, manmade and natural harbours and an active RAF base, ending at the mouth of one of Scotland's most famous rivers.

Inverness, recently granted city status, is the capital of the Highlands and always seems to be in a state of major development as new shopping malls are installed. You can still find touches of the old style though, away from the corporate logos. Record shops have little space for mainstream pop or classical music, concentrating instead on local, traditional groups and singers. There is an excellent secondhand bookshop and café, in a converted church, which usually holds several shelves of old bird books.

For anyone passing through Inverness, it is often worth taking a quick detour along the A96. At the first roundabout, there is a huge Tesco's supermarket. Apart from stocking up on provisions, the petrol here tends to be the cheapest in the area and it is well worth filling up.

The massive complex at Fort George, built to counter any further rebellions after Bonnie Prince Charlie had been defeated, never actually saw a shot fired in anger and so seems something of a waste of a billion or so pounds in today's money. However, there is an excellent museum here and anyone visiting should take the opportunity to indulge in a spot of seawatching.

Culbin Sands now cover the fertile coastal estate that was desroyed by sandstorms in 1694. Over-harvesting of marram grass was probably responsible for all the erosion and this was banned by an act of the Scottish Parliament in 1695. The area was only stabilised when the Forestry Commission acquired the land in 1922 and planted many thousands of trees though it took until the 1960s before the dunes stopped shifting.

Though you can easily spend the whole day birding along the coast, this trip fits in well if you want to broaden your horizons, or other family members want to take in a bit of shopping or culture.

Some of the sites here might only take half an hour or so to cover: some half a day. To a large extent you are dependent on the tide too, so that has to be taken into account. As ever, the birds are closest either side of high tide.

Continues on page 150

How to get there

Nearest large town: Inverness is the starting point for this tour.

Take A82 towards city centre. At Harbour Roundabout turn R into Harbour Road, then R at traffic lights into Longman Drive. Park in lay-by on L, next to the hide and just before the bridge.

Continue under the bridge, past Inverness Caledonian Thistle football ground. Park carefully here and view the firth. Continue and turn L at roundabout back onto A9, proceeding S until L turn onto A96 towards Nairn and Aberdeen. All other sites can be easily accessed from this road.

Carry straight on at the next roundabout (Tescos) and after half a mile, turn L signed Milton of Culloden. Pass under railway bridge and park immediately on L.

For Alturlie, continue along A96 for another 1.5 miles and turn L (signed Alturlie). Follow the road to the shore and park without blocking the road.

Continuing E on A96 past Inverness Airport, the crossroads with B9006 leads to Fort George.

At Nairn, turn R at roundabout into St Ninian Road (still A96) then first L into Harbour Street. If you cross the river, you have gone too far. Continue to the large car park at the harbour.

Leaving the harbour, cross a bridge over River Nairn to East Beach and the Caravan Park. Park at the far end of the car park and continue E through dunes to Culbin Sands. Alternatively, retrace your steps to A96, turn L, cross the river and take the second on L into Lochloy Road. Stay on this minor road, which leads along the southern edge of Culbin Forest. Ignore the first picnic site at Cloddymoss and continue E, following signs for Welhill and the large picnic site there.

Findhorn Bay is N of Forres. From A96, take B9011 to Kinloss and Findhorn. The

Continues on page 151

Key points

- **Best viewpoints for Ospreys are Longman Point (distant views), Findhorn Bay and Spey Bay**

- **Wildlife cruises from Inverness and Spey Bay (east bank)**

- **Seaducks and waders can turn up anywhere along the coast in winter**

- **Fort George (and Chanonry Point) best sites for passage seabirds**

- **Bottle-nosed dolphins common**

From page 149

Non-birding attractions are plentiful. Anyone who has ever read Macbeth at school will want to visit Cawdor Castle, while Culloden was the site of the last battle on

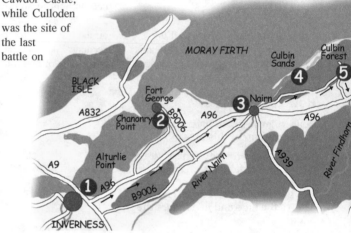

British soil in 1746, when the Jacobite forces led by Bonnie Prince Charlie made their last, futile stand. The National Trust for Scotland's excellent visitor centre is always crowded.

You never know who you will meet either. Our guide at Brodie Castle seemed especially helpful, showing us letters from Mary Queen of Scots that weren't on general display. It was only when we recognised a portrait in the hall that we realised that it was the laird himself showing us round.

Ancient history is well represented too with Clava Cairns dating back to the Bronze Age, and Sueno's Stone in Forres being one of the best examples of Pictish culture. Mediaevalists will no doubt prefer the ruined cathedral in Elgin. If Inverness is 'bustling', then the only way to describe the likes of Nairn and Elgin is 'genteel', as both exhibit much understated Georgian and Victorian elegance. The people of Elgin pride themselves as speaking the best English in the whole of Britain.

All these attractions will provide a good selection of commoner bird species and none is more than a few miles from one of the major birding sites detailed later.

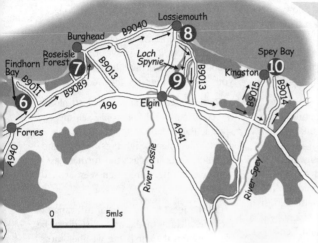

From page 149

hide is well signposted on L, at far end of the RAF base. For the beach, continue into Findhorn itself and follow signs to car park.

Retrace your steps to Kinloss and turn L onto B9089 towards Burghead. Look for signs on L towards the Forestry Commission's picnic site at Roseisle. The B-road continues into Burghead and down to the harbour.

As you leave Burghead, turn L onto B9040 to Lossiemouth. As you enter the town, you will see the golf course and car park for the West Beach on L. Carry on into town centre, picking up signs for the harbour and East Beach.

Leave Lossiemouth on A941 towards Elgin. On the edge of town, turn L onto B9103. Cross the canal and turn R onto a minor road just before the river at Arthur's Bridge. After about a mile, take the first R towards Scarffbanks on a very minor road. Park on R as you arrive in the farmyard and walk down the path to the hide overlooking Loch Spynie.

Back at B9103 turn R to reach A96. Turn L and continue E for six miles. For Kingston and the west bank of the Spey, turn L on B9015 and continue to picnic site at end of road. For the east bank of the Spey, stay on A96 for another 0.5 mile, over the river and then turn L onto B9014. Follow the road down to the river mouth.

Inverness to Spey Bay is about 52 miles.

On the coast itself, non-breeding waders start to arrive back from late summer. Numbers of waders and wildfowl start to build steadily as autumn turns into winter and the firth holds internationally important numbers of Knot, Bar-tailed Godwits, Curlews, Oystercatchers, Redshanks and Dunlin. Look for Ringed Plovers, Turnstones and Purple Sandpipers on rocky outcrops and Sanderling along the tide line. Late spring sees a few stragglers still remaining as birds head north again.

The sea holds auks, Common and Velvet Scoters, Long-tailed Ducks, divers, grebes, Goosanders and Red-breasted Mergansers, often in spectacular numbers. Geese feed inland and huge skeins can be seen flying over at dawn and dusk.

Continues on page 152

From page 151

There are usually flocks of Snow Buntings wintering in the dunes, though these can range far and wide. Any flock of passerines is likely to attract the attentions of Merlins and Sparrowhawks while waders and ducks are the preferred food of Peregrines.

Spring and autumn are dynamic as you never know what you might find, while winter offers huge numbers of birds. Summer has plenty to offer as well though. There are three good spots to watch Ospreys fishing, tern colonies are active, all the migrants have settled in to breed and there are always resident species such as Crested Tits and Red Kites to watch.

Timing is fairly crucial and if you want to get the best out of your wader watching, then an hour either side of high tide is going to prove most productive as it brings the birds closer to you, and concentrates the flocks.

Bottle-nosed dolphins patrol all along the coast here and you could see these spectacular creatures from any of the coastal sites here. Sightings of grey and common seals increase the further east you go and otters are often seen around Spey Bay.

All the local towns offer a full range of facilities. Many of the areas listed can be viewed from the car if the weather turns inclement or you have limited mobility.

---

❶ Longman Point and the Inner Moray Firth
Background information

LYING in the shadow of the spectacular Kessock Bridge, the sewage outfalls at Longman Point offer a nutrient-rich diet to a variety of birds. Winter sees good numbers of gulls, waders and wildfowl. Spring and autumn sees an ever-changing population as birds stop en route to or from their breeding grounds.

Summer is the quietest period, but even so, there is a good chance of seeing an Osprey or two fishing at low tide (Apr-Sep). As you look over to the Black Isle, Red Kites and Buzzards can be seen throughout the year.

A road at the north end of the Inverness industrial estate snakes along the southern edge of the firth. A lay-by and small hide give excellent views of the shore, though there is little need to actually use the hide unless it is raining. If you want to use the hide, you will need to get a key from Inverness Service Point, Church St, Inverness Tel. 01463 703999, open 9-5 (Mon-Fri) and 9.30-1 (Sat). Refundable deposit.

Winter wildfowl include good numbers of Goldeneye and Teal. Check all the Teal for the occasional Green-winged Teal. Grebes, Red-throated Divers, Red-breasted Mergansers, and Long-tailed Ducks are occasionally seen from here, but the other three vantage points are probably better for these species. Numbers of gulls build up and are worth scanning for Iceland and Glaucous Gulls or even something rarer: Ross's Gull and Ivory Gull have both been recorded.

A Peregrine is the likeliest hunter, attracted by the wintering waders including Black- and Bar-tailed Godwits, Dunlin, Curlews, Redshanks, Ringed Plovers and Turnstones. Ruff and Spotted Redshanks are most likely on spring passage, whereas Little Stints and Curlew Sandpipers move through in autumn.

This is when seawatching can be productive, especially in easterly winds though if you have the choice, Chanonry Point (page 168) or Fort George (see below) are likely to give you better views of the same birds.

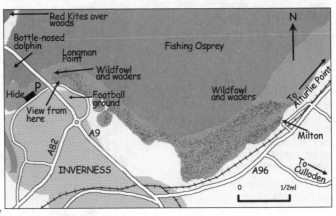

As you head east, the road swings past Inverness Caledonian Thistle's football ground. Park carefully here and again, scan the firth. The species here will be the same as those mentioned above, but you might get much better views, depending on the state of the tides. High tides bring the waterfowl closer, whereas exposed mud makes for the best wader watching.

There are another couple of sites that offer excellent and different views of this stretch of the firth, both easily accessed and signed off the A96. Milton of Culloden is a much prettier viewpoint than Longman, enhanced by areas of scrub and gorse, which in turn attract a selection of small birds including Yellowhammers. Listen out for the scratchy song of Whitethroats in spring.

Waders and wildfowl are similar to Longman, though you have a better chance of catching

up with Goosanders and Red-breasted Mergansers than you do further along the firth. A Green-winged Teal, the North American cousin of our own Teal, and now deemed to be a separate species, has been a regular along the coast here in recent winters. Look out for Slavonian and Little Grebes in winter.

The road out to Alturlie Point follows the curve of the bay and you can get excellent views of the firth from the car if it is raining. This is a particularly good spot for Red-breasted Mergansers; our last May visit produced a raft of more than 30, very close inshore. The bay here is a traditional wintering site for Scaup and Shelducks are ever-present. All the hirundines are present in summer, though it always seems incongruous to see Sand Martins feeding over the sea.

Likely bird species/other fauna

All year	Slavonian Grebe	Dunlin	Curlew Sandpiper
Shelduck	Wildfowl numbers	Curlew	Seabirds in easterlies
Common wildfowl	increasing	Redshank	including
Buzzard	Scaup	Turnstone	Skuas
Red Kite	Long-tailed Duck		Shearwaters
Gulls	Goosander	*Summer*	Terns
Yellowhammer	Red-breasted	Osprey	Auks
	Merganser		
Winter	Peregrine	*Autumn*	*Other wildlife*
Red-throated Diver	Both godwits	Little Stint	Bottle-nosed dolphin

153

❷ Fort George
Background information

FORT GEORGE is built on the southern of two 'tooth-like' projections that almost meet in the middle of the Moray Firth, Chanonry Point on the Black Isle being the other. Any birds blown into the firth during autumnal easterly gales automatically have to fly right in front of you, making this an excellent seawatching spot. See the section on Chanonry Point (page 168) for a full description of typical species.

This is an excellent spot to see bottle-nosed dolphins and harbour porpoises. There are usually a few grey and common seals offshore.

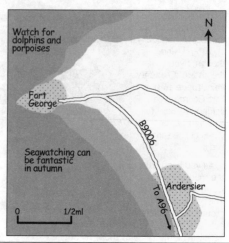

Watch for dolphins and porpoises

Fort George

Seawatching can be fantastic in autumn

B9006

To A96

Ardersier

N

0   1/2ml

Likely bird species/other fauna

All year	Shearwaters (autumn)	Common Scoter	Common waders
Meadow Pipit	Gannet	Velvet Scoter	
Rock Pipit	Kittiwake	Goldeneye	*Other wildlife*
Yellowhammer	Auks	Red-throated Diver	Bottle-nosed dolphin
	Fulmar	Sanderling	Harbour porpoise
Spring/autumn		Purple Sandpiper	
Terns	*Winter*	Bar-tailed Godwit	
Skuas	Long-tailed Duck	Turnstone	

❸ Nairn Harbour
Background information

THE HARBOUR makes an excellent vantage point for a spot of seawatching. Walking out to the end of the harbour wall affords a good all-round view of the firth, but if the weather turns nasty you can always use your car as a hide.

If there have been severe storms, especially in autumn and winter, check the harbour itself for birds taking shelter from the gales. You could get excellent close-up views of auks, divers, grebes and seaducks.

Eiders are ever-present and this is a good place to check the large rafts of Common Scoters for Velvet Scoters, with the outside chance of a Surf Scoter turning up in winter. Good numbers of Purple Sandpipers roost in winter, check any of the rocks on the beaches. They usually feed with Turnstones and Dunlin.

Other species could include flocks of waders from nearby Culbin Sands moving to newly exposed bits of mud, or, if the tide is coming in, being forced off to a new temporary roost site. Seabirds include a similar range of species to those seen all along the coast; terns in summer (the quietest season here) with skuas and shearwaters appearing in autumn.

From the harbour, you can follow signs for East Beach. Drive through the caravan site to the car park at the end and explore the dune systems for the likes of Sky Larks, Linnets and Whitethroats. Merlins and Peregrines hunt the area in late autumn and winter.

If you really want a good walk, you can continue from here to Culbin Sands.

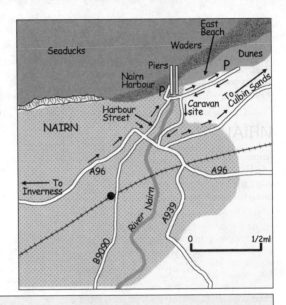

Likely bird species

All year	*Spring/autumn*	Seabirds including	*Winter*
Eider	Waders including	Terns	Wader and wildfowl
Common Scoter	Godwits	Skuas	numbers increase
	Knot	Shearwaters (autumn)	Purple Sandpiper
Summer	Dunlin	Gannets	Merlin
Terns	Redshanks	Auks	Peregrine

➍ RSPB Culbin Sands
Background information

PROBABLY one of the least visited and unspoilt RSPB reserves, Culbin Sands offers you a walk of many miles along the beach and you will have to hike if you get the tides wrong! This is one of the largest shingle and sand dune bars in Britain and there is also an extensive area of saltmarsh for the waders to feed.

The sands stretch out behind Culbin Forest, all the way to Findhorn Bay, about ten miles away, but fortunately, most of the waders roost towards the west end of the beach, the end where you will park.

Winter is far and away the best time of year to visit. As well as the huge wader flocks Knot, Dunlin, Bar-tailed Godwit, Curlew, Redshank, Sanderling and Ringed Plover etc, you can also expect to see a good range of ducks on the sea with Eiders, Red-breasted Mergansers, Common and Velvet Scoters, Long-tailed Ducks and Shelducks all present in good numbers. Feeding parties of Greylag Geese regularly fly over.

Small birds include flocks of Snow Buntings, Sky Larks and Meadow Pipits, which in turn attract the attentions of Merlins and Sparrowhawks. Panic among the waders and wildfowl usually mean that a Peregrine is hunting.

Bird numbers start to build up from late summer and there are usually wintering birds present as late as May. It is only really summer that it is quiet, though even then, you have a good chance of seeing an Osprey fly over and Little and Common Terns fishing along the shoreline.

Even if you are not planning to spend any time in Culbin Forest itself, it is worth walking back along the edge of the forest to see what woodland birds you can add to your list. Indeed, you might even find the forest easier to work this way. The edge between two disparate habitats is often a productive area. See below for more details on the forest itself. Pools on the saltmarsh are well worth checking too.

Boots are strongly recommended if you visit

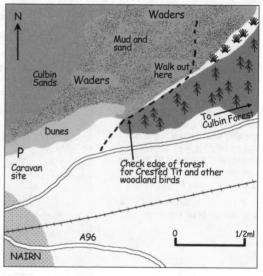

and a telescope is a good idea if you want to get good views of the roosting waders without disturbing them. A final word of warning about the tides, they can be treacherous, so take care not to get cut off.

Likely bird species

Autumn/winter/ spring	Red-breasted Merganser	Curlew	Snow Bunting
Greylag Goose	Long-tailed Duck	Knot	
Common Scoter	Merlin	Sanderling	*Summer*
Velvet Scoter	Peregrine	Redshank	Osprey
		Bar-tailed Godwit	Common Tern
			Little Tern

❺ Culbin Forest
Background information

THIS VAST stretch of largely coniferous forest stretches all the way from Nairn to Findhorn Bay and it can prove a daunting prospect for the first-time visitor. The best area to explore is probably the Welhill picnic site towards the eastern end of the forest.

There are Crested Tits around the car park area. Following the blue trail from here, you soon arrive at a largish pond. Because fresh water is in such short supply here, the pond acts as a magnet for all sorts of creatures.

156

If you want to explore further, you are strongly advised to pick up one of the Forestry Commission's leaflets, which has a map of all the various trails. There are numbered posts throughout the forest to help you work out where you are. Because much of this massive wood looks exactly the same as the next bit, it is very easy to get lost.

The forest has a good range of typical woodland species, including Scottish Crossbills and Capercaillie but the words 'needle' and 'haystack' spring to mind and there are better places to look for the 'horse of the forest' – the translation of the Gaelic name for Capercaillie. You are far more likely to see Great Spotted Woodpecker, Siskins, Goldcrests, Coal Tits and Treecreepers. You would be unlucky indeed if you failed to see a Sparrowhawk here.

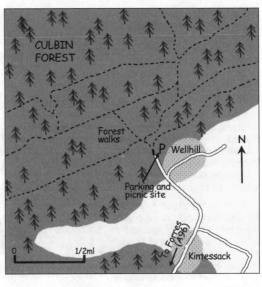

Summer brings migrants such as Willow Warbler, which is widespread. You will be lucky to see a Cuckoo though you will no doubt hear one.

Keep your eye on the sky whenever you come to a clearing. As well as the ever-present Buzzards, you could pick up an Osprey flying over as it heads to the coast to fish.

Winter here can be pretty desolate. The birds form feeding flocks and if you don't connect with one of these, you could walk for hours without seeing a single bird. A better bet would be Culbin Sands, with the aim of working the edge of the forest. Other wildlife includes roe deer, red squirrels, badgers, pine martens and wildcats.

Likely bird species/other fauna

All year	Treecreeper	*Summer*	*Other wildlife*
Capercaillie (rarely	Crested Tit	Osprey	Red squirrel
sighted)	Siskin	Cuckoo	Roe deer
Sparrowhawk	Scottish Crossbill	Willow Warbler	Pine marten

❻ Findhorn Bay
Background information

SIGNS on hides may instruct you to 'be quiet as birds have ears', but just the other side of the road from the hide at Findhorn Bay is RAF Kinloss where noisy ocean-patrolling Nimrods are continually taking off.

The birds have got used to the engine noise and ignore the planes totally, but drop your tripod, as I managed to do on my last visit, and you can see all the heads suddenly pop up as they look around for any danger.

157

Findhorn Bay is a huge tidal basin. At low tide, you can watch the Oystercatchers trying to prise some food away from the mussel beds, while Red-breasted Mergansers and Cormorants fish in the deeper channels. A telescope is recommended.

It has to be said that this is not the most salubrious hide in the Highlands. There are plenty of signs of extra-curricular activities, none of them involving birding, but the hide is worth using either side of high tide as any waders get forced up in front of you.

This is a good all year round place to visit. Spring and autumn produce the greatest variety of species and offers your best chance of finding something slightly out of the ordinary. Many of the waders stay over winter when wildfowl numbers also increase dramatically. Spring regularly produces a few Pintails.

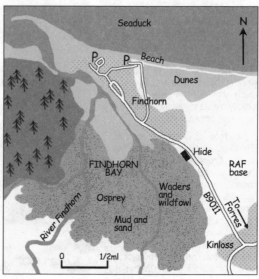

This is a particularly good place to catch up with Knot and you can watch the full cycle of plumage changes as they arrive, brick red, from their breeding grounds in autumn, change to pale grey in winter and then start to attain their breeding plumage again in the spring.

Other wintering waders include Redshanks, Curlews, Grey and Golden Plovers, Bar-tailed Godwits, Dunlin and Ringed Plovers. Passage times might bring the likes of Greenshanks, Green Sandpipers, Whimbrel, Black-tailed Godwits, Little Stints and Curlew Sandpipers. Numbers are usually at their highest in early spring as birds gather prior to migrating north to breed.

Ospreys are seen regularly in summer. Late summer, when the young are on the wing is the best time to see them and up to ten have been recorded fishing in the Bay. Yellowhammers, Sky Larks, Meadow Pipits and Linnets can be heard in the car park, even above the noise of the jets. We have even seen Short-eared Owls displaying here, presumably getting in a bit of practice

before moving onto their breeding territories on nearby moorland.

When you have finished scanning the Bay, continue into Findhorn itself. Park at the picnic site in the dunes and go and have a look at the sea (scope recommended). Eiders are present all year round. Common and Velvet Scoters can usually be found and you may be lucky enough to find a wintering Surf Scoter or King Eider.

Winter also brings Long-tailed Ducks and a few Scaup. There are always plenty of divers and grebes, many lingering into spring, by which time they will usually have moulted into their breeding finery. Up to 3,000 Greylag Geese roost in the area and winter at dusk can provide a great spectacle as skeins of birds flight in. By the early spring, there are usually some 3,000 Pink-footed Geese in the area too, their last stop before they fly back north.

One of the problems with scanning the sea is that the birds don't seem to favour any one particular area and can be found anywhere in Burghead and the adjoining Spey Bays, so don't be put off if you don't see much from your first vantage point; try several other places further along the coast.

In summer, you should also get a good passage of gulls and terns – Common, Arctic. Little and Sandwich all breed locally. A few Gannets usually cruise past, transforming themselves from fairly slow, lumbering birds into guided missiles if they find a shoal of fish to feed on. Rock Pipits are along the beach.

Mammals include bottle-nosed dolphins, both common and grey seals and otter.

Merlins are on the look-out for small birds in the Culbin Sands area

Likely bird species/other fauna

Winter	Grey Plover	Green Sandpiper	Common Tern
Divers	Golden Plover	Whimbrel	Arctic Tern
Greylag Goose	Bar-tailed Godwit	Black-tailed Godwit	Sandwich Tern
Common Scoter	Peregrine	Little Stint (autumn)	Little Tern
Velvet Scoter	Merlin	Curlew Sandpiper	
Long-tailed Duck		(autumn)	*Other wildlife*
Knot	*Spring/autumn*		Bottle-nosed dolphin
Curlew	Pintail (spring)	*Summer*	Grey seal
Redshank	Greenshank	Osprey	Common seal
			Otter

7 Roseisle Forest and Burghead
Background information

THE Forestry Commission's picnic site (fee payable) is good for Crested Tits and, if you are really lucky, Scottish Crossbills though you will need excellent views to determine exactly which species of crossbill you are looking at.

An additional bonus is that it is only a short stroll through to the large sandy beach where you can have another scan across the whole of Burghead Bay for waders and seaducks, the latter usually present in spectacular numbers.

The fields around here are good for flocks of feeding geese in winter, mostly Greylags but with the occasional Pinkfoot or Whitefront among them.

The drive along this stretch of coast between Findhorn and Lossiemouth passes through some prime farmland and it is one of the best areas locally to find Corn Buntings. Check the telegraph wires along the edge of the road for these chunky, but otherwise fairly anonymous buntings.

Continue into Burghead itself and head towards the harbour. Check the rocks and beach as well as the sea. Purple Sandpipers winter here in good numbers and can linger on into May. The beach is good for waders; few in number but you are likely to get a good assortment. This is another good spot for scanning for wintering seaducks, divers and grebes. Stormy weather is likely to force birds to shelter in the harbour.

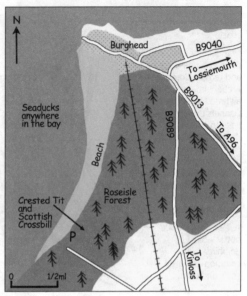

Likely bird species/other fauna

All year	*Autumn/winter/*		
Crested Tit	*Spring*	Common Scoter	Purple Sandpiper
Scottish Crossbill	Divers	Velvet Scoter	Roosting waders
Corn Bunting	Grebes	Long-tailed Duck	
		Peregrine	

❽ Lossiemouth
Background information

THREE areas here are worth checking. The West Beach car park (well signposted), by the golf course is another good vantage point for seaducks. As ever, check any scoter flocks for Surf Scoter and eiders for King Eider.

The harbour can hold all manner of seabird flocks, especially after severe weather in autumn and winter. It is worth checking the outer wall too for the occasional auk and diver as they linger into spring. Strong north and north-easterly winds are most likely to produce good seawatching conditions.

The mouth of the river can be explored from the East Beach area. Plenty of gulls loaf and wash here and you might pick out the occasional Glaucous or Iceland Gull in winter.

There are Wigeon aplenty in winter with smaller numbers at other times. An American Wigeon has been seen sporadically in recent years, though there are plenty of other suitable sites in the area where it can hide.

This is another good spot for waders with the usual range of species at passage times and in winter. In summer, there are good numbers of Ringed Plovers breeding. The dunes hold a flock of Snow Buntings in winter.

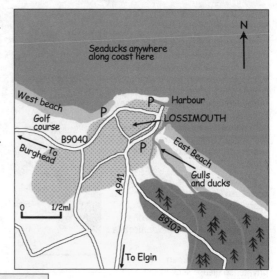

Likely bird species

Autumn/Winter/	Gulls
Spring	Snow Bunting
Seaducks	
Wigeon	*Summer*
	Ringed Plover

---

❾ Loch Spynie
Background information

AVOID this place if you are scared of very large mosquitoes; the place always seems to be crawling with them in summer and you are guaranteed to come out of the hide feeling itchy all over.

The woods leading to the hide hold Long-tailed, Great, Blue and Coal Tits, Goldcrests and Siskins. The occasional Brambling winters while spring brings the ubiquitous Willow Warbler and Spotted Flycatchers. Though Crested Tits are in the nearby woods, none has made use of the nest boxes as yet.

Winter sees an excellent range of wildfowl on the shallow, nutrient-rich loch. Almost anything can turn up, depending on the severity of the local weather. Recent sightings have included Green-winged Teal, American Wigeon, Scaup, Whooper Swan and Smew together with the more usual Wigeon, Goldeneyes, Pochards and Goosanders. A few thousand Greylag and Pink-footed Geese roost and can be seen flighting in at dusk.

There is a large, and very noisy, Black-headed Gull colony in summer. A few Common Terns brave their unwanted attention and try to nest among the gulls on the platforms. Apart from Mallards and Tufted Ducks, wildfowl numbers decrease dramatically though there is

161

always the chance of turning up something slightly unusual.

Water Rails are present but you are more likely to hear one squealing rather than see it. Look for Sedge Warblers (summer) and Reed Buntings (all year) in the reedbeds. Sightings of otters are regularly recorded in the logbook. Total panic, followed by all-out aggression among the gulls will alert you to their presence. Several species of bat come out at dusk in summer.

Buzzards and Sparrowhawks patrol and Marsh Harriers pass through most years. Spring and summer sees good numbers of hirundines and Swifts feeding over the loch; those mozzies do have their uses.

The farm and surrounding area are private, so please stick to the path through the woods down to the hide and nowhere else.

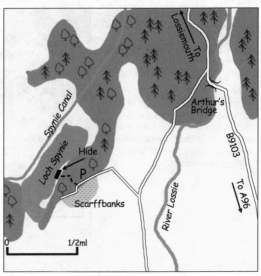

Likely bird species/other fauna

Winter	Whooper Swan (rare)	Common Tern	*Other wildlife*
Greylag Goose	Brambling	Swift	Otter
Pink-footed Goose		Swallow	Daubenton's bat
Wigeon	*Spring*	House Martin	Pipistrelle
Pochard	Marsh Harrier	Sand Martin	Long-eared bat
Tufted Duck		Spotted Flycatcher	
Smew (rare)	*Summer*	Sedge Warbler	
	Black-headed Gull		

⑩ Kingston and Spey Bay
Background information

SOMETIMES, a single incident can ensure that a particular place becomes a firm favourite. The first time we came here, we hadn't even turned off the car engine when an Osprey caught a flounder, about 20 yards in front of us. A definite 'magic moment'.

The mouth of the Spey is an excellent place to see these spectacular birds feeding, even if you can't always guarantee to be so close. There are several pairs in the area and by late summer, when the young are on the wing, you can often see several birds in the air at once. Look for mobbing gulls, always a good sign that Ospreys are in the area. Ospreys are present between April to September.

You can watch the mouth of the River Spey

162

from either the west or the east bank, and each has its own merits, though most birders stick to the west bank at Kingston. Unfortunately, there is no convenient bridge so to visit the opposite bank involves backtracking five miles to the main road, crossing the river, and five miles out again.

The reserve on the western bank is accessed from the village of Kingston. The picnic site gives good views over the estuary and you should see a good selection of waders and wildfowl, throughout the year, according to the state of the tide.

All the little channels mean that birds can stay hidden for long periods. At the end of our last visit a raft of 31 Goosanders sailed into view. I've no idea where they had been hiding as I thought we had worked the area thoroughly and seen everything.

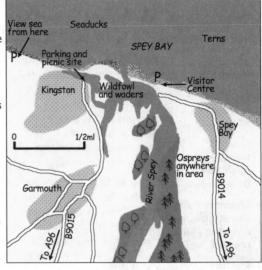

The gorse holds a good range of small birds such as Linnets and Yellowhammers and there is a breeding colony of Common Terns on the shingle ridge. Sandwich and Little Terns are usually present too.

Autumn and spring are the most dynamic times to visit, with birds constantly moving through. Numbers of passage waders are never huge but you do get a good variety, which can include Greenshanks, Whimbrel, Curlew Sandpipers and Little Stints.

From the picnic site, head west along the coast for about half a mile to another large car park. From here, take the path through the shingle ridge to view the sea. Look for flocks of scoters, Eiders, Red-breasted Mergansers, gulls, Fulmars and Gannets all year with terns (Arctic, Common, Sandwich and Little) flying past in summer, large numbers of Red-throated Divers in autumn and an increase in seaducks in winter.

The main reason for visiting the east bank is to visit the Moray Firth Wildlife Centre (01343 820339 www.mfwc.co.uk) which, as well as having all sorts of interpretative displays, is also an excellent viewpoint for bottle-nosed dolphins, grey and common seals and otters. There are also full facilities and you can organise a boat trip to view the wildlife.

Likely bird species

All year			Winter
Eider	Gulls	Sandwich Tern	Long-tailed Duck
Red-breasted	Skuas	Little Tern	Goosander
Merganser	Linnet		Peregrine
Common Scoter	Yellowhammer	Spring/Autumn	Merlin
Common wildfowl		Red-throated Diver	
Fulmar	Summer	Greenshank	
Gannet	Osprey	Whimbrel	
Common waders	Common Tern	Little Stint (autumn)	
	Arctic Tern	Curlew Sandpiper (autumn)	

Key points

- Toilets and petrol available at various towns en route, also Inverness

- Plenty of places for food on Black Isle

- Hides at Munlochy Bay, Udale Bay and Orrin Lodge

- Chanonry Point and Strathconon often busy with tourists

- Red Kites common on the Black Isle and as far as the entrance to Strathconon

- Rising tide seems to be best for dolphins

- Dolphin cruises available from Inverness and Avoch on Black Isle

- Fairy Glen and Orrin Lodge not suitable for wheelchair users

- Rest of Black Isle and Strathconon can be watched from car

IT'S NOT BLACK and it's not an island, but apart from that, the Black Isle is perfectly named! Lying between the Moray and Cromarty Firths, the name is thought to derive from either the rich soil, ideal for farming, or from a corruption of St Duthac, the Gaelic word for black being dubh. Neither explanation is particularly convincing.

This is the area where the first tranche of Red Kites were reintroduced to Scotland and with about 30 pairs in the area, you would have to be very unlucky not to see one on a casual drive round. Failing that, a quick visit to the Tourist Information centre, just north of the Kessock Bridge on the A9 heading out of Inverness could point you in the right direction.

Though there are several nature reserves in the area, most visitors are set on seeing something other than birds. This is the best place to find our most northerly population of bottle-nosed dolphins, which often give superb close-up views of their aquanautic displays. Chanonry Point, accessed from Fortrose, is the best place to see them and has the advantage of being an excellent seawatching spot as well.

A cairn here is dedicated to the Brahan Seer, a sort of Mystic Meg of his day. Though many of his predictions, such as the Caledonian Canal and the Highland Clearances, seem to have come true (at least with the benefit of hindsight), he failed to foresee his own fate. When he mentioned his employer's adultery to his employer's wife, the outcome was his own demise. He was supposedly burnt to death in a tar barrel.

History buffs will find Fortrose of interest, because of its ruined cathedral. Why such a small community was blessed with such an edifice is a mystery, but it seems linked to Euphemia, Countess of Ross. One of her many husbands was the notorious Wolf of Badenoch, a well known outlaw with castles dotted round several of the prime birding spots (see Lochindorb and Loch an Eilean etc.) who was known to have destroyed Elgin cathedral.

Nearby, Rosemarkie has an excellent museum at Groam House, devoted to the mysterious Picts, well worth a look if only for the bird carvings in their so-far undeciphered pictorial language. Rosemarkie is also where you find the RSPB's Fairy Glen, a delightful woodland walk to some waterfalls.

Cromarty lies at the tip of the Black Isle and is a fabulously picturesque Georgian town. Parking on the front for great views over the firth. A two-car ferry operates here May to September, taking you over to Nigg and the Nigg Bay RSPB reserve, currently being developed and boasting a new hide.

Alternatively, if you stay on the Black Isle, you can view the firth from the southern side at Udale Bay where again, there is a large hide next to the lay-by.

To finish your day off, Strathconon, a nearby valley and local beauty spot, offers a chance for Golden Eagles and Red-throated Divers. Nearby, there is a hide overlooking a fish farm where Ospreys regularly come to feed during the spring and summer months. Birding on the Black Isle is best in spring, autumn and winter. Strathconon and Muir of Ord are best from April to September. Red Kites are present all year.

How to get there

Nearest large town: The tour begins at Inverness.

Leave Inverness N on A9. After crossing Kessock Bridge look for Tourist Information Centre on L. Continue N, turning R onto B9161, then R at A832. Car park for Munlochy Bay is immediately on R.

At Fortrose look for signs for Chanonry Point on R at far end of town. Leaving Fortrose towards Cromarty, there is a large car park on R after road turns sharp L, which is the start of the Fairy Glen walk.

At Cromarty a minor road on R as you face the sea leads up to the Sutors. Leave Cromarty on B9163 and continue through Jemimaville. The road follows the edge of Udale Bay and you are looking for the lay-by and hide on R.

Follow B9163 W and turn R on A862 towards Dingwall. Turn L at

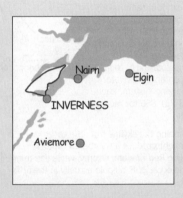

roundabout onto A835 and then L again after three miles onto A832 towards Muir of Ord. After half a mile, you reach Marybank where you turn R into Strathconon or continue towards Muir of Ord, stopping off at Glen Orrin Lodge if you want the Osprey hide. Stay on A832 through Muir of Ord until you rejoin A9 at the Tore roundabout.

Approximate length of loop from Inverness is 100 miles.

❶ Kessock Bridge

Background information

THE TOURIST Information Centre immediately on your left after crossing the Kessock Bridge is no longer manned by the RSPB, but their display material remains. So, you can watch live pictures from a Red Kite nest (or a video of last year's birds), but it depends on the availability of the centre staff. There used to be a recent sightings board here too, but this seems also to have disappeared.

The centre is open from Easter to October with live pictures likely from May to August. Phone 01463 731 505 for more details.

The Dolphin and Seal Visitor Centre is in the hut next door (admission free, open from June) where scientists will explain their projects and you can listen to the mammals calling to each other on an underwater microphone system. Phone 01463 731 866 for more details.

Scanning the skyline from the car park might produce a number of raptors, including Red Kite and Osprey, while you might see the occasional dolphin actually in the firth.

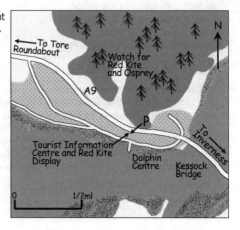

Likely bird species

All year
Red Kite
Buzzard

Spring/summer
Osprey

❷ Munlochy Bay
Background information

A SMALL hide in the car park overlooks the bay, though even at high tides the birds are fairly distant and you will probably need a telescope to get the best out of the area. In fine weather, you will do better to stay outside as you get a better all-round view as you look for raptors.

Scan the skyline for Red Kite, Buzzard, Peregrine and Osprey. The bay itself should produce a few waders such as Curlew, Oystercatcher and Redshank and you could pick out a Red-breasted Merganser or Grey Heron working the channels. Swallows and Sand Martins are overhead.

Telegraph wires and surrounding scrub often hold a selection of small birds including Yellowhammers and Whitethroats. Flocks of Greylag Geese feed here in late autumn.

Tore roundabout:
This is the first roundabout you reach north of Inverness on the A9, having crossed the bridge. It is a good spot for Red Kites and a short stop to look around is worth doing if you are heading north.

Likely bird species

All year	Redshank
Red-breasted	Sky Lark
Merganser	Yellowhammer
Grey Heron	
Red Kite	**Spring/summer**
Peregrine	Osprey
(occasional)	Whitethroat
Curlew	

❸ Chanonry Point

Background information

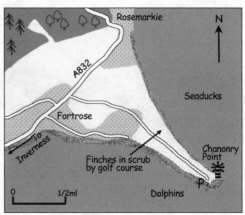

JUST PAST the cathedral ruins in Fortrose, a road leading to the Point passes right through a golf course, so there is a good chance to study the local Yellowhammer, Linnet and Meadow Pipit population as you watch the golf balls whistle over the bonnet of your car.

Chanonry Point juts into the Moray Firth and you can get excellent views of passing birds as they get funnelled between here and Fort George, less than a mile away on the opposite shore. Park by the lighthouse, preferably overlooking the sea so you can watch from inside the car if weather is inclement.

This is the spot to watch for the resident bottle-nosed dolphins though you might get closer views if you walk a couple of hundred of yards round the lighthouse to the very tip of the promontory. A rising tide seems to be the best time to visit though local advice depends on who you ask!

There are about 100 dolphins in the area and they are a great attraction, so you might want to avoid obviously busy times such as weekends and bank holidays. Look out too for the much smaller harbour porpoises - the dolphins have been known to attack them. Seals often investigate the proceedings - there are about 1,200 common and 100 grey seals in the area.

The birding here is pretty good too, though summer is probably the quietest time. The Meadow Pipits of the golf course are replaced by Rock Pipits foraging around the beach and you might also see a Turnstone.

There are usually a few auks on the sea though Black Guillemots are rare here. Cormorants, Shags, Red-breasted Mergansers, Wigeon and Shelducks are often seen. Fulmars, gulls, Gannets and Kittiwakes, can all pass in varying numbers.

This is a great seawatching spot. Spring terns (Arctic, Common, Sandwich and Little) and waders are joined in autumn by shearwaters, skuas and seaducks. North-easterly winds are best and you get the added bonus of seeing the birds twice as they are blown into the Moray Firth and then have to fly out again.

Winter brings plenty of Common and Velvet Scoters, Goldeneyes and Long-tailed Ducks. Red-throated Divers and Guillemots are abundant and Sanderling, Purple Sandpiper and Bar-tailed Godwit increase dramatically in numbers.

Likely birds species/other fauna

All year	Shearwaters (autumn)	Common Scoter	Common waders
Meadow Pipit	Gannet	Velvet Scoter	
Rock Pipit	Kittiwake	Goldeneye	**Other wildlife**
Yellowhammer	Auks	Red-throated Diver	Bottle-nosed dolphin
	Fulmar	Sanderling	Harbour porpoise
		Purple Sandpiper	Seals
Spring/autumn		Bar-tailed Godwit	
Terns	*Winter*	Turnstone	
Skuas	Long-tailed Duck		

4 RSPB Fairy Glen

Background information

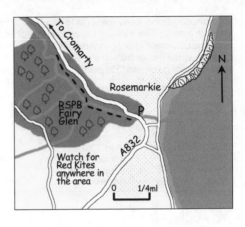

THIS IS ONE of the RSPB's least known reserves and offers a delightful walk to two waterfalls through broad-leaved woodland, a welcome change after all the coniferous woodland in the Highlands.

Dipper and Grey Wagtail can often be seen from the car park, but that's as far as wheelchair users can go. The walk, about a mile and a half, should produce a good selection of common woodland species, possibly with a Buzzard or Red Kite over-head. Fulmars nest on the upper reaches of the glen.

Likely birds species

All year	Buzzard	Grey Wagtail	Tits
Fulmar	Great Spotted	Dipper	Treecreeper
Red Kite	Woodpecker		

5 Cromarty

Background information

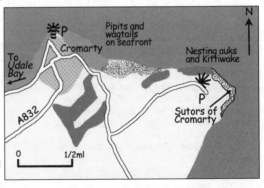

SUMMER VISITORS can usually be assured of sighting the occasional auk at Cromarty as there is a small breeding colony on the nearby Sutors of Cromarty. You can walk or drive up here (head east from the town) and the extra elevation affords spectacular views of the surrounding area. Guillemot, Razorbill, Fulmar and Kittiwake all nest here.

Aberdeen University runs the Lighthouse Field Station here with ongoing projects into seal, dolphin and Fulmar ecology. Visit http://www.abdn.ac.uk/~nhi519/lighthse/index.hti for more details.

Pipits and wagtails are likely along the seafront, with maybe the occasional pair of Ringed Plovers. Terns are plentiful in summer, though you will need a telescope to pick out the finer identification details as they perch on the buoys.

Red-breasted Mergansers are usually on the

169

sea, joined by Eiders, Long-tailed Ducks and divers in autumn. There always seems to be at least one Cormorant or Shag in the air at any given time, the former from one of Scotland's largest breeding colonies (250 pairs).

If you want even closer views of the dolphins, you can take a boat trip into the Moray Firth from here. Contact Dolphin Ecosse at Bank House, High Street, Cromarty IV11 8UZ. Phone 01381 600 323 or visit http://www.dolphinecosse.co.uk/ for more details. Many other coastal villages around the Forth also offer boat trips.

Likely bird species

All year		*Winter*	Red-throated Diver
Red-breasted	Ringed Plover	Long-tailed Duck	
Merganser	Rock Pipit	Common Scoter	*Summer*
Cormorant	Meadow Pipit	Velvet Scoter	Terns
Shag	Grey Wagtail	Goldeneye	Auks
	(occasional)		

❻ Udale Bay

Background information

TIMING is crucial to get the best from this site. You want to be in the hide (plenty of disabled access, direct from the lay-by) about an hour either side of high tide. Winter is the best time to visit, when all the seaducks are present, but spring and autumn passage can be pretty spectacular.

Passage and wintering waders include good numbers of Knot, Bar-tailed Godwits, Curlews, Dunlin and Redshanks. Look for Greenshanks, Spotted Redshanks, Black-tailed Godwits and Ruff in passage periods, but in mixed wader flocks, anything can turn up. You also have a good chance of finding it yourself; a quick look at the sightings book shows that there aren't too many visitors. Some excellent display boards in the RSPB hide show where the birds have come from and why the area is so attractive to them.

The large numbers of winter wildfowl include up to 5,000 Wigeon, but look out too for Scaup and Slavonian Grebes. Whooper Swans and Greylags also winter. Peregrines find the sheer numbers irresistible, while the regularly-seen Merlins find the finch and pipit flocks more to

their liking. Ospreys can often be seen fishing in late summer.

In summer you may sight either a late departing bird or an early arrival. We watched a pair of Pink-footed Geese in late May. One had a badly broken wing and was never going to fly, but its mate didn't want to split the pair bond.

Generally, this season can be very quiet at Udale, ditto if you get the tides wrong, but it

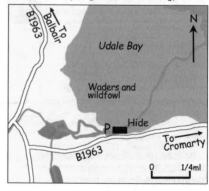

is always worth a quick look. With the hide right next to the lay-by, this makes an excellent spot for a coffee break or somewhere to avoid heavy rain.

Likely bird species

Spring /autumn			
Pink-footed Goose	Greenshank	Teal	Dunlin
Greylag Goose	Osprey (autumn)	Scaup	Bar-tailed Godwit
Ruff		Slavonian Grebe	Curlew
Black-tailed Godwit	*Winter*	Merlin	Redshank
Spotted Redshank	Whooper Swan	Peregrine	
	Wigeon	Knot	

⑦ Strathconon and Glen Orrin

Background information

A FEW MILES inland from the Black Isle, and totally different in character, is Strathconon, another of those wonderful long, winding single-track roads seemingly leading into the middle of nowhere.

A leisurely drive here provides a whole new range of habitats and you should add several species to your day list. This is a well-known, well-signposted drive, so avoid the obviously busy times.

Look for Red Kites at the entrance to the strath if you haven't seen them already – the A832 between Marybank and the Tore roundabout gives you a good opportunity of seeing birds from the car.

Summer migrants include Redstarts, Wheatears and Tree Pipits. Scanning the peaks might produce a Golden Eagle among the commoner raptors and you might be lucky enough to see Red-throated Divers on one of the three lochs. There is a large car park at the end of the road.

The Glen Orrin Osprey Hide is at Orrin Bridge, off a minor road north-west of Muir of Ord. Open from dawn to dusk, tickets can be bought at Glen Orrin Lodge and there is a discount for RSPB members. Phone 01997 433 219 for more details.

Likely bird species

All year	Osprey
Red Kite	(Glen Orrin)
Golden Eagle	Tree Pipit
	Redstart
Summer	Wheatear
Red-throated Diver	

Key points

- Café and toilets at Inverewe

- Toilets at reserve centre, Gairloch and Corrieshalloch Gorge

- Petrol in Kinlochewe and Gairloch

- Long distance route with plenty of birding spots

- Check the visitor centre for guide books etc.

- Expect busy roads close to Inverewe gardens

- Check weather before climbing high and dress appropriately

- Wildlife cruises available in Gairloch

- No wheelchair access on nature trails at Beinn Eighe. Rest of route can be worked from the road

- Birdwatching hide at Loch Maree Hotel

THIS DRIVE through a corner of Wester Ross takes in a glorious mix of mountain, loch and coast. Besides the scenery, there are world famous tropical gardens and the most romantic place name in Britain, as well as the scene of Britain's wartime experiments into biological warfare and currently one of the best places on the British mainland to see the massive White-tailed Eagle.

The selected route is the middle of the three major loop roads of north-west Scotland, with Inverpolly to the north and Applecross to the south. Pronounced to rhyme with 'hay', Beinn Eighe was Britain's first National Nature Reserve, established in 1951.

For the first part of this drive, the road picks its way between the shadow of the 3,313-foot high mountain that gives the reserve its name and the edge of the massive Loch Maree. The Loch is described on the website of Ramsar (dealing with wetlands of international importance) as having 'The single most important breeding population of Black-throated Divers in Britain,' and goes on to talk about other important wildlife including 'a nationally outstanding assemblage of dragonflies.'

The reserve itself has an excellent visitor centre, overlooking the loch with the unmistakeable profile of Slioch dominating the background and this makes a good starting point for learning about the rest of the drive. Displays at the centre describe the geography, natural history, conservation and geology of the reserve. There is a good selection of guide books on sale.

Continuing along the road, there are many places from which to look for birds, including two very different nature trails and a hide overlooking the loch. Passing through Gairloch, and maybe making a detour for a bit of seawatching, you will reach the gardens at Inverewe. Run by the National Trust for Scotland and attracting 130,000 visitors a year, they offer a mix of tropical and sub-tropical plants, the whole area existing in its own micro-climate warmed by the Gulf Stream.

The view on this stretch of the road, across to the Isle of Ewe, will undoubtedly score plenty of Brownie Points from your partner if you tell him/her that you brought them here specially. (Say the name out loud if you can't work out why.)

Hunting raptors swoop down off the hills and on our visits we have had both Peregrine and Buzzard practically brushing the car windscreen with their wingtips.

Gruinard Island is the site of Britain's experiments into biological weapons. Back in 1942, anthrax spores were released and the island became so contaminated that it was put out of bounds for nearly 50 years. The island was decontaminated in 1986 and declared safe in 1990, though it would take a brave man to visit. Today, the island is one of the best places in Scotland to look for White-tailed Eagles. If you ask the staff at Loch Garten where to see these spectacular raptors, this is where they always send you.

This final stretch of road, beyond Dundonnell, is known as Destitution Road, and was built in 1851 to provide relief and much needed work after the potato famine. This is another great spot for eagles, Golden this time.

When you reach Braemore Junction, stop off to admire the impressive Corrieshalloch Gorge. There are spectacular views from a suspension bridge, though it is not for the faint-hearted. Strangely, every time we have visited, it seems obligatory for the male of the species to bounce up and down on the bridge in an attempt to scare the female of the species. These attempts are usually successful. Look for common woodland birds including Wood Warbler. The National Trust for Scotland owns the area. It is well signed and there is a large car park.

How to get there:

Nearest large town: Inverness is 32 miles SE from Garve (the start of the route).

Leave Inverness on A835 towards Ullapool. At Garve, turn L onto A832 and follow road round to Braemore Junction. Turn R onto A835 for return to Inverness.

The only detours are if you want to head out to one of the seawatching points listed with this drive, both accessed by B-roads, either side of Gairloch.

The loop from Garve is 102 miles long.

❶ Beinn Eighe

Background information

FROM THE AULTROY visitor centre the road heads left, following the shore of Loch Maree. There are several lay-bys and picnic sites where you can scan the loch and the mountains. Ravens, Hooded Crows and Buzzards are usually overhead and persistence is likely to be rewarded with a Golden Eagle over one of the ridges. The first picnic site you come to is the start of both the woodland and mountain trails.

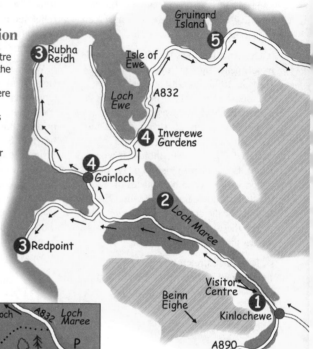

A. Woodland trail

LOOPING THROUGH a mixture of pine and birch woods, this walk takes about an hour, with just a moderate amount of climbing involved. Wildlife is abundant, whether you are interested in flowers, insects, mammals or birds, though you are more likely to see droppings of wildcat and pine marten than the creatures themselves. Pine martens apparently investigate the rubbish bins in the picnic sites after dark.

Star avian attraction is the

Scottish Crossbill. Listen for their *'chup, chup'* calls as they fly over, or the sound of pine cones hitting the floor. They really are noisy birds. Numbers fluctuate dramatically, depending on the success of the previous year's pine crop.

Other birds to look out for include Siskin, Goldcrest and Great Spotted Woodpecker with Spotted Flycatcher, Wood Warbler and Redstart in summer. Thirteen species of dragonfly have been recorded including azure hawker, golden-ringed dragonfly, Highland darter and northern emeralds.

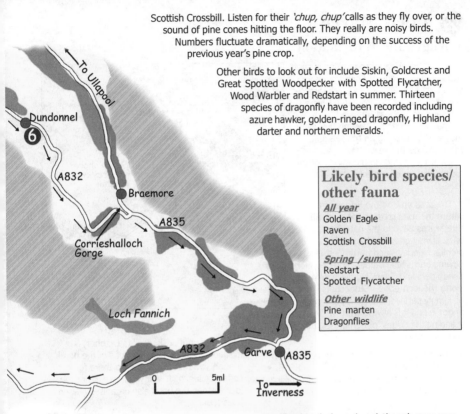

Likely bird species/ other fauna

All year
Golden Eagle
Raven
Scottish Crossbill

Spring /summer
Redstart
Spotted Flycatcher

Other wildlife
Pine marten
Dragonflies

B. Mountain trail

THIS IS A FOUR mile walk and will take between three and four hours to complete. There are some quite steep sections as the path climbs to 1,800 feet. As always, make sure you are properly equipped for changeable weather.

Starting in the woods, you should find a few

Likely bird species

All year	
Red Grouse	Merlin
Ptarmigan	Peregrine
Golden Eagle	Meadow Pipit
Buzzard	*Spring/summer*
Kestrel	Wheatear
	Ring Ouzel

woodland birds (see above) though once you are out in the open, the number of species and quantity of birds will drop dramatically. Meadow Pipits are omnipresent and the heather holds Red Grouse. A white flash of rump indicates a Wheatear while the gullies hold white-bibbed Ring Ouzels. Look out for red deer too.

By the time you reach the plateau, you should be seeing Ptarmigan and mountain hares. On a clear day, your view includes 31 peaks above 3,000 feet, so there are plenty of ridges to scan for raptors including Golden Eagle. Agitation among the Ravens is always a good clue that a raptor has entered their territory. Lunar Loch on the plateau holds palmate newts and common hawker dragonflies.

❷ Loch Maree
Background information

USE THE car parks and pulling in spots along the edge of Loch Maree to scan the water. As well as Black-throated Divers, there are Red-throated Divers, Goosanders and Red-breasted Mergansers breeding, though the divers may well be feeding on the sea during the day (see the seawatching section below). The islands in the middle of the loch are relics of ancient Caledonian forest.

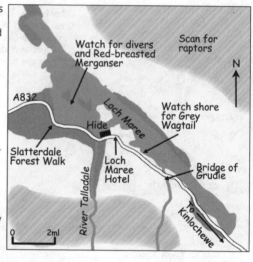

The area around the Bridge of Grudie, where the road crosses the river, about three miles beyond the nature trails car park, is very good for dragonflies, orchids, sundews and butterflies. Fast-flowing burns hold Dippers and Common Sandpipers and Grey Wagtails bob merrily along the loch edge. Stonechats obligingly perch on seemingly any clump of gorse and it is always worthwhile scanning the ridges for Peregrines, Buzzards and Golden Eagles.

There is a hide at the Loch Maree Hotel on the A832, run in conjunction with the RSPB. As you face the hotel, take the path on your left for a couple of hundred yards. The hide (open from 8am until dusk, April to October) is available to all, not just patrons of the hotel, though you may want to stop there for a coffee or lunch. If you want to explore the loch further, the hotel also organises guided boat tours.

Likely bird species/other fauna

All year	Golden Eagle	Black-throated Diver
Red-breasted	Raven	Common Sandpiper
Merganser	Dipper	
Goosander		*Other wildlife*
Peregrine	*Spring/summer*	Otter
Buzzard	Red-throated Diver	Dragonflies and butterflies

❸ Redpoint and Rubha Reidh seawatching viewpoints

Background information

A S THE road leave the shores of Loch Maree, the B8056 on your left leads to a great seawatching viewpoint at Redpoint, about eight miles away. Our last visit produced 30-40 Red- and Black-throated Divers, Eiders, Fulmars and a few auks, including Black Guillemots. Cetaceans are possible throughout the year and whales are almost guaranteed on calm days in September, though these are the exact opposite of the conditions needed for a good seabird passage, when onshore gales are preferred.

The other seawatching area is from the lighthouse at Rubha Reidh, (Pronounced roo ray. Ironically this is Gaelic for Redpoint!) accessed on the B8021 from Gairloch, which again offers a similar range of species. At both sites, you will need a telescope.

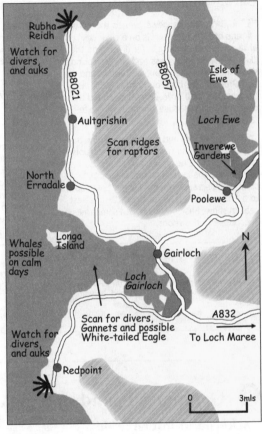

This map covers Red Point and Rubha Reidh seawatching viewpoints and also Gairloch Bay and Inverewe Gardens (details overleaf).

Likely bird species/other fauna

All year	*Autumn to spring*	Terns
Black Guillemot	Great Northern Diver	Skuas
Rock Pipit		
	Passage	*Other wildlife*
Spring/summer	Shearwaters	Whales and dolphins
Red-throated Diver	Gannets	
Black-throated Diver	Gulls	

❹ Gairloch Bay and Inverewe Gardens

Background information

THE BAY, with its views over to the north end of Skye (also Lewis on a clear day), is always worth a quick scan for divers and the like. A few Gannets pass and waders round the shore include Ringed Plovers, Curlews and the odd Greenshank. Look out for Great Skuas harrying the local gulls. Anywhere round the coast here can produce sightings of White-tailed Eagles.

Common lizards and slow worms are in the area. This is a good spot for harbour porpoises and grey seals. One grey seal, nicknamed 'Sammy' by the locals has got the art of scrounging scraps from the fishing boats down to a fine art - just look for the fattest, laziest seal on show. Basking sharks can sometimes be seen close to the shore.

You can also take a wildlife cruise. Contact the Gairloch Marine Life Centre, Pier Road, Gairloch, Ross-shire IV21 2BQ. Tel 01445 712636 or visit www.porpoise-gairloch.co.uk

Trips run from Easter to the beginning of October, though September has the dual advantage of losing both the school kids and midges!

At Inverewe Gardens, look for common woodland species among the plants and trees, including Chiffchaff and Garden Warbler in summer. The gardens drop down to the shores of Loch Ewe where you can expect a similar range of species to those listed for Gairloch. Looking inland from the car park, scan the ridges for Buzzards, Peregrines and Golden Eagle.

Likely bird species/other fauna

All year			*Other wildlife*
Red-breasted Merganser	Golden Eagle	Common woodland birds	Seals
Goosander	Oystercatcher		Harbour porpoise
Grey Heron	Ringed Plover	*Passage*	Common lizard
White-tailed Eagle (rare)	Curlew	Whimbrel	
	Redshank	Greenshank	

❺ Gruinard Island and Bay

Background information

THE ISLAND is best viewed from a lay-by overlooking the south-eastern side of Gruinard. White-tailed Eagles can sometimes be seen sitting on the island's beach or in one of the fields.

Despite their massive size - they are often compared to flying barn doors or bedspreads - they are not always easy to pick up on the ground. We watched one for over an hour, convinced it was a boulder in a field. It was only when a Hooded Crow started tweaking its tail

that the 'boulder' moved. This seems to be a favourite occupation of Hoodies. Often, working in pairs, they take it in turn to annoy the eagle. When the eagle eventually turns round, the other one moves in.

When the eagles fly, they attract a lot of attention from mobbing birds, resulting in huge aerial battles between the eagle, Hoodies, Ravens, Buzzards and gulls. Seen together, they make Buzzards look very small, but there is no guarantee of seeing one though. Talking to birders over the years, some get lucky and see one fly within a few minutes of arriving. Others come back two or three times and still fail miserably.

The bay often holds all three species of diver from late summer through to late spring and White-billed Divers have been recorded several times on the coast from here back

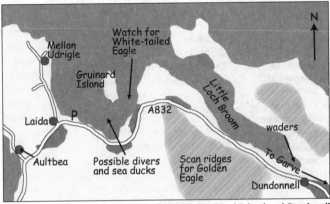

Map for Gruinard Island and Dundonell

to Gairloch. Mellon Udrigle is a good place to check in winter. Black Guillemots are ever present.

Great and Arctic Skuas are occasionally seen in spring and autumn and these are the best times to pick up a Manx Shearwater or similar, though

Redpoint and Rubha Reidh are generally better for seawatching.

Seaducks overwinter in small numbers and you might pick up the occasional Velvet Scoter in the Common Scoter flock or catch up with a Long-tailed Duck feeding actively.

Likely bird species/other fauna

All year	Black Guillemot	Common Sandpiper
Eider	Rock Pipit	
Shag	Raven	*Winter*
White-tailed Eagle		Long-tailed Duck
Golden Eagle	*Spring/summer*	Common Scoter
Buzzard	Dunlin	Great Northern Diver

❻ Dundonnell

Background information

THE MUDDY shallows at the end of Little Loch Broom can be good for wildfowl and waders, including Greenshanks, depending on the state of the tide. You might also find Great Northern Divers hanging on until well into May, by which time they will have acquired their fine summer plumage. Black Guillemots sometimes swim right up to the head of the loch.

Likely bird species

All year	*Passage*
Grey Heron	Greenshank
Golden Eagle	
Hooded Crow	*Winter*
	Great Northern Diver

The mountain ridges along the opposite shores of the loch are well worth scanning for Golden Eagles.

See map above for location

Key points

- Facilities (food, toilets and petrol) in Ullapool and Lochinver
- Toilets and café at Inverkirkaig
- Spectacular scenery throughout
- Important geology
- Excellent seawatching from Reiff and Stoer
- Limited off-road parking – don't block passing places
- Interior difficult to work – dress appropriately
- Wildlife cruises from Ullapool, Achiltibuie and Lochinver
- Much of the area can be explored from the road
- Some tricky driving on twisty, narrow roads

EVEN AMONG all the scenic grandeur of the west coast, Inverpolly is almost impossibly beautiful. The combination of loch, boggy moorland, mountain, native woodland and coast makes for a magical mix.

There are spectacular views of three of the best-known Scottish mountains – Suilven, Canisp and Quinag, all sitting strangely isolated, rather than part of a major range. We have seen more double rainbows here than the rest of Britain put together, especially in the northern part of this tour. Sea views over the islands and sunsets to die for are mere icing on what is already a pretty fantastic cake.

This tour starts at Ullapool and explores the area of Assynt, immediately to the north.

Though Ullapool is small by most people's standards, it is far and away the main centre of population in these parts and would make an excellent base for anyone wanting to explore the north-west. As well as all local amenities, there are plenty of places to stay and eat, outdoor clothes shops and a thriving local music scene. You can also catch the ferry to the Isle of Lewis.

The first thing that strikes you as you head north is the amazing change in the rock formations of the area, obvious to even the biggest geological ignoramus. At the Knockan visitor centre, you can pick up all the latest news and information on the local natural history though you are more likely to meet geologists rather than birders. This is one of the most important areas in Britain

Black Guillemots can be found at Ullapool and other coastal sites.

for studying rocks. A trail helps you explore and is ideal if you don't know your Lewisian gneiss from your Moine schist.

Also in the area is Inchnadamph NNR. Limestone caves here have revealed evidence of some of Britain's earliest human settlements. Sawn-off deer antlers date back over 8,000 years. As well as the human remains, bones were also found of creatures long since lost from Britain such as polar bear, Arctic fox, lynx and lemming.

Again, this area is better known for its interesting geology and botany (the UK's largest area of alpine willow scrub) rather than its bird life, though you should find a typical range of moorland and montane species. Both sites are well worth exploring if you have the time and are easily accessed directly from the main road back to Ullapool if you follow the tour as written.

A minor road skirts the southern edge of Inverpolly NNR. On your left is Loch Lurgainn, best viewed from a large car park where a well-worn path opposite leads up Stac Pollaidh. Keep to your left

Continues on page 182

How to get there

Nearest large town: The tour starts at Ullapool.

From Ullapool, head N on A835. Ardmair is on L about three miles out of town. There is obvious parking overlooking the bay. Another six miles further on, turn L at Drumrunie following signs for Achiltibuie. Note where the Wee Mad Road to Lochinver starts as you will be returning here.

Continue to next junction and turn L for Achiltibuie. When you reach the coast, you can either turn L for views over the Summer Isles or R and park almost immediately just in front of the pier. Return to the Wee Mad Road and head for Lochinver.

When you cross the River Kirkaig, there is a car park on L or you can turn R and drive up the hill to the bookshop/café. Continue into Lochinver and either take A837 back to Ledmore and then Ullapool or continue on B869 coast road.

For the Point of Stoer, turn L at Rienachait, signed to the lighthouse. Otherwise, continue round the coast until you reach A894 where you turn R back towards Ullapool. Look for Inchnadamph centre on L, one mile S of junction of A894/A835 and the Knockan visitor centre on L about three miles S of Ledmore.

Total mileage of the tour is approximately 130 miles

From page 181

and follow the road round towards Achiltibuie. This road goes round the Scottish Wildlife Trust reserve of Ben Mor Coigach, after the mountain of the same name.

Achiltibuie is famous for its Hydroponicum, a place where plants are grown in solution rather in soil. Guided tours are available. There is also a smoke house where you can buy all sorts of delicately smoked meat and fish. This is prime diver country and you should find birds both on the local lochs and sea here.

After exploring the coast looking out to the Summer Isles, you are ready to undertake another of the great Scottish drives, the road to Lochinver, known locally as the 'Wee Mad Road.'

Twisting, turning, climbing, falling, along the narrowest of roads, the view changes constantly – but only for the passenger! Pity the poor old driver who has to concentrate so much, he is unlikely to see much of what's around him.

The only slightly disappointing feature is that there are relatively few places to stop and take in the birds and scenery. If you do stop in a passing place, stay by your car and be ready to move instantly. There is always a horrible sinking feeling when you see another car coming towards you and you wonder how you are going to get past each other. Caravans and other large vehicles are banned, but it doesn't seem to stop them trying – we have met one on all but one of our trips here and it is not fun.

Cars aren't the only potential source of accidents. It is hard to keep your attention on the road when a Buzzard glides majestically over your bonnet, its wing tip brushing the windscreen. At least our similar encounters with a Peregrine and a pair of Merlins were briefer and slightly more distant.

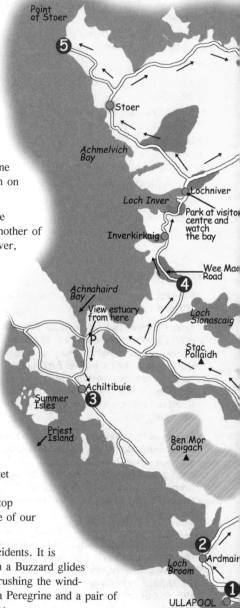

Point of Stoer

5

Stoer

Achmelvich Bay

Loch Inver

Lochniver

Inverkirkaig

Park at visitor centre and watch the bay

Wee Mad Road

4

Achnahaird Bay

View estuary from here

Loch Sionascaig

Stac Pollaidh

P

Achiltibuie

3

Summer Isles

Priest Island

Ben Mor Coigach

2

Ardmair

Loch Broom

1

ULLAPOOL

From Lochinver, you can either take the fast road out if time is pressing, or, and much better if you can manage it, follow the coast round through increasingly remote moorland, possibly making a detour to the lighthouse at Stoer.

As well as some excellent seawatching at Stoer, you can walk another two miles to the rock formation known as the Old Man of Stoer, a 200 foot high pillar, just offshore where you can watch the climbers attempting to scale the stack and ponder on the folly of such a strange hobby while they look at you and your collection of telescopes and other optical equipment and think exactly the same.

Winter here is fairly quiet. Apart from a few Barnacle Geese and Whooper Swans, there isn't a lot to see. As ever, spring is the most dynamic season to visit and there is plenty to see in summer. Things will start to quieten down in autumn as the migrants disappear from the interior, but the changing colours and excellent seawatching more than make up for the absence of a few Wheatears.

Whenever you come though, just sit back and take your time. This is a reserve to savour.

Postscript

After this chapter was finished, the landowners announced that Inverpolly was no longer going to be a National Nature Reserve. Formerly managed by Scottish Natural Heritage, the Vestey family have decided that they now want to run the estate themselves in accordance with their preferred business interests.

While the bird life should not be affected in the immediate future, it is not known at the time of writing what is going to happen to the various visitor centres, information panels, signs and notice boards.

① Ullapool

Background information

THE HARBOUR OFTEN holds a few auks, including Black Guillemot, and seaducks. Winter usually produces a couple of Glaucous and Iceland Gulls. If the boats are out fishing, a better bet is the river mouth at the north edge of town (walk along West Terrace until the junction with Castle Terrace). Gulls come here to loaf and bathe and the occasional bird, usually a young Glaucous Gull, stays all summer.

You can usually see a good selection of waders here in spring and autumn, such as Redshank, Greenshank, Common Sandpiper, Curlew, Dunlin and Oystercatcher. West Terrace is a good spot for Twite.

There are several boat companies in the harbour offering wildlife cruises. These usually head towards the Summer Isles and concentrate

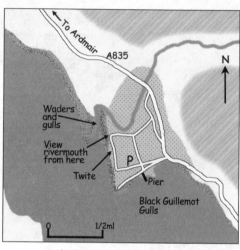

on the larger mammals – seals and porpoises etc – but you should get some good views of breeding seabirds too. Check the notice boards for details of what's been seen recently and choose accordingly.

Likely bird species/other fauna

All year	Black Guillemot	Glaucous Gull	*Other wildlife*
Eider	Twite		Grey seal
Red-breasted		*Passage*	Common seal
Merganser	*Winter*	Greenshank	Harbour porpoise
Gulls	Iceland Gull		

② Ardmair

Background information

ARDMAIR HAS A FINE sandy beach looking out to Isle Martin. Park just before the caravans and scan Loch Kanaird. We have actually managed to see all three species of diver and Black Guillemot in the same field of view through a telescope, the only minor disappointment being that the Great Northern Diver was still in winter plumage!

Likely bird species

All year	Shag
Red-throated Diver	Black Guillemot
Black-throated Diver	Peregrine
Great Northern Diver	Rock Pipit
(not summer)	

Look out too for Shags, auks, seaducks and Rock Pipits. Peregrines can sometimes be seen hunting over the island.

The beach here often turns up semi-precious stones such as agates, various quartzes and cornelians, though you might not recognise them as such in their unpolished form.

Eiders and Red-breasted Mergansers are ever-present and the gulls from Ullapool are often seen loafing here and are worth checking for lingering Glaucous and Iceland Gulls.

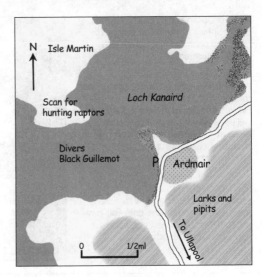

❸ Achiltibuie area
Background information

IT IS WORTH SCANNING all the lochs round here for divers, though they will often be feeding at sea during the day. Remember, they are highly susceptible to disturbance so watch from a distance and move on to the next lay-by if necessary. Keep checking the mountain ridges for raptors, including Golden Eagle.

Looking across Badentarbat Bay towards the Summer Isles is one of the classic views, especially if you are staying nearby and can wait long enough for the sunset.

One special bird that you might see along this stretch of coast, especially from June onwards, is the diminutive Storm Petrel, pit-pit-pattering across the surface of the sea.

With their white rumps flashing, they look like a flock of pelagic House Martins. Towards dusk is the best time to see these nocturnal

nesters as they return to their large breeding colony on Priest Island.

Look out too for more divers on the sea and plenty of Red-breasted Mergansers and Rock Pipits along the shore. Mammals include both grey and common seals, otter, minke whale, porpoise and common and white-beaked dolphins. A few Barnacle Geese are present in winter with the occasional Whooper Swan on larger lochs.

Retrace your steps and continue to the small pier. Boats leave here to the Summer Isles (10.30 and 2.15 at the time of writing) and allow you an hour ashore.

Alternatively, park on the large grassy area in front of the pier, probably the best viewing place along this stretch of coast, and scan the bay. Check the grass and beach for foraging flocks of Dunlin and Ringed Plovers, totally unfazed by your presence. The fields and pools behind you are also worth a quick check.

If you want to try a spot of seawatching and don't have time to get to Stoer Point, then you can continue along the minor road here to Reiff. You will see a similar range of species to those at Stoer (see below) with a good chance of cetaceans if the weather is calm in summer and late autumn.

Otherwise, retrace your steps and find a good place to stop and scan the estuary and Achnahaird Bay (see main map). Depending on the tide, you can get some excellent views of waders here, including Greenshanks.

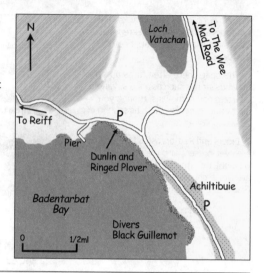

Likely bird species/other fauna

All year	Rock Pipit	Petrels	Great Northern Diver
Red-breasted		Gannet	
Merganser	Spring/summer	Skuas	Other wildlife
Red-throated Diver	Storm Petrel	Gulls	Grey seal
Black-throated Diver	Seabirds	Terns	Common seal
Shag	Greenshank	Auks	Whales
Golden Eagle	Wheatear		Dolphins
Black Guillemot		Winter	Porpoises
Ringed Plover	Autumn	Whooper Swan	
Dunlin	Shearwaters	Barnacle Goose	

---

❹ The Wee Mad Road
Background information

MUCH OF YOUR BIRDING is likely to be done from the car along this stretch. Even if you do manage to pull off the road safely, access to the interior is never easy and shouldn't be undertaken lightly.

Working the lochs isn't easy either, with so many hidden bays and inlets to hide the birds. For example, Loch Sionascaig, one of the

biggest and deepest lochs in Inverpolly, is only three miles long but has 17 miles of shoreline.

Nevertheless, there is still plenty to see and typical birds in the area include Stonechat, Whinchat, Meadow, Tree and Rock Pipits, Twite, Raven, Wheatear, Ring Ouzel, Wigeon, Greylag Goose and Common Sandpiper. Greenshanks and Dunlin breed on the moors, but are just as likely to be encountered at a lochside or beach. Ringed Plovers breed along the shore.

Grey Herons often fish in the bays – unusual for those of us who only think of them as inland birds. Cormorant, Shag and Red-breasted Merganser can be seen out to sea. Goosanders favour lochs and rivers and are less common than their cousins. Arctic and Common Terns fish all round the coast and Eiders and Black Guillemots are common.

Golden Eagles drift into the area, so it is always well worth scanning the skyline. Cuckoos, Golden Plovers and Red Grouse are on the moors with Ptarmigan on the tops of Cul Mor, Cul Beg and Stac Pollaidh. Redwings occasionally breed. Red and roe deer are common, as are badgers though you will be lucky to see a pine marten or wildcat.

There is a small car park as the road crosses the River Kirkaig. From here, a three mile walk along the north side of the River Kirkaig -which is the border between Ross-shire and Sutherland - should produce Dippers on fast-flowing streams with Redstart, Wood Warbler, Woodcock and Spotted Flycatcher in the woods. The path leads to the

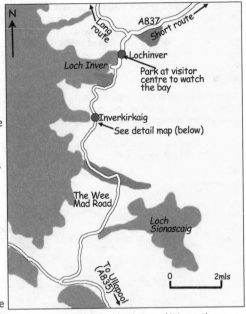

spectacular Falls of Kirkaig and it is worth continuing another 500 yards or so to view Fionn Loch and Suilven, Assynt's 'sugar-loaf' mountain. The most unusual sighting at Inverkirkaig is an excellent book and music shop, miles from anywhere. There are café and toilet facilities here.

Lochinver is a bustling little village complete with a craft shop and the award-winning Assynt Visitor Centre. Among the displays of local geology and wildlife, there is live CCTV footage from a local heronry. You can get good views of the Loch Inver sea loch from here and take a wildlife cruise too – the visitor centre has details.

You now have a choice of routes. You can turn right onto the A837 across moorland and along the edge of Loch Assynt. Scan here again for more divers and look out for the ruins of Ardvreck Castle where the Scottish hero, Montrose, staunch defender of the Catholic Stuart line, was betrayed. This area abuts the Inchnadamph NNR, famous for its geology and botany.

Alternatively, and much better if you have the time, continue north on a minor road that hugs the coast towards Drumbeg, passing more moorland, lochans and isolated beaches and coves. Achmelvich Bay can be good for divers and terns. A ranger service provides guided walks.

The coast road continues past a series of lochans and any number of spectacular sea views before ending up in a desolate stretch of moorland, skirting the northern edge of Quinag. Red-throated Divers fly over as they commute between small lochans and the sea. Merlins hunt and Wheatears flash their white rumps. There is always the chance of something unusual turning up. We came across a field full of what we thought were feeding Linnets. It was only when we stopped for a closer look that we found least 200 Lesser Redpolls and a couple of Mealy Redpolls coming down to take seeds from the field.

Likely bird species

All year			
Greylag Goose	Golden Eagle	Barnacle Goose	Wheatear
Wigeon	Merlin	Great Northern Diver	Ring Ouzel
Red-breasted	Peregrine		Wood Warbler
Merganser	Raven	*Spring/autumn*	
Red and Black-throated	*Winter*	Breeding waders	
Divers	Whooper Swan	(including Greenshank)	
		Whinchat	

⑤ Stoer
Background information

IF YOU CAN, take a detour at Stoer, one of my favourite seawatching spots. The minor roads here can be good for Merlin. Roadside Wheatears and Meadow Pipits are abundant.

Kittiwakes breed on the cliffs at Stoer.

Ravens are usually right over your head when you park at the picnic site just in front of the lighthouse.

Seabirds constantly stream past the cliffs here as they fly between Handa and their feeding grounds. Most are Razorbills and Guillemots though you should see a few Puffins too, especially if you have use of a telescope (recommended).

Great Skuas regularly patrol the cliffs and you shouldn't have too much trouble finding Arctic Skuas too. But what about finding Pomarine and Long-tailed Skuas in spring? The trouble is, there are not enough local birders to cover the area so you have a chance to cover yourself in glory.

There is a large spring passage of skuas at Balranald in the Western Isles, including good numbers of Long-tailed Skuas, and birds have been seen passing Handa just to the north. So who is going to be the first person to find a major mainland watchpoint?

Other birds that you can expect to see include Gannets, Fulmars, Kittiwakes, Shags, gulls and terns. Look for divers on the sea.

There are usually one or two Manx Shearwaters moving through in spring, though numbers start to increase in late summer. Autumn itself can produce some spectacular seabird movements in strong onshore winds

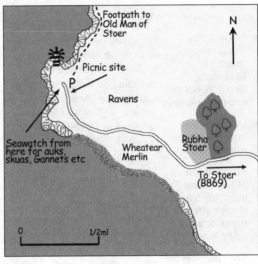

with many tens of thousands of birds per hour passing the lighthouse, mostly Gannets, Kittiwakes and auks. Additional species that you might see in autumn include both Storm and Leach's Petrels plus the two rarer skuas (see above). In calmer weather in late summer and autumn sightings of whales and dolphins are almost guaranteed.

At the risk of stating the obvious, it can get very windy here, so take care not to venture too close to the edge of the cliff. In inclement weather, you can still get reasonable views from the comfort of your own car.

Likely bird species/other fauna

All year	Storm Petrel	Gannet	*Other wildlife*
Shag	Leach's Petrel	Arctic Skua	Whales
Merlin	Pomarine Skua	Great Skua	Dolphins
Raven	Long-tailed Skua	Kittiwake	
		Guillemot	
Autumn	*Spring to autumn*	Razorbill	
Manx Shearwater	Fulmar	Puffin	

Key points

- **Full facilities (food, petrol, toilets) in Inverness, Dornoch, Golspie and Bonar Bridge**

- **Loch Fleet of interest all year round**

- **Worth stopping at Loch Fleet for anything from a short coffee break to a full day's exploring**

- **The Mound is the best place for a short stop**

- **Embo is best from autumn to spring**

- **Moorland best from spring to autumn**

- **A9 and Struie viewpoint can get busy**

- **Easy driving conditions with relatively flat terrain**

- **Much of this tour can be explored from the car**

WITH THE the SNH – managed Loch Fleet at its centre, this drive takes in a wide range of habitats. There is prime Hen Harrier moorland, a wonderful valley, a tidal basin attracting terns, passage waders and wintering wildfowl and Crested Tit-enriched conifers.

Head north from Inverness on the A9, checking for Red Kites en route, until you cross the Cromarty Firth – an excellent place to see seals. You soon leave all the lorries behind as you take the scenic route to Bonar Bridge. After a bit of farmland, you pass through some excellent moorland, though stopping places are few and far between and you have to resort to looking out for birds as you drive along.

The one place you can't miss though is the Struie viewpoint. The lay-by here offers a fantastic panoramic view over the Dornoch Firth and most of south and central Sutherland. The locals call it the 'million dollar view' and it's easy to see why.

The downside is that unless you are there first thing in the morning or in the evening, you are likely to find your birding interrupted by coach-loads of tourists all demanding to know what you are looking

at and wanting to try your telescope.

Just before you reach Bonar Bridge, you come to Ardgay, pronounced 'Ordguy' where a minor road leads off down Strathcarron (not to be confused with Strathcarron on the west coast) towards the church at Croick. This is another of those delightful little valleys to be explored at leisure.

The road ends at the church, which featured prominently in the Highland Clearances. Landowners realised that they could make more money from grazing sheep and so forcibly evicted the local population. They all gathered outside the church – they weren't even allowed in – and many of them scratched their names into the church's windows, a very poignant reminder of man's inhumanity to man.

From Bonar Bridge, a minor road – very minor in places with plenty of grass growing in the middle – leads across more moorland past Loch Buidhe (pronounced byou-ee) before dropping down to Loch Fleet, one of those fantastic places that you can watch for anything from ten minutes to a whole day.

The internationally important loch is effectively cut in two by the A9. This causeway is known as the Mound and was built by Thomas Telford back in 1816. Sluices control the flow of water and the whole area is tidal.

There is a car park on the north-west corner of the Mound and this is by far the best area to stop if you are just calling in for a quick break. Alternatively, there are many different habitats to explore here if you have the time.

As you work your way along the

southern shore of the loch, past the ruined 14th Century Skelbo Castle, you reach the tiny settlement of Embo, hardly big enough to even be called a hamlet. Whereas most towns and villages twin themselves with a similar-sized place in France or Germany, someone in Embo has decided to try for a bit of one-upmanship. The result is that this tiny village is twinned with somewhere in Hawaii. Now that's style. The pier here makes an excellent place to scan the sea

Continues on page 192

How to get there

Nearest large town: Inverness (50 miles).

From Inverness, head N on A9. Cross Cromarty Firth and look for lay-bys immediately on R. Continue on A9 and after five miles turn W onto A836 signed 'Scenic route'. This road is 14 miles long, with the Struie viewpoint (well signposted) about a mile from the end. Turn L when you rejoin A9 towards Bonar Bridge.

To explore Strathcarron, turn L in Ardgay about 50 yards after the war memorial, following signs for Croick Church. Retrace your steps and continue on A9 to Bonar Bridge.

Cross bridge and at crossroads take minor road that goes straight on (slightly staggered) which is signposted Migdale and hospital.

Continue on this minor road and pass Loch Buidhe on L to rejoin A9 at western edge of Loch Fleet.

Turn L, cross the causeway, (the Mound) and look for the picnic spot on L. To explore the northern part of Loch Fleet, continue N on A9 into Golspie and

turn R towards Littleferry.

For Embo, return along A9 and re-cross the Mound. Take first L along loch's southern shore, stopping opposite castle en route. Follow road for two miles then turn L on a minor road to Embo. Continue through the village to the caravan site and pier.

To return, turn L out of Embo towards Dornoch and from there, back to A9 where a bridge over the Dornoch Firth saves you a lot of time on your return journey to Inverness.

Total mileage of this tour from Inverness 130 miles

From page 191

for ducks and the surrounding rocks for waders.

If you are looking for other attractions in the area, then Dunrobin Castle is just north of Loch Fleet. Beware if you see any strange raptors in the area as they have falconry displays here where they fly a variety of birds including some pretty odd hybrids such as a Merlin-Gyrfalcon cross!

Just to the south of Embo is Dornoch, complete with its cathedral (site of Madonna's wedding) and a good selection of craft shops. There are toilets and a petrol station here too.

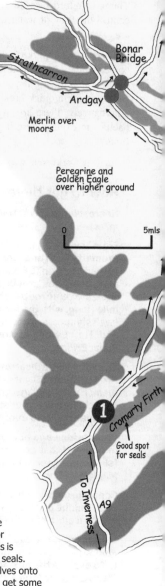

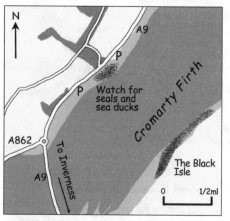

❶ Cromarty Firth

Background information

IMMEDIATELY AFTER you cross the Cromarty Firth heading north, look for some large lay-bys on your right.

Likely bird species/ other fauna	
All year	*Other wildlife*
Shelduck	Common seal
Red-breasted	Grey seal
Merganser	

Though the bird life is likely to be restricted to the occasional Shelduck, Eider or Red-breasted Merganser, this is an excellent place to watch seals. Good numbers haul themselves onto the sandbanks and you can get some

very close views, depending on the state of the tide.

Buzzards hang on the air currents over the woods and are often seen hunting above the short grass here, much to the annoyance of the breeding Lapwings and Oystercatchers.

❷ Struie viewpoint and area
Background information

THE AREA AROUND the lay-by is all moorland and in quieter moments you might find a Stonechat and Whinchat using a bit of heather as a lookout, or Cuckoos looking for suitable nests to parasitise. Merlins and Hen Harriers hunt in the area, though Buzzards and Kestrels are more likely.

For a more thorough exploration of the area, stop about six miles south of here where the road crosses the River Rory and explore the surrounding strath.

Likely bird species

All year	Meadow Pipit	Merlin
Red Grouse	Stonechat	Curlew
Buzzard	*Summer*	Cuckoo
Kestrel	Hen Harrier	Whinchat

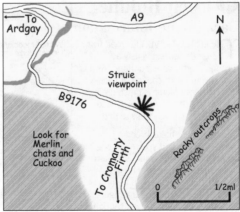

❸ Strathcarron and Croick church

Background information

THE RIVER BLACKWATER holds Dippers, Grey Wagtails and Common Sandpipers while the woods support Siskins, Spotted Flycatchers and a range of warblers including Wood Warbler. Look for Twite and Linnets along the first stretch of the road. Buzzards are usually overhead.

As you get towards the end of the valley, it opens out into moorland with the bubbling calls of Curlews filling the air and Wheatears flitting along the road edge. Any small raptor flying low and fast will almost certainly be a Merlin. Look out for Ring Ouzels on rocky outcrops or even the occasional summering Redwing.

Likely bird species

All year		*Summer*	
Golden Eagle (rare)	Dipper	Merlin	Whinchat
Buzzard	Stonechat	Curlew	Ring Ouzel
Grey Wagtail	Twite	Common Sandpiper	Redwing (rare)
	Linnet		Wood Warbler
			Spotted Flycatcher

❹ Loch Buidhe

Background information

THE LITTLE-TRAVELLED road from Bonar Bridge winds its way through more prime moorland. As it is a lot quieter, your chance of seeing a Hen Harrier or Merlin is much greater than at the Struie viewpoint. Red Grouse are relatively easy to find.

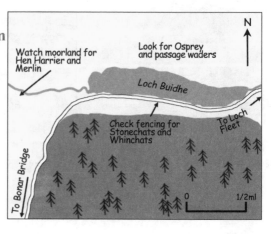

Loch Buidhe holds breeding Greylag Geese and you might see the occasional passage wader such as a Greenshank along the shoreline, though it is more likely to be one of the breeding Common Sandpipers. An Osprey could drift over, though don't worry if you don't see one, they are relatively easy to find at Loch Fleet.

The fencing on the opposite side of the road to the loch seems to be a favoured perch for family parties of Stonechats and Whinchats. Yellowhammers are

---

Likely bird species

All year	Summer	
Red Grouse	Osprey	Common Sandpiper
Greylag Goose	Hen Harrier	Whinchat
Stonechat	Merlin	
Yellowhammer	Greenshank	

---

present around the pasture at either edge of the moor.

---

❺ Loch Fleet National Nature Reserve

Background information

AROUND TEN pairs of Osprey are in the Dornoch Firth area and can be seen fishing from spring through to autumn. Note that there are lots of Grey Herons in the area too, so don't automatically assume that every distant silhouette of a large bird with a slow, flapping flight is an Osprey. Buzzards and Kestrels are common, with Peregrines and Golden Eagles noted occasionally.

Either side of high tide, the area west of the A9, where the River Fleet feeds into the loch, gets covered last and uncovered first and is the best place to check for passage waders such as Greenshanks feeding in the channels. Common Sandpipers breed.

Internationally important numbers of Bar-tailed Godwits, Curlews, Redshanks, Dunlin, Knot and Oystercatchers overwinter, arriving in late summer/early autumn and staying through to late spring. The three best sites to watch the high tide roosts are the river mouth, Skelbo Point and Balblair Bay. Autumn is the best bet for unusual bird species.

The area round this part of the lagoon is alder carr, the largest area of estuarine alders in Britain. Though there is no immediate access to the woods from the Mound causeway, small birds can often be seen flying in and out, while the bushes immediately in front of the car park often hold a foraging Willow Warbler, Coal Tit or Stonechat. Listen for Siskins and Lesser Redpolls flying over.

The best place to explore this habitat is just before you rejoin the A9 after coming down from Loch Buidhe. Park sensibly and check out the fantastic lichen-covered trees. As well as the species mentioned above, Redstarts and Spotted Flycatchers arrive in spring.

One seemingly incongruous species is the cliff-nesting Fulmar. To watch this maritime species appear out of the woods is most strange. These birds are present all year round, save for a month or so in winter.

Of the waterbirds, Shelducks are ever-present and Red-breasted Mergansers are often seen. A few pairs of Eiders and Wigeon remain throughout the year. You can get really close views of Eiders from the southern edge of the loch where a minor road leads past Skelbo Castle towards Embo.

There are plenty of small parking spots and one larger car park complete with interpretative

Likely bird species/other fauna

All year	Scottish Crossbill	Greenshank	Divers
Eider	Woodland birds	Curlew Sandpiper	Grebes
Shelduck		(autumn)	Merlin
Wigeon	*Summer*	Little Stint (autumn)	Peregrine
Red-breasted Merganser	Osprey		Curlew
Common wildfowl	Common Sandpiper	*Winter*	Knot
Fulmar	Arctic Tern	Greylag Goose	Bar-tailed Godwit
Golden Eagle (rare)	Common Tern	White-fronted Goose	Dunlin
Buzzard	Little Tern	(occasional)	Oystercatcher
Sky Lark	Redstart	Pink-footed Goose	Redshank
Meadow Pipit	Spotted Flycatcher	(occasional)	Seaducks
Goldcrest	Waders – passage and	Whooper Swan	
Treecreeper	winter	(occasional)	*Other wildlife*
Crested Tit		Long-tailed Duck	Grey and common seals
Siskin	*Spring and autumn*	Common Scoter	Otter
Lesser Redpoll	Whimbrel	Velvet Scoter	Butterflies

board by the castle itself. Look out for summering Arctic, Common and Little Terns. This is a good place to see common seals, though you will be lucky to find an otter.

On the northern edge of the loch, around Littleferry, there are two further habitats to explore - Balblair Woods and Ferry Links, a dune system. The woods hold Crested Tits, Redstarts and crossbills of one variety or another. Park at Balblair Bay, overlooking the loch (check here too for passage waders) and retrace your steps

for a couple of minutes. Please keep to the paths in the woods. Alternatively, continue to the end of the road and park at Littleferry, the best site for exploring the dunes.

As well as typical dune species such as larks and pipits, this area is good for butterflies, with green hairstreaks, green fritillaries and graylings present. The sea here is particularly good for Common Scoters, Velvet Scoters, Long-tailed Ducks, divers and grebes from autumn through to spring and it is worthwhile finding a

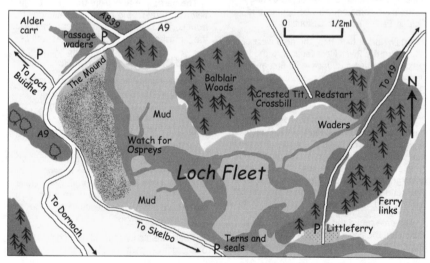

sheltered spot in the dunes and settling down for a bit of seawatching.

Wintering wildfowl includes good numbers of Wigeon and Teal, plus a thousand or so Greylag Geese. Their flock is always worth checking for the occasional White-fronted Goose. Pinkfeet and Whooper Swans might only stay for a few days, en route to their wintering and summering grounds.

With the exception of the dunes, there shouldn't be any difficulty for wheelchair users to get a good view at any of the spots mentioned above.

⑥ Embo
Background information

A S YOU DRIVE through the village, you reach a small dune system where a pier, used mostly by local fishermen, juts into the Dornoch Firth. This makes for a good seawatching spot, the best time being autumn through to early spring. This is when the seaducks are still present, including Long-tailed Ducks, Common and Velvet Scoters, divers, grebes and Eiders.

This used to be a regular spot for King Eider and though there have been no recent sightings, that and Surf Scoter remain the most likely rarities. There shouldn't be any problems in getting a wheelchair from the car to the pier. Small waders, such as Dunlin, Ringed Plovers, Purple Sandpipers and Turnstones gather on the rocky outcrops over winter, with a few birds still hanging around to mid May.

Summer is fairly quiet with maybe the occasional tern, auk or Gannet drifting past. The dunes hold a typical assortment of larks,

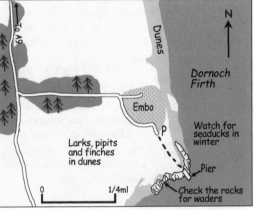

pipits and wagtails with Linnets ever present. The rich birdsong is often accompanied by a distant 'crump, crump' of shells being fired on MOD ranges over the firth.

Easterly or north-easterly winds in autumn make this an excellent seawatching spot with auks, skuas, shearwaters and rare gulls all likely to appear in suitable conditions.

Likely bird species

All year	Autumn		
Oystercatcher	Manx Shearwater	Great Skua	Surf Scoter (rare)
Ringed Plover	Sooty Shearwater	Arctic Skua	King Eider (rare)
Sky Lark	Gannet		Divers
Meadow Pipit	Gulls	*Winter*	Grebes
Linnet	Terns	Long-tailed Duck	Dunlin
	Auks	Common Scoter	Purple Sandpiper
		Velvet Scoter	Turnstone

Key points

- **Full range of services in Helmsdale, Wick and Thurso, but note opening hours**

- **Recommended route the best way to explore the Flow Country**

- **Fantastic seabird cliffs including breeding skuas**

- **Amazing botany, geology and archaeology**

- **Bird hides at Dunnet Forest, St John's Loch and Loch of Mey**

- **Wildlife cruises available from John o'Groats**

- **Disabled birding best from car along the Strath of Kildonan/ Strath Halladale road**

- **Limited disabled seawatching from the car parks at Dunnet and Duncansby Heads**

THE FLOW COUNTRY in the far north-east of Scotland is one of the most specialised habitats in Britain, full of bogs, deep, black pools, carnivorous plants and some of our rarest breeding birds.

Combine that with a visit to the seabird colonies on the most northerly point in Britain, a couple of super little straths and a loch just waiting to be discovered and you can expect a spectacular day's birding.

Starting from Helmsdale, the road follows the River Helmsdale through the Strath of Kildonan. There was a goldrush here in Victorian times and though you are not likely to meet many prospectors today, you can still try your hand at panning.

The single-track road is surprisingly busy. Your journey towards RSPB Forsinard – surely the only bird reserve that doubles up as a working railway station – will take a lot longer than you might imagine as you are constantly pulling into passing places to let the locals go past. Never mind. Take your time and use the opportunity to scan for birds.

Having been used to the mountainous scenery of the west coast, I always assumed

that I would find the flat landscape of the Flow Country something of an anti-climax. As usual, I was completely wrong.

The Patterned Lands – a beguiling mix of peat and pools – is a fascinating area, whatever your interest in wildlife. This is somewhere you just have to experience, especially the strange feeling when you step off the boardwalk onto the peat and feel the whole surface sinking down with you on board.

The road beyond Forsinard now follows Strath Halladale. It is worth spending time looking over the sea at Dunnet Bay. All three species of diver, Common and Velvet Scoters, Eiders, Red-breasted Mergansers and Long-tailed Ducks spend the winter here, lingering into spring.

Along the shoreline you should find a range of feeding waders before they set off on migration to their Arctic breeding grounds. Terns can be seen from spring and the bay is used by feeding auks.

As you reach the coast, you turn right and continue past the Dounreay nuclear power station Visitor Centre towards John o'Groats, where you will find another myth shattered! John o'Groats is not the most northerly point on the British mainland. That honour goes to Dunnet Head's 300-foot high cliffs which provide an excellent spot for seabirds.

On a clear day you can see the southern islands of Orkney as well as dramatic views all along the north Scottish coast as far as the lighthouse at Strathy Point – about 25 miles away. The weather is not always that kind though and you are just as likely to see the Old Man of Hoy looming in and out of the mist faster than a Bonxie can rob a Kittiwake.

Dunnet Head and nearby Duncansby Head both offer a similar range of

seabird species, but are totally different in feel. So, which should you choose if you only have time to visit one?

I have always had better views of skuas at Dunnet and the approach road is far more interesting. However, if the spectacle of numbers is what you want, then Duncansby takes a lot of beating.

Between Dunnet Head and the Queen Mother's beloved castle of Mey is the Loch of Mey, a wonderful spot for birdwatching and yet, because of its remoteness, sadly underwatched.

There is a decidedly old-fashioned feel to this part of Scotland. Towns are small

Continues on page 200

How to get there

Nearest large town: Inverness is 60 miles S of Helmsdale.

From Helmsdale, take A897 W towards Melvich. Follow this to Forsinard railway station and RSPB reserve.

Continue N through Strath Halladale to A836. Turn R and go through Thurso until you see Dunnet Bay signed on L.

Just after Dunnet Bay, turn L on B855 towards Dunnet Head (well signposted). Large, free car park at the lighthouse.

Back on A836, continue towards Mey and take minor road on L along eastern edge of Loch of Mey. Park on R by ruined croft, just before turn to Harrow Harbour.

Retrace your steps to A836, towards John o'Groats. Duncansby Head is well signed from here. Pick up A99 and A9 back towards Helmsdale. At Auckengill, eight miles S of John o'Groats, there is a sign to Iron Age brochs.

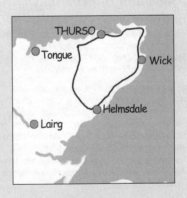

Just beyond Ulbster, seven miles S of Wick, turn right following signs for the chambered cairn. Park overlooking Loch Watenan and follow the signed footpath towards the cairn. The Hill o' Many Stanes is another three miles S on A99.

Total mileage for the tour, about 138 miles.

From page 199

and though they have a full range of amenities, they tend to stick to traditional opening hours. We found one Tourist Information Office closed all day on Saturdays!

The return journey follows the coast southwards and past the main Caithness Glass factory (of interest to those with non-birding partners in need of some retail therapy). There are also three archaeological sites, giving you the chance to catch up on some of Britain's most ancient history.

Spring through to autumn is the best time to visit the whole area. The seabird colonies are at their best in May and June. Autumn brings seawatching and passage waders on the coast. Loch of Mey and Dunnet Bay are the best places to visit in winter.

① RSPB Forsinard
Background information

CONSTANTLY HAVING to pull over to let someone pass gives you the chance to have a quick scan for birds and you should pick up Wheatear, Stonechat and Whinchat as you drive along the edge of the River Helmsdale.

Cuckoos are present in good numbers and Greylag Geese breed. There is a chance of a Merlin zipping through, especially a couple of miles either side of the reserve centre. They often perch on fence-posts or large boulders. There are otters on the river and red deer are often seen close to the road, especially in spring and early summer. In the last few years, a Black Kite has been summering near Loch an Ruathair.

Park at Forsinard station, which also doubles up as the reserve's visitor centre. It is open from April to October, 9am to 6pm. Here you can get details of the latest sightings and watch live video footage from a Hen Harrier nest. There are various interpretative displays explaining the significance of the habitat.

A self-guided walk takes you round the Dubh Lochan (Black Lochan) trail, roughly a mile long and taking

Map labels: A836 · Strath Halladale · Check for Golden Plovers and Dunlin · Forsinard · ① · Dubh Lochan Trail · Loch an Ruathair · A897 · 0 5mls · Helmsdale

Likely bird species/ other fauna	
All year	
Hen Harrier	Greenshank
Merlin	Dunlin
Short-eared Owl	Golden Plover
Divers	
Common Scoter	*Other wildlife*
	Red deer

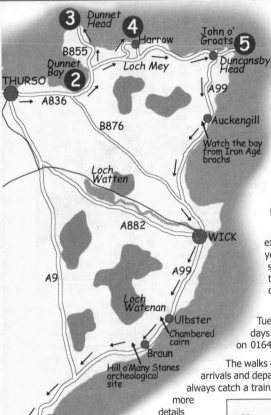

Watch the bay from Iron Age brochs

Chambered cairn

Hill o'Many Stanes archeological site

about an hour. Here you get to experience the incredible bouncing blanket bog, full of the strangest plants including sphagnum mosses and *drosera* - the flesh-eating sundews. This is a good spot for dragonflies in summer.

This is the most amazing habitat, though you are not likely to see a great number of bird species here. Listen out for Red Grouse, the tri-syllabic *'tu tu tu'* of a Greenshank and the plaintive *'pyoo'* of a Golden Plover. Other breeding waders include Lapwings, Dunlin, Curlews, Redshanks and Oystercatchers. Be alert for raptors or Short-eared Owls flying low over the ground.

The habitat makes for very difficult exploration away from the boardwalk, so if you want to see some of the rarer species such as Common Scoters, Black and Red-throated Divers, it is best to book yourself onto one of the longer guided walks.

At the time of writing, these run on Tuesdays and Saturdays, 2pm to 5pm but the days are liable to change so phone the reserve on 01641 571 225 to check.

The walks are usually scheduled around the train arrivals and departures, so if you don't fancy driving, you can always catch a train from Inverness. Phone 0345 484 950 for more details

Continue north through Strath Halladale. About a mile north of the station, fields on the right often hold small groups of feeding waders and this might be your best chance for connecting with Golden Plovers and Dunlin.

The landscape is spoilt by blocks of coniferous forest, once planted by the rich and famous as a tax avoidance scheme. The RSPB is buying some of these near Forsinard, removing the trees and trying to return the landscape to what it once was. As it stands, all you are likely to see is a pair of Buzzards over each wood.

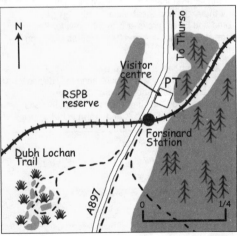

② Dunnet Bay and Forest

Background information

A S YOU APPROACH the wide sweep of Dunnet Bay, there are Forestry Commission signs off on your right for Dunnet Forest complete with several nature trails and a small hide. Expect to see a typical range of woodland species, sometimes including Crossbills if there has been an irruption from the continent the previous winter. Also here are various orchids and dark green fritillaries.

Continuing on to Dunnet Bay, there is a large car park, caravan site and visitor centre on your left. The centre is open regularly in summer though there is a programme of guided walks starting here throughout the year – see the local tourist offices for details.

Park here and explore the huge dune system. All three divers, especially Great Northern Divers, which are sometimes present in good numbers (86 in Nov 97) overwinter in the bay. Look for seaducks too, such as Long-tailed Ducks, Common and Velvet Scoters and Goldeneyes. All these species often linger into May. You will probably need a telescope.

Common and Arctic Terns fish in the bay in summer, or at least they do if not being harried by the Arctic and Great Skuas. Little Terns have bred and Eiders are ever present. Look for Red-breasted Mergansers and Red-throated Divers on the sea.

Autumn gales are a feature of this part of Scotland. Birds passing Dunnet Head may decide to take temporary shelter from the storms. The bay is well worth visiting after the weather eases and you may find Leach's and Storm Petrels,

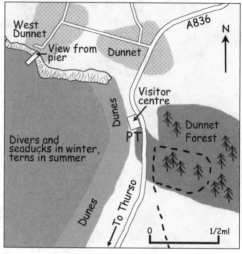

Manx Shearwaters and even Sabine's Gulls taking advantage of the calm water.

Waders build up from August and remain through to the spring, though there is also some passage in spring and autumn. The Rock Doves here are reckoned to be relatively pure. The dunes themselves hold Sky Larks and assorted pipits and finches.

For an alternative viewpoint, and probably the better choice for anyone in a wheelchair, use the pier in the tiny settlement of West Dunnet. This is a good spot for all three divers, dolphins and porpoises. From the B855 to Dunnet Head, turn left on a minor road through Dunnet to West Dunnet and then turn left at the T-junction down to the sea front.

Likely bird species

Autumn to spring	Great Northern Diver	Petrels	Crossbill
Long-tailed Duck	Waders	Scarce gulls	Common woodland birds
Common Scoter		Auks	
Velvet Scoter	Autumn		
Goldeneye	Storm-blown seabirds	All year	Summer
Red-throated Diver	including	Eider	Red-throated Diver
Black-throated Diver	Shearwaters	Rock Dove	Common Tern
			Arctic Tern
			Little Tern

❸ Dunnet Head

Background information

IMMEDIATELY AFTER you turn off the main road towards Dunnet Head, you get glimpses of St John's Loch on your right. At the top end of the loch, look for signs on your right to the 'Artsmith Exhibition', an art gallery featuring paintings of local wildlife and landscapes (limited summer opening, www.artsmith-caithness.co.uk).

About 200 metres from the gallery is the newly reopened John Corbett memorial hide. Nearly 200 species have been recorded here, including a good selection of rarities and the loch is well worth a visit at any time of year. The range of species roughly mirrors that of the Loch of Mey (see page 204).

The road continues over the moors and past several small lochs. These are worth a quick scan for Red-throated Divers, wildfowl, waders, Twite and chats. Whimbrel move through the area in May.

As you arrive at the Head, you will see signs for the viewpoint. For some strange reason, the display map shows the area that you have come from, not what you are looking at – obviously designed for pillaging Vikings. However, this spot is useless for birding. Instead, park by the left side of the lighthouse and watch from the cliffs there.

All the auks breed, though, as usual, Puffins are the hardest to see as they nest in burrows rather than on the cliffs. Black Guillemots are present, but you will find them easier to see on the west coast.

Great Skuas are obvious and you should get good views looking down on them, their powerful build and large white wing flashes being immediately apparent. Arctic Skuas are regularly seen here too with good

numbers of Kittiwakes and Fulmars. Gannets can be seen in large numbers in autumn with smaller counts for the rest of the year. Peregrines patrol the cliffs.

This is another good site for whale and dolphin watching though you are more likely to pick up harbour porpoises. Look for seals, both grey and common, anywhere around the headland, especially at Brough Bay where you can often see them sunning themselves on the rocks, looking for all the world like giant slugs. If you are in the area at dawn or dusk, look out

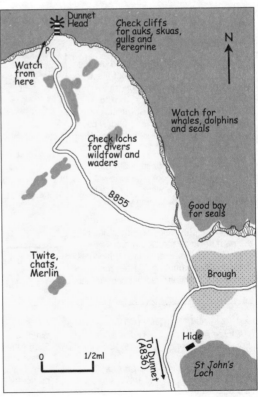

too for otters around the coastline.

Mid April to July are the best times for breeding seabirds. Autumn can produce some spectacular seabird passage with many thousands of birds moving past the headland including shearwaters, petrels and the scarcer skuas – Pomarine and Long-tailed. The cliffs are largely empty in winter.

Likely bird species/other fauna

Spring/summer		*Autumn*	
Red-throated Diver	Gulls	Wildfowl	Skuas
Fulmar	Auks	Shearwaters	Gulls
Peregrine	Whinchat	Petrels	Terns
Great and Arctic Skuas	Stonechat	Gannets	Auks
Kittiwake	Wheatear	Waders	
	Twite		

❹ Loch of Mey
Background information

YOU MIGHT STRUGGLE to find the hide here, but it's worth it. Look for a track leading down to the loch, opposite a ruined croft, just before the turn to Harrow harbour. This is just the sort of place I would love to have as a local patch – a good range of habitats with something of interest all year round.

And boy, is it underwatched! From the sightings in the logbook, the hide gets visited about once a week, so there is plenty of chance for finding your own birds.

In summer, the fields on either side of the path down to the hide are alive with displaying waders, Stonechats, Whinchats, Twite and Reed Buntings. Listen for Sedge Warblers and reeling Grasshopper Warblers. If

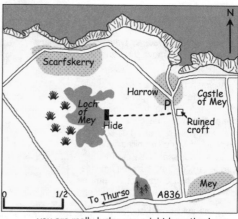

you are really lucky, you might hear the *'crex crex'* of a calling Corn Crake - the occasional bird breeds along this stretch of coast.

Likely bird species

All year	*Spring/autumn*		*Winter*
Common wildfowl	Passage waders	Whinchat	White-fronted Goose
Stonechat		Sedge Warbler	Whooper Swan
Twite	*Summer*	Grasshopper Warbler	Hen Harrier
Reed Bunting	Arctic Tern	Corn Crake (outside chance of hearing)	

Spring and autumn are dynamic times here. The combination of geographical location and shallow margins act as a magnet for migrating waders.

There is always the chance of something out of the ordinary among the commoner species. For instance, our first visit turned up a superb summer-plumaged Spotted Redshank, only the second spring Caithness record. There is a reasonable chance of an American wader in autumn.

There is a colony of 20-30 Arctic Terns on the loch in summer, though breeding success is poor. Winter attracts various wildfowl, including Greenland White-fronted Geese and Whooper Swans as well as a good selection of hunting raptors, including Hen Harriers.

Other attractions in the area include the Castle of Mey, once the Queen Mother's favourite home, and now open to the public on a seasonal basis.

⑤ Duncansby Head
Background information

THOUGH THE CLIFFS hold a similar range of species to Dunnet, minus the Peregrines, Duncansby Head feels totally different. It is much easier here to see the cliffs themselves, so the number of birds on view increases dramatically. And it's not just a visual experience either. Your senses of hearing and smell get equally assailed.

You can easily study the dynamics of a breeding seabird colony, with Fulmars at the top of the cliffs, seemingly flying for fun, down through the Kittiwakes and the auks, to the Shags at the very bottom of the cliffs.

Many of the Guillemots here, and at Dunnet, are of the bridled form, their eyes picked out by a pair of white 'spectacles'. Great and Arctic Skuas breed on the surrounding moorland.

The Head is well signposted out of John

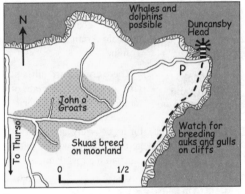

o'Groats. Though there is a cliff immediately by the car park, your best bet is to head south (ie to your right as you are driving in to the car park).

A short walk brings you back to the coastal path and some amazing rock formations, known as geos, with what appear to be huge stone daggers sticking out of the sea.

Again, look for whales and dolphins offshore, though this is not as good a site as Dunnet Head for cetaceans.

Likely bird species/other fauna

Spring/summer	Kittiwake	Gannets
Auks		
Great Skua	*Autumn*	*Other wildlife*
Arctic Skua	Shearwaters	Cetaceans
Gulls	Petrels	Seals
Fulmar	Skuas	

Key points

- Facilities (food, toilets, petrol) in Lairg, Tongue and Durness

- Wildlife cruises available in Durness

- Mostly single-tracked road – very narrow round the Kyle of Tongue

- Excellent conditions with the sun mostly behind you

- Excellent botany and geology as well as birds

- Guided walks organised out of the Ferrycroft Centre in Lairg

- Main tour is wheelchair-friendly, with roadside viewing throughout

- No wheelchair access to Salmon Leap or Ravens Rock Gorge

CUTTING A SWATHE right through the centre of Sutherland, this part of Scotland is about as remote as it gets on Britain's 'main' roads. This isolation offers visitors the chance to explore a rich mix of moorland and coastal habitats that are rarely disturbed.

With luck, you will see all three species of diver, resplendent in their breeding finery. You should also pick up a good selection of breeding waders on both moor and coast, and a fantastic Arctic Tern colony at Tongue.

There are seabird cliffs to visit and a good selection of raptors in the area. Deer, seals and salmon add non-birding variety and the geologist and botanist will find much to interest them.

When you reach Raven Rock Gorge, you may be puzzled by the presence of a life-size sculpture of a bear, carved out of wood in the middle of one of the most inaccessible parts of the site. In recent times there has been talk of re-introducing all sorts of once-native wildlife into Britain. Most likely is the beaver, but there have also been calls for the likes of wolf, lynx and bear. Perhaps that explains why the carving is here – or maybe not. What is

less of a mystery is the human history of the area. It is positively dripping with archaeology and anyone who enjoys a bit of history with their birding will be well pleased.

With the area being so remote, you can get really close to the wildlife. Driving across the moors at dusk, we twice came across Merlins taking grit from the road, just feet in front of the car. Vehicles make excellent hides and these tiny falcons were totally oblivious to our presence.

Deer bound in front of you and all you can see is their eyes, reflecting an eerie *X-Files* shade of green in your headlights. It has to be said that the moors are really spooky after dark and it is perhaps not the best place to start telling each other ghost stories. If a deer does run in front of you, stop immediately. The police reckon that most accidents are caused by collision with the second animal in the herd.

The strangest behaviour we saw from the car was demonstrated by Wheatears, which totally panicked when caught in the light beams, careering wildly from side to side, freezing in the middle of the road but never once flying out of the light. Stonechats and Meadow Pipits were totally unfazed by the light, but several times we had to stop and turn off the lights so that the Wheatears could escape.

One advantage of being so far north is that this is one of the first areas wintering bird migrants reach in autumn and one of the last that they leave in spring, so visits in May and September can produce the best of both worlds with winter and summer migrants present at the same time.

Spring and summer are the best times to visit, though autumn seawatching from Faraid Head could well be rewarding. Seaducks and Great Northern Divers will be present around the coast from autumn through to late spring and if you do visit in winter, I would suggest that you stick largely to the coast.

How to get there

Nearest large town: Lairg is about 50 miles N of Inverness.

Start the loop at Lairg where the Ferrycroft Centre (NC579061) is well signposted off A839.

For the Falls of Shin, leave Lairg SW on A839 and turn L onto B864 after a mile. Large visitor centre and car park are on R after about five miles (NC498008).

For Ravens Rock Gorge, take A839 SW out of Lairg. After eight miles, turn L on minor road towards Altass and the car park is on your right after a mile (NC498008).

For Loch Loyal, head N from Lairg on A836 for 30 miles and the loch is on R.

For Tongue, continue N on A836 for 12 miles to Tongue. Turn L onto A838 and L again onto a minor road round the Kyle when A838 hairpins back on itself. Follow minor road until it rejoins A838, then turn R over the causeway and park in the well-signed car park on R (NC574587).

Leave car park heading W towards Durness. For short route, turn L on minor road at Hope and follow this until

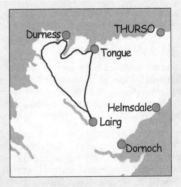

it crosses A836 at Altnaharra. Turn R and return to Lairg.

Alternatively, continue on A838 round Loch Eriboll until you reach Durness. Balnakeil is well signed just to W of village and you can access Faraid Head either from here (park at NC392687) or from Durness itself. The ferry to Cape Wrath leaves from Keoldale, a couple of miles to the S, off A838.

Continue SW on A838 to Laxford Bridge (19 miles) and turn L, still on A838, for 37 miles towards Lairg. Turn R when you reach A836 for the last three miles.

Total mileage for the long route is 135 miles.

❶ Lairg

Background information

A SMALL, PICTURESQUE town at the southern end of Loch Shin, Lairg makes an excellent centre for anyone wanting to explore Sutherland. Ospreys have recently recolonised the area and regularly fish in Little Loch Shin and Black-throated Divers can often be seen at the southern end of Loch Shin.

The Ferrycroft Countryside Visitor Centre (open April - September) has excellent interpretative displays about the wildlife, geology and history in the area, as well as toilets and an Internet café. The Centre is well signposted on the western side of Little Loch Shin.

The rangers here run an assortment of guided walks throughout the year and there is usually a week of special wildlife-related events organised across the whole of Caithness, Sutherland and Wester Ross around the last week in May.

Walks are designed for all levels of fitness and include visits to Black Grouse leks, badger, pine marten and otter watches, treks over the moors looking for divers or up some of the higher mountains in search of Ptarmigan. Telephone the centre on 01549 402160 or visit http:// www.highlandwildencounters.info/ for further details.

The Centre is also the starting point for the Ord Hill archaeological trail, a walk that allows you to learn about some 6,000 years of habitation. The 90-minute stroll should also produce a good range of species ranging from hirundines and finches round the Centre to Meadow Pipits, Wheatears and Cuckoo up on the hill.

Cape Wrath

A838

Kinlochbervie

Long route

❾ Laxford Bridge

Loch Stack

A838

Loch More

0   5mls

A837

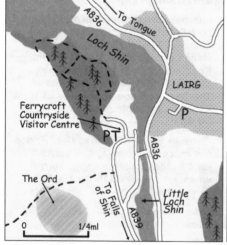

A836

To Tongue

Loch Shin

LAIRG

P

Ferrycroft
Countryside
Visitor Centre

PT

A836

The Ord

A839

Little
Loch
Shin

To Falls
of Shin

0   1/4ml

Likely bird species

Summer
Black-throated Diver
Osprey
Cuckoo

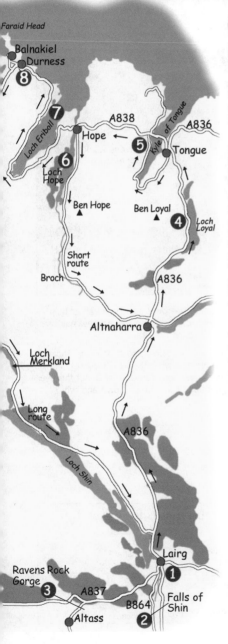

❷ Falls of Shin
Background information

A FEW MILES SOUTH of Lairg, the main attraction of this popular tourist attraction is not birds, but fish. This is a well-known salmon run and fish can be seen trying to leap up the waterfalls at any time between June and September.

Of course, there is plenty of bird interest, too. Dippers forage around the base of the falls and Grey Wagtails fly up and down the river. Buzzards are usually overhead and the woods hold Willow Warblers (summer), Goldcrests, Treecreepers and other common woodland birds. There are way-marked woodland walks behind the car park.

Likely bird species/ other fauna
All year
Buzzard
Grey Wagtail
Dipper
Common woodland birds
Other wildlife
Salmon

The influx of visitors attracted by the massive tourist centre shop and restaurant means your chances of seeing the likes of deer and otters are going to be best at dawn and dusk, when the coaches are at home. The walk from the car park to the viewing platforms is short, but there are plenty of steps so it is not suitable for wheelchair access.

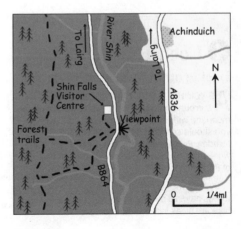

❸ Ravens Rock Gorge
Background information

THIS SITE has to be one of the Forestry Commission's best-kept secrets, but if you give it a try you'll find it offers you a wonderful walk along the edge of Allt Mor (Big Burn), full of primeval, moss-covered trees and boulders. Living up to its name, Ravens can be heard calling, though you are just as likely to hear the mewing of a Buzzard overhead.

Smaller birds can be difficult to hear over the roar of the fast-moving water in the river, but rest assured, there is a good range of typical woodland species present.

Crossbills' *'chip chip'* calls are never hard to hear though and you will always be alerted to the presence of flocks either feeding or flying over. Look for Dippers and Grey Wagtails anywhere along the burn.

The walk takes about an hour and is steep and slippery in parts though there are plenty of

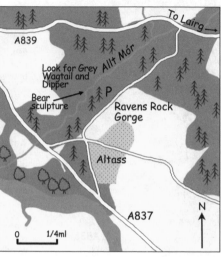

good quality boardwalks and handrails to help you. Even so, there is no way a wheelchair-user could get round the site.

The walk is worth doing at any time, though early mornings, when the birds are most active are best. And don't forget to seek out the bear sculpture and ask yourself 'how?' and 'why?'

Likely bird species

All year	
Grey Wagtail	Coal Tit
Dipper	Common Crossbill
Goldcrest	Raven

---

❹ Loch Loyal
Background information

AS YOU HEAD NORTH from Lairg, the surrounding countryside alternates bits of moorland with blocks of conifers. In summer, you should see Wheatears, Stonechats, Meadow Pipits and Cuckoos in the former while most of the woods have a resident pair of Buzzards.

By the time you reach Altnaharra, the woods have all but disappeared. The moors here are bleak indeed and birding is hard

Likely bird species/other fauna

All year	
Greylag	Hen Harrier
Golden Eagle	Merlin
Buzzard	Greenshank
Red Grouse	Golden Plover
Stonechat	Cuckoo
	Wheatear

Summer	*Other wildlife*
Black-throated Diver	Red deer

210

going. A Red Grouse might stick its head up and a stop might produce the occasional calling wader – Curlew, Dunlin, Golden Plover or Greenshank – but you might as well drive on to Loch Loyal, taking whatever birds happen to fly in front of the car. This may be a Merlin or, if you are really lucky, a Hen Harrier.

Greylag Geese breed around the loch and Common Sandpipers creep and bob round the edges, occasionally flying over the water with their characteristic burst of flapping interrupting stiff-winged glides.

Look for red deer on the slopes of Ben Loyal on your left and scan the mountain ridges for Golden Eagle. The larger bodies of water sometimes hold Black-throated Divers while Greenshanks can often be seen feeding at the edges of smaller lochans.

⑤ Kyle of Tongue
Background information

BEFORE 1971'S CAUSEWAY was built across the inlet you had little choice but to drive round a very minor road skirting the Kyle. Today, nobody gives the original road a second glance, making it ideal for some undisturbed birding.

Passing places are scarce, so park carefully. Siskins and Reed Buntings make unlikely bed-fellows, but you are just as likely to find either in the scrub along the eastern edge of the road, together with Willow Warblers and Stonechats.

Most of the best birding is to be found along the western edge of this minor road where you can get superb views over the estuary. What you see is obviously going to be dependant on the tide, but this is an excellent place for waders.

Breeding birds that come here to feed

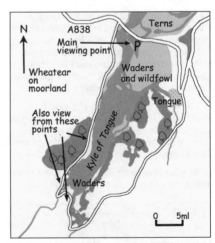

include Greenshanks – our last visit produced 12 at low tide – together with good numbers of Common Sandpipers and small flocks of Dunlin, Redshanks and Ringed Plovers. As with all estuaries, spring and autumn are the dynamic times as passage birds swell the numbers and range of species.

Shelducks and Mallards swim in the channels and Wheatears are common. With the moorland coming right down to the edge of the estuary, this is a good place to study the differences between Meadow and Rock Pipits. Otters are sometimes seen and stoats also hunt the area.

Likely bird species/other fauna

All year	Siskin	Ringed Plover	Bar-tailed Godwit
Eider	Reed Bunting	Greenshank	
Shelduck		Arctic Tern	*Other wildlife*
Red-breasted Merganser	*Summer*		Grey and common seals
Grey Heron	Common Sandpiper	*Spring/autumn*	Otter
Stonechat	Dunlin	Whimbrel	

❻ Loch Hope
Background information

THIS IS THE SHORT cut back to Lairg. A minor road takes you in the shadow of Ben Hope along the edge of Loch Hope. Various lay-bys give you good opportunities to scan the loch for waterfowl including Black-throated Divers or maybe a Whooper Swan, lingering well into the spring before heading off north.

The ridges here are again well worth scanning for raptors such as Buzzard, Peregrine and Golden Eagle. Ravens are regularly seen and heard. Check the gullies on Ben Hope for Ring Ouzels.

As you continue down the road, there is an extremely well preserved Iron-age broch on

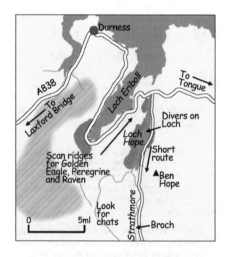

Likely bird species

All year	Peregrine
Golden Eagle	Cuckoo
Raven	Wheatear
	Whinchat
Summer	
Black-throated Diver	*Winter*
Wigeon	Whooper Swan (rare)

your right. Stop here, and as well as brushing up your ancient history, look for the likes of Whinchats on the surrounding fences. The road continues through moorland back to Altnaharra and from there, back to Lairg.

⑦ Loch Eriboll
Background information

IF YOU WANT a longer drive, the main road continues round Loch Eriboll, christened, with amazing wit, Loch 'Orrible by British troops in the Second World War. This is where the German U-boat fleet surrendered; it is one of the few sea lochs deep enough to hold them. The Brahan Seer back in the 17th century (see Chanonry Point on page 164) supposedly prophesied that a war would end here but like many of the prophecies of Nostradamus, this seems to be one of those amazing pieces of insight that was made up much later.

The loch itself is an excellent place to see divers, not least Great Northern Divers, which linger on well into late spring and attain their full

Likely bird species

Summer	Winter
Black-throated Diver	Great Northern
Red-throated Diver	Divers (Sep-May)
Merlin	
Cuckoo	

breeding finery. We've counted nearly 30 birds on occasions complete with Black- and Red-throated Divers. Viewing is best from the western edge of the loch. Merlins and Cuckoos often give good views, usually in pursuit of either a Meadow Pipit itself, in the case of the former, or its nest in the case of the latter.

⑧ Durness Area
Background information

THIS SMALL VILLAGE makes an excellent base for exploring the extreme north-west of Scotland and the tourist office, complete with ranger service, will give you lots of advice on the best places to visit. They organise a range of guided walks. Wildlife cruises are also available. Contact Cape Sea Tours, Tel 01971 511284 or 511259 for details.

There are some amazing seabird colonies here - tens of thousands of birds - though getting access to them is no easy matter. A ferry and minibus service operates from Keoldale to Cape Wrath, but only when the Ministry of Defence bombing ranges are closed. The easy option is to carry on to the café at Cape Wrath itself, and watch the birds streaming past the headland.

If you want to visit the breeding cliffs, you have to tell the bus driver where you want to get to (Clo Mor) so he can drop you off. You then face a 45-minute walk across very difficult terrain before you even get to cliffs. Not surprisingly, you won't see many other people here. You should bank on spending the best part of a day at Clo Mor, if not camping overnight. If you want an easier trip to see seabird cliffs, you will probably do a lot better at Handa (see page 216)

If you do make it here, there are fantastic numbers of Puffins and Fulmars as well as huge numbers of the other auks, Kittiwakes etc. There are genuine Rock Doves, Peregrines patrol the cliffs and Ravens are plentiful. As you walk over the moorland, look out for Great and Arctic Skuas defending their territories, as well as Red Grouse and low-level Ptarmigan. Breeding waders include Greenshanks.

The ferry runs between May and September and there are snacks and toilet facilities at the lighthouse.

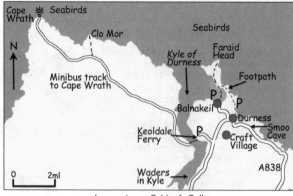

More easily accessible is Faraid Head, a mix of limestone outcrops, dunes, coastal grassland and cliffs, which sticks out two miles into the Atlantic Ocean, beyond the craft village of Balnakeil. The buildings here were designed as early warning centres in case of nuclear attack. They were never finished and now house a variety of craft shops and cafés.

The beaches are fantastic and there is plenty of interesting botany and geology too. As for the Head, it makes for an excellent seawatching spot, with thousands of seabirds flying in and out of their breeding colonies in the summer. Puffins breed and you might also see otters, seals, whales and dolphins. Arctic and Common Terns return in early May and need careful separation.

It is in the autumn though that seawatching really comes into its own, and as well as any numbers of auks, Kittiwakes and Gannets, you will now start to pick up Manx and Sooty Shearwaters, Leach's and Storm Petrels, Pomarine and Long-tailed Skuas as well as the chance of something rarer, such as a scarce

shearwater or Sabine's Gull.

A circular walk – Balnakeil to the Head to Durness and back to Balnakeil - along well-worn paths will take about two hours plus any time for birding, but obviously you can shorten this if you return the way you came. Check the beach for passage waders such as Whimbrel in spring and Sanderling, Dunlin and Redshanks in the autumn – which can start as early as late July. Long-tailed Ducks arrive back in October, staying through to early May – there are usually a few in Balnakeil Bay. Barnacle Geese overwinter in the area.

The other main attraction here is Smoo Cave, and there are tours concentrating on the geology and natural history of the area, though these are not for the claustrophobic. As with all the northern coast of Sutherland and Caithness, Twite flit around the crofts and a few pairs of Corn Crakes hang on. Returning in the second half of May, you may hear their repetitive and ventriloquial calls at any time of day.

Likely bird species/other fauna

All year		*Autumn*	*Winter*
Red Grouse	Greenshank	Manx Shearwater	Barnacle Goose
Ptarmigan	Kittiwake	Sooty Shearwater	Long-tailed Duck
Peregrine	Arctic Tern	Storm Petrel	Sanderling
Rock Dove	Common Tern	Leach's Petrel	Dunlin
Twite	Puffin	Gannet	Redshank
	Guillemot	Great Skua	
	Razorbill	Arctic Skua	
Summer	Black Guillemot	Pomarine Skua	*Other wildlife*
Corn Crake (rare)	Great Skua	Long-tailed Skua	Seals
Fulmar	Arctic Skua		Cetaceans

⑨ Laxford Bridge and Loch Shin
Background information

A S YOU HEAD SOUTH towards Laxford
Bridge, you can't fail to notice a massive
change in the geology of the land. Whereas
further south, the landscape looks fairly green,
here you get massive boulders of bare rock, like
some Scottish moonscape. The centre at
Knockan (see Inverpolly trip page 181 for
directions) has all the details.

There's nothing avian to particularly detain
you here so your birding is likely to be from the
car only – a few Wheatears and chats or a
raptor or two. If you are really lucky, a Red-
throated Diver might fly over, en route from its
breeding grounds on small inland lochans to the
sea where it feeds.

The B-road to Kinlochbervie is only worth a
detour in winter. The Russian fleet uses the
harbour here and the trawlers attract good
numbers of gulls, including Iceland and Glaucous
Gulls though in variable numbers.

At Laxford Bridge, a 37-mile single track road
leads back to Lairg. Fans of National Hunt racing
will immediately be drawn to the names of the
two peaks that dominate the landscape here;
Foinavon, which won the Grand National when
just about every other horse fell, and Arkle,
possibly the greatest steeplechaser of all time.

The first three lochs you come across –
Stack, More and Merkland are by far the most
productive and can produce an assortment of
wildfowl, waders feeding round the muddy
margins and various small birds in the
surrounding heather. They also offer a good
chance for finding Black-throated Divers. Scan

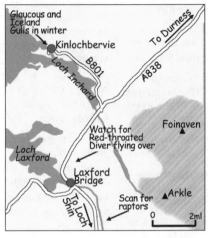

the high ridges over Reay Forest for Buzzards
and Golden Eagles. These are the best places
to linger along this road.

The valley here is steep and V-shaped,
complete with dark, brooding moorland. A
typical range of species occur, though if you are
following the route in this direction, you
probably won't be here at the best time of day
for maximum activity. The areas round human
habitation are likely to be best for a few garden
birds to boost your day list.

Loch Shin, which is about 14 miles long, is
too large and deep to hold many birds. The
fringes are likely to be most productive with the
likes of breeding Wigeon and Common
Sandpipers, or the occasional feeding Snipe.

Likely bird species

All year	Summer
Common wildfowl	Black-throated Diver
Buzzard	Red-throated Diver
Golden Eagle	Cuckoo
Stonechat	Wheatear

215

Key points

WHEN I STARTED researching this chapter, I looked back at the notes I had written after my first trip to Handa, a site managed by the Scottish Wildlife Trust. They simply said 'Magic.' Not a great deal of help ornithologically, but a pretty fair summation of a fantastic place.

It seems strange this far north to be entering Sutherland, which is Old Norse for 'the South Lands', but I suppose that reflects accurately the perspective of Viking invaders.

Handa provides a seabird spectacular! Nearly 200,000 birds offer a full frontal assault on your senses. The sound and smell of massive colonies are just as memorable in their own way as the fantastic sights. Not only do you get the chance to view some amazing breeding colonies, but you also have to brave crossing the breeding grounds of the fiercely defensive Great and Arctic Skuas.

Skuas get their food by the simple method of 'encouraging' other seabirds to part with their catch. There is the Arctic Skua, dashing, handsome and very much of the gentleman highwayman 'Stand and deliver' school of persuasion.

The Great Skuas, known locally as Bonxies, are bigger and brutish. Being attacked by one of them is more akin to a full broadside by a marauding pirate ship. Henry Morgan would be proud. This trip will give you close encounters with both species: a lot closer than some of you might prefer.

The boat to Handa leaves from the harbour in Tarbet. You approach along a minor road with ever-increasing amounts of grass growing up the middle, being chomped by ever-increasing numbers of sheep. Just as you think that the place can't possibly get any more remote, you drop down to the harbour and there, already parked, are likely to be more cars than you have seen in the whole of the last three hours. The minor road skirts Loch nam Brach and is well worth a quick drive round as you leave the area.

The village on the island was occupied until 1847 when a catastrophic potato famine forced everyone off Handa. You can still see the remains of the cottages today, a poignant reminder of a time of hardship.

Now, the Scottish Wildlife Trust manages the island and its warden will meet you when you land. It is best to stick to the three and a half mile footpath, which offers a good tour round the island. Remember to take food and drink with you and note that there are no toilet facilities on the island; the nearest ones are in Tarbet. Suitable bushes are in short supply too! The island is unsuitable for wheelchair access, though most of the species can be seen, albeit distantly, from Tarbet Harbour.

About three miles south of Handa, Scourie is probably the largest of the small crofting communities that lie along the main road here. It has a full set of amenities i.e. shop, petrol and toilets and likes to boast that it has the most northerly palm trees in the world, but there is more to it than that.

Like several other villages (see Abriachan and Boat of Garten), a community hide has been built and this offers a real alternative to anyone with a pathological fear of boats. It is also fully wheelchair-friendly. A lovely little picnic site in the village allows you to add many species of small birds to your day list.

May and June are the best times to visit Handa for maximum numbers of seabirds. Birds arrive back in April and start to leave the cliffs in mid-July. June is the best time to see the abundant wildflowers.

How to get there

Nearest large town: Ullapool is about 40 miles S of Scourie on A894.

Once in Scourie, turn L on a road signed 'Beach'. Hide is halfway down on R. Continue down to cemetery and view from there. Retrace to main road and continue N. Take next road on L signed 'Jetty' for boat trips. Look for toilet block at N end of Scourie on A894. Park in lay-by here and view picnic site behind toilet block.

For Handa, continue N on A894. After three miles, turn L on minor road to Tarbet. Park at harbour. Leave harbour to L and loop round on minor road. Rejoin A894.

Access details for Handa
Ferries to Handa run from April until early September, weather permitting. As is usual in this part of Scotland, they do not run on Sundays. The first boat leaves at 9.30am with regular

departures until about 2.00pm. The last return boat is at 4.30pm.

Ferry crossings take about 15 minutes and you should aim to spend between three and six hours on the island to do it justice.

Prices (2004) were £7.50 return for adults and £4 for children.

Total mileage from Ullapool is 110 miles

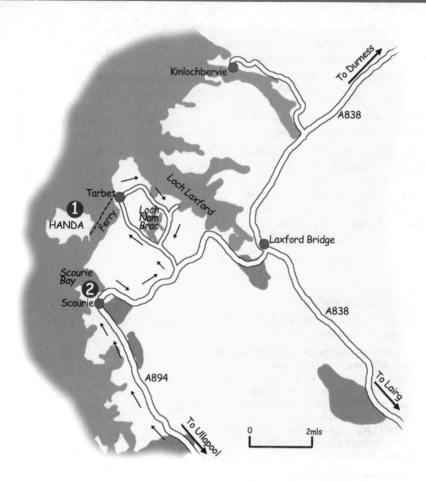

① Handa Island

Background information

SET YOUR TELESCOPE up while you wait for your ferry and already you will start to feel the first tingle of excitement. Look for Rock Pipits around the shore and Red-breasted Mergansers, Shags and divers, particularly Red-throated, on the sea.

If you can't face the boat trip, you can see many of the species from the harbour here, but the views will be distant and you will need a telescope.

As you sail over, the highlight is likely to be the close encounters with Black Guillemots, or Tysties, as they are known locally. These are relatively easy to see all along the west coast but there is something special about seeing their bright red feet paddling like mad as one swims close by.

Once on the island, you have to follow the well-marked path. After an initial, fairly steep climb, you arrive at an area of moorland, slap bang in the middle of the Bonxies' breeding area. Though they are relatively tolerant of your intrusion, they can still remind you of their presence as they launch themselves at you in well-aimed dive-bombing attacks, even going to the extent of making physical contact as they clip you with trailing legs.

These are big birds and even if they don't actually make contact, they will certainly put the fear of God into you. The Arctic Skuas – there are fewer of them – tend to keep their distance. There are great photographic opportunities here, without the need to spend thousands of pounds on huge telephoto lenses.

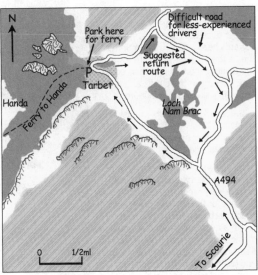

Check the lochans for Red-throated Diver, though they will probably be feeding out at sea. Your best chance of seeing one could well be as it flies over. Golden Plovers and Snipe breed in the boggier parts. Wheatears and Stonechats flit among the boulders and Sky Larks sing from high above you. The occasional Red Grouse seems somehow out of place.

The path continues towards the Great Stack, a huge rock rising out of the sea. The sandstone cliffs here reach over 400 feet and this is where you will find most of the seabird activity. On a clear day, you can see Cape Wrath to the north and Lewis to the west.

There are about 9,000 Guillemots here, the largest breeding colony in Britain. This far north, you can expect to see good numbers of the 'bridled' form, looking as if some avian graffiti artist has gone round during the night drawing white spectacles on their black faces.

There are good numbers of Razorbills too though far fewer Puffins. These were largely wiped out by brown rats getting into their

burrows, but the rats were eradicated in 1997 and Puffin numbers are beginning to increase as a result. Kittiwakes and Fulmars breed abundantly and the Rock Doves here are considered to be pretty pure.

On the beaches, look out for breeding Oystercatchers and Ringed Plovers or an otter if you are lucky. Whimbrel and Greenshanks move through on passage.

Look for other seabirds moving through in spring and, especially, autumn. Typical species include Gannets, divers, shearwaters, skuas and petrels. North-westerly winds in autumn are likely to be the best conditions for spectacular seabird passage. The island is totally underwatched at these times as the main attraction, the breeding seabirds, are largely absent. Ardent seawatchers may prefer to save themselves the boat trip and visit a headland such as the nearby Stoer Head instead.

Arctic and Common Terns, which breed nearby, fish offshore and need careful separation before you clinch their identification. One useful identification tip is to look at the body shape. Common Terns have their centre of gravity towards the middle of their body, and this is where their bodies appear thickest, tapering evenly towards head and tail. In Arctic Terns, the centre of gravity is more towards the front of the bird and their bodies look thickest at the chest, a noticeably skewed distribution.

Seals, dolphins and the occasional whale can be seen offshore, calm days in late summer and autumn being most productive.

As you come off the island, turn left out of the harbour. The minor road – very steep, narrow and twisty and not for the nervous driver – loops round Loch nam Brach. It is well worth a quick drive round as you leave the area, looking for wildfowl such as Red-breasted Mergansers on the loch and lochans, Common Sandpipers round the loch fringes and more moorland species.

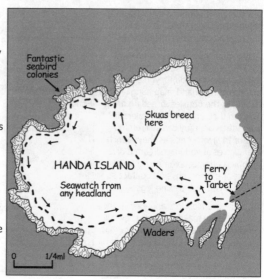

Likely birds/other flora and fauna

Summer	Arctic Tern	Sooty Shearwater	Skuas
Red-throated Diver	Common Tern	Storm Petrel (autumn)	
Fulmar	Great Skua	Leach's Petrel	*Other wildlife*
Kittiwake	Arctic Skua	(autumn)	Seals
Guillemot		Gannet	Otter
Razorbill	*Spring/autumn*	Whimbrel	Whales and dolphins
Puffin	Divers	Greenshank	Wildflowers
Black Guillemot	Manx Shearwater	Terns	

❷ Scourie

Background information

AS YOU DRIVE DOWN towards the cemetery, the hide is on your right, about half way down the beach road. It overlooks the tidal part of Scourie Bay and what you see is to some extent limited by a combination of the moon's position and the local dog walkers.

Nevertheless, there is usually a fair bit around, including a pair of Red-throated Divers that often feeds in front of you. Shags and Red-breasted Mergansers also fish here. The beach attracts a number of waders including Dunlin, Ringed Plover, Redshank and Curlew, with

Whimbrel the most likely passage bird. Even when they are flushed by dogs, the birds are pretty unfazed and soon return to their favoured feeding areas.

Eiders loaf in the bay along with an assortment of gulls (Bonaparte's Gull in 2004) and Buzzards and Peregrines patrol the mountain ridges opposite. Hooded Crows try to break the shells of stubborn seafood by dropping them on the rocks. Look for Linnets and Twite in the fields behind you.

Seabirds do appear in front of the hide, but you will probably get better views if you continue down the beach road. Park by the cemetery and walk through a couple of gates to explore the main part of Scourie Bay. Most of the birds that appear on Handa can be seen here – divers, auks, skuas, Gannets, Fulmars, Kittiwakes etc. –

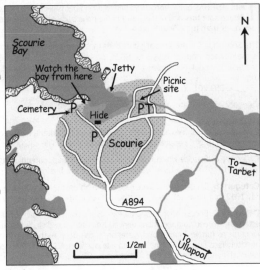

but the views tend to be distant unless bad weather forces the birds into the bay. You will definitely need a telescope.

Be careful as you walk over the grass here. If you see any Ringed Plovers getting agitated, including their famous 'broken wing' display, then they are trying to tell you that their nest is nearby and lure you out of the area. Just move away 50 yards or so.

The next road north from the beach road is signed to the jetty and here you can hire a boat to take you round Handa. The views gained by sailing round the island rather than watching from Handa itself, are equally as

spectacular and you will get some amazing close-up views of birds sitting on the water, as well as being able to study the Great Stack from the bottom up rather than top down.

Toilets are at the north end of the village. Check out the picnic site, which leads off the parking area here. An area of scrubby gorse overlooks the river feeding into the bay. The combination of telegraph wires, plenty of nesting sites and a ready supply of water proves irresistible to small birds. Siskins and Redpolls are common and listen out for what must be one of the most north-westerly Sedge Warblers in Britain.

Likely bird species/other fauna

All year			
Shag	Ringed Plover	Greenshank	*Other wildlife*
Eider	Dunlin	Seabirds after autumn	Otter
Red-breasted	Siskin	gales (see Handa)	
Merganser	Redpoll		
Oystercatcher	Twite	*Summer*	
Redshank		Red-throated Diver	
Curlew	*Spring/autumn*	Seabirds as for Handa	
	Whimbrel	Sedge Warbler	

THE SCOTTISH BIRD LIST

THIS LIST HAS been reproduced with the kind permission of The Scottish Ornithological Club. Please note that bird names used in the main body of the book are the popular names and may differ from the official Scottish List.

The Scottish List is the 'official' list of birds that have been reliably recorded in Scotland. It is maintained and reviewed by SBRC on behalf of SOC. Since 1994, the committee has regularly published updates to the list, together with details of all records of species that have occurred in Scotland less than five times (see *Scottish Birds* 17: 146-159, 18: 129-131, 19: 259-261, 21:1-5).

Category A: 479, Category B: 9, Category C: 6, Total: 494

SOC

CATEGORIES

Each species has been categorised, depending on the criteria for its admission to the Scottish List and the category (A, B or C) appears after the scientific name. The categories are defined as follows:

Category A. Species which have been recorded in an apparently wild state in Scotland at least once since January 1, 1950. An asterisk denotes that there are five or less accepted records.

Category B. Species which were recorded in an apparently wild state in Scotland at least once up to December 31, 1949, but have not been recorded subsequently.

Category C. Species that, though originally introduced by man, either deliberately or accidentally, have established breeding populations derived from introduced stock that maintain themselves without necessary recourse to further introduction. Category C has been further subdivided to differentiate between various groups of naturalised species. (C1 naturalised introductions. C2 naturalised establishments. C3 naturalised re-establishments. C4 naturalised feral species. C5 vagrant naturalised species.)

THE SCOTTISH ORNITHOLOGISTS' CLUB

AFTER nearly 70 years in existence, the Scottish Ornithologists' Club (SOC) has 2,200 members and 14 branches around Scotland. It plays a central role in Scottish birdwatching, bringing together amateur birdwatchers, keen birders and research ornithologists with the aims of documenting, studying and, not least, enjoying Scotland's varied birdlife. Above all the SOC is a club, relying heavily on keen volunteers and the support of its membership and welcomes applications from regular visitors from outside Scotland.

The network of branches organises field meetings, a winter programme of talks and social events.

SOC is due to open a brand new 4000 sq. ft. Resource Centre at Aberlady in East Lothian in July 2005. The new building known as Waterston House will be the new HQ for SOC and will house its famous 10,000 Library of bird books and various exhibition displays. The new Resource Centre will be open to the public and will also have an extensive wildlife garden with some special waterfeatures.

Waterston House is at the centre of a very pleasant network of 20 miles of coastal and woodland walks. The Centre will also sell optics and bird books, new and second hand. etc, and is the ideal place to drop into if you are going North or having a birdwatching break in East Lothian.

Contacts

Bill Gardner MBE, SOC Manager
Postal address: SOC, Scottish Birdwatching Resource Centre, Waterston House, Aberlady, East Lothian EH26 6PY, Scotland.
Office hours: 9am to 5pm. Monday to Friday, except Bank Holidays.
Tel : 01875 871330
Fax : 01875 871335
email : mail@the-soc.org.uk
website : www.the-soc.org.uk

A	Red-throated Diver	*Gavia stellata*							
A	Black-throated Diver	*Gavia arctica*							
A	Great Northern Diver	*Gavia immer*							
A	Yellow-billed Diver	*Gavia adamsii*							
A	Pied-billed Grebe	*Podilymbus podiceps*							
A	Little Grebe	*Tachybaptus ruficollis*							
A	Great Crested Grebe	*Podiceps cristatus*							
A	Red-necked Grebe	*Podiceps grisegena*							
A	Slavonian Grebe	*Podiceps auritus*							
A	Black-necked Grebe	*Podiceps nigricollis*							
A*	Black-browed Albatross	*Thalassarche melanophris*							
A	Northern Fulmar	*Fulmarus glacialis*							
A*	Madeira/Soft-plumaged/Cape Verde Petrel								
		Pterodroma madeira/mollis/feae							
A	Cory's Shearwater	*Calonectris diomedea*							
A	Great Shearwater	*Puffinus gravis*							
A	Sooty Shearwater	*Puffinus griseus*							
A	Manx Shearwater	*Puffinus puffinus*							
A	Balearic Shearwater	*Puffinus mauritanicus*							
A*	Little Shearwater	*Puffinus assimilis*							
A*	Wilson's Storm-petrel	*Oceanites oceanicus*							
B*	White-faced Storm-petrel	*Pelagodroma marina*							
A	European Storm-petrel	*Hydrobates pelagicus*							
A	Leach's Storm-petrel	*Oceanodroma leucorhoa*							
A*	Swinhoe's Storm-petrel	*Oceanodroma monorhis*							
A	Northern Gannet	*Morus bassanus*							
A	Great Cormorant	*Phalacrocorax carbo*							
A	European Shag	*Phalacrocorax aristotelis*							
A*	Magnificent Frigatebird	*Fregata magnificens*							
A	Great Bittern	*Botaurus stellaris*							
A	American Bittern	*Botaurus lentiginosus*							
A	Little Bittern	*Ixobrychus minutus*							
A	Black-crowned Night Heron	*Nycticorax nycticorax*							
A*	Green Heron	*Butorides virescens*							
B*	Squacco Heron	*Ardeola ralloides*							
A*	Cattle Egret	*Bubulcus ibis*							
A	Little Egret	*Egretta garzetta*							
A	Great Egret	*Ardea alba*							
A	Grey Heron	*Ardea cinerea*							
A	Purple Heron	*Ardea purpurea*							
A	Black Stork	*Ciconia nigra*							
A	White Stork	*Ciconia ciconia*							
A	Glossy Ibis	*Plegadis falcinellus*							
A	Eurasian Spoonbill	*Platalea leucorodia*							
A,C	Mute Swan	*Cygnus olor*							
A	Tundra Swan	*Cygnus columbianus*							
A	Whooper Swan	*Cygnus cygnus*							
A	Bean Goose	*Anser fabalis*							
A	Pink-footed Goose	*Anser brachyrhynchus*							
A	Greater White-fronted Goose	*Anser albifrons*							
A	Lesser White-fronted Goose	*Anser erythropus*							
A,C	Greylag Goose	*Anser anser*							
A	Snow Goose	*Anser caerulescens*							
A,C	Canada Goose	*Branta canadensis*							
A	Barnacle Goose	*Branta leucopsis*							
	Sub total								

A	Brent Goose	*Branta bernicla*							
A	Red-breasted Goose	*Branta ruficollis*							
B	Ruddy Shelduck	*Tadorna ferruginea*							
A	Common Shelduck	*Tadorna tadorna*							
C	Mandarin Duck	*Aix galericulata*							
A	Eurasian Wigeon	*Anas penelope*							
A	American Wigeon	*Anas americana*							
A,C	Gadwall	*Anas strepera*							
A	Eurasian Teal	*Anas crecca*							
A	Green-winged Teal	*Anas carolinensis*							
A,C	Mallard	*Anas platyrhynchos*							
A	American Black Duck	*Anas rubripes*							
A	Northern Pintail	*Anas acuta*							
A	Garganey	*Anas querquedula*							
A	Blue-winged Teal	*Anas discors*							
A	Northern Shoveler	*Anas clypeata*							
A	Red-crested Pochard	*Netta rufina*							
A	Common Pochard	*Aythya ferina*							
A	Ring-necked Duck	*Aythya collaris*							
A	Ferruginous Duck	*Aythya nyroca*							
A	Tufted Duck	*Aythya fuligula*							
A	Greater Scaup	*Aythya marila*							
A	Lesser Scaup	*Aythya affinis*							
A	Common Eider	*Somateria mollissima*							
A	King Eider	*Somateria spectabilis*							
A	Steller's Eider	*Polysticta stelleri*							
A	Harlequin Duck	*Histrionicus histrionicus*							
A	Long-tailed Duck	*Clangula hyemalis*							
A	Black Scoter	*Melanitta nigra*							
A	Surf Scoter	*Melanitta perspicillata*							
A	Velvet Scoter	*Melanitta fusca*							
A*	Bufflehead	*Bucephala albeola*							
A*	Barrow's Goldeneye	*Bucephala islandica*							
A	Common Goldeneye	*Bucephala clangula*							
A	Smew	*Mergellus albellus*							
A	Red-breasted Merganser	*Mergus serrator*							
A	Goosander	*Mergus merganser*							
C	Ruddy Duck	*Oxyura jamaicensis*							
A	European Honey-buzzard	*Pernis apivorus*							
A	Black Kite	*Milvus migrans*							
A,C	Red Kite	*Milvus milvus*							
A	White-tailed Eagle	*Haliaeetus albicilla*							
A	Eurasian Marsh Harrier	*Circus aeruginosus*							
A	Hen Harrier	*Circus cyaneus*							
A*	Pallid Harrier	*Circus macrourus*							
A	Montagu's Harrier	*Circus pygargus*							
A,C	Northern Goshawk	*Accipiter gentilis*							
A	Eurasian Sparrowhawk	*Accipiter nisus*							
A	Common Buzzard	*Buteo buteo*							
A	Rough-legged Buzzard	*Buteo lagopus*							
A	Golden Eagle	*Aquila chrysaetos*							
A	Osprey	*Pandion haliaetus*							
A*	Lesser Kestrel	*Falco naumanni*							
A	Common Kestrel	*Falco tinnunculus*							
A*	American Kestrel	*Falco sparverius*							
	Sub total								

A	Red-footed Falcon	*Falco vespertinus*						
A	Merlin	*Falco columbarius*						
A	Eurasian Hobby	*Falco subbuteo*						
A*	Eleonora's Falcon	*Falco eleonorae*						
A	Gyr Falcon	*Falco rusticolus*						
A	Peregrine Falcon	*Falco peregrinus*						
A	Willow Ptarmigan (Red Grouse)	*Lagopus lagopus*						
A	Rock Ptarmigan	*Lagopus mutus*						
A	Black Grouse	*Tetrao tetrix*						
B,C	Western Capercaillie	*Tetrao urogallus*						
C	Red-legged Partridge	*Alectoris rufa*						
A,C	Grey Partridge	*Perdix perdix*						
A	Common Quail	*Coturnix coturnix*						
C	Common Pheasant	*Phasianus colchicus*						
C	Golden Pheasant	*Chrysolophus pictus*						
A	Water Rail	*Rallus aquaticus*						
A	Spotted Crake	*Porzana porzana*						
A*	Sora	*Porzana carolina*						
A*	Little Crake	*Porzana parva*						
A	Baillon's Crake	*Porzana pusilla*						
A	Corn Crake	*Crex crex*						
A	Common Moorhen	*Gallinula chloropus*						
A	Common Coot	*Fulica atra*						
A	Common Crane	*Grus grus*						
A*	Sandhill Crane	*Grus canadensis*						
A	Little Bustard	*Tetrax tetrax*						
B*	Macqueen's Bustard	*Chlamydotis macqueenii*						
A	Great Bustard	*Otis tarda*						
A	Eurasian Oystercatcher	*Haematopus ostralegus*						
A	Black-winged Stilt	*Himantopus himantopus*						
A	Pied Avocet	*Recurvirostra avosetta*						
A	Stone-curlew	*Burhinus oedicnemus*						
A*	Cream-coloured Courser	*Cursorius cursor*						
A	Collared Pratincole	*Glareola pratincola*						
A*	Black-winged Pratincole	*Glareola nordmanni*						
A	Little Plover	*Charadrius dubius*						
A	Ringed Plover	*Charadrius hiaticula*						
A	Killdeer	*Charadrius vociferus*						
A	Kentish Plover	*Charadrius alexandrinus*						
A*	Greater Sand Plover	*Charadrius leschenaultii*						
A*	Caspian Plover	*Charadrius asiaticus*						
A	Eurasian Dotterel	*Charadrius morinellus*						
A	American Golden Plover	*Pluvialis dominica*						
A	Pacific Golden Plover	*Pluvialis fulva*						
A	European Golden Plover	*Pluvialis apricaria*						
A	Grey Plover	*Pluvialis squatarola*						
A*	Sociable Lapwing	*Vanellus gregarius*						
A	Northern Lapwing	*Vanellus vanellus*						
A*	Great Knot	*Calidris tenuirostris*						
A	Red Knot	*Calidris canutus*						
A	Sanderling	*Calidris alba*						
A	Semipalmated Sandpiper	*Calidris pusilla*						
A*	Western Sandpiper	*Calidris mauri*						
A*	Red-necked Stint	*Calidris ruficollis*						
A	Little Stint	*Calidris minuta*						
Sub total								

A	**Temminck's Stint**	*Calidris temminckii*						
A*	**Least Sandpiper**	*Calidris minutilla*						
A	**White-rumped Sandpiper**	*Calidris fuscicollis*						
A	**Baird's Sandpiper**	*Calidris bairdii*						
A	**Pectoral Sandpiper**	*Calidris melanotos*						
A*	**Sharp-tailed Sandpiper**	*Calidris acuminata*						
A	**Curlew Sandpiper**	*Calidris ferruginea*						
A	**Purple Sandpiper**	*Calidris maritima*						
A	**Dunlin**	*Calidris alpina*						
A	**Broad-billed Sandpiper**	*Limicola falcinellus*						
A*	**Stilt Sandpiper**	*Micropalama himantopus*						
A	**Buff-breasted Sandpiper**	*Tryngites subruficollis*						
A	**Ruff**	*Philomachus pugnax*						
A	**Jack Snipe**	*Lymnocryptes minimus*						
A	**Common Snipe**	*Gallinago gallinago*						
A	**Great Snipe**	*Gallinago media*						
A*	**Short-billed Dowitcher**	*Limnodromus griseus*						
A	**Long-billed Dowitcher**	*Limnodromus scolopaceus*						
A	**Eurasian Woodcock**	*Scolopax rusticola*						
A	**Black-tailed Godwit**	*Limosa limosa*						
A*	**Hudsonian Godwit**	*Limosa haemastica*						
A	**Bar-tailed Godwit**	*Limosa lapponica*						
B*	**Eskimo Curlew**	*Numenius borealis*						
A	**Whimbrel**	*Numenius phaeopus*						
A	**Eurasian Curlew**	*Numenius arquata*						
A	**Upland Sandpiper**	*Bartramia longicauda*						
A	**Spotted Redshank**	*Tringa erythropus*						
A	**Common Redshank**	*Tringa totanus*						
A	**Marsh Sandpiper**	*Tringa stagnatilis*						
A	**Common Greenshank**	*Tringa nebularia*						
A*	**Greater Yellowlegs**	*Tringa melanoleuca*						
A	**Lesser Yellowlegs**	*Tringa flavipes*						
A*	**Solitary Sandpiper**	*Tringa solitaria*						
A	**Green Sandpiper**	*Tringa ochropus*						
A	**Wood Sandpiper**	*Tringa glareola*						
A	**Terek Sandpiper**	*Xenus cinereus*						
A	**Common Sandpiper**	*Actitis hypoleucos*						
A	**Spotted Sandpiper**	*Actitis macularia*						
A*	**Grey-tailed Tattler**	*Heteroscelus brevipes*						
A	**Ruddy Turnstone**	*Arenaria interpres*						
A	**Wilson's Phalarope**	*Phalaropus tricolor*						
A	**Red-necked Phalarope**	*Phalaropus lobatus*						
A	**Grey Phalarope**	*Phalaropus fulicarius*						
A	**Pomarine Skua**	*Stercorarius pomarinus*						
A	**Arctic Skua**	*Stercorarius parasiticus*						
A	**Long-tailed Skua**	*Stercorarius longicaudus*						
A	**Great Skua**	*Catharacta skua*						
A	**Mediterranean Gull**	*Larus melanocephalus*						
A	**Laughing Gull**	*Larus atricilla*						
A	**Franklin's Gull**	*Larus pipixcan*						
A	**Little Gull**	*Larus minutus*						
A	**Sabine's Gull**	*Larus sabini*						
A	**Bonaparte's Gull**	*Larus philadelphia*						
A	**Black-headed Gull**	*Larus ridibundus*						
A	**Ring-billed Gull**	*Larus delawarensis*						
	Sub total							

A	Mew Gull	*Larus canus*							
A	Lesser Black-backed Gull	*Larus fuscus*							
A	Herring Gull	*Larus argentatus*							
A	Iceland Gull	*Larus glaucoides*							
A	Glaucous Gull	*Larus hyperboreus*							
A	Great Black-backed Gull	*Larus marinus*							
A	Ross's Gull	*Rhodostethia rosea*							
A	Black-legged Kittiwake	*Rissa tridactyla*							
A	Ivory Gull	*Pagophila eburnea*							
A	Gull-billed Tern	*Sterna nilotica*							
A	Caspian Tern	*Sterna caspia*							
A*	Royal Tern	*Sterna maxima*							
A*	Lesser Crested Tern	*Sterna bengalensis*							
A	Sandwich Tern	*Sterna sandvicensis*							
A	Roseate Tern	*Sterna dougallii*							
A	Common Tern	*Sterna hirundo*							
A	Arctic Tern	*Sterna paradisaea*							
A*	Forster's Tern	*Sterna forsteri*							
A*	Bridled Tern	*Sterna anaethetus*							
A*	Sooty Tern	*Sterna fuscata*							
A	Little Tern	*Sterna albifrons*							
B*	Whiskered Tern	*Chlidonias hybrida*							
A	Black Tern	*Chlidonias niger*							
A	White-winged Tern	*Chlidonias leucopterus*							
A	Common Guillemot	*Uria aalge*							
A	Brünnich's Guillemot	*Uria lomvia*							
A	Razorbill	*Alca torda*							
B	Great Auk	*Pinguinus impennis*							
A	Black Guillemot	*Cepphus grylle*							
A	Little Auk	*Alle alle*							
A	Atlantic Puffin	*Fratercula arctica*							
A	Pallas's Sandgrouse	*Syrrhaptes paradoxus*							
A,C	Rock Pigeon	*Columba livia*							
A	Stock Pigeon	*Columba oenas*							
A	Common Wood Pigeon	*Columba palumbus*							
A	Eurasian Collared Dove	*Streptopelia decaocto*							
A	European Turtle Dove	*Streptopelia turtur*							
A*	Oriental Turtle Dove	*Streptopelia orientalis*							
A*	Mourning Dove	*Zenaida macroura*							
A*	Great Spotted Cuckoo	*Clamator glandarius*							
A	Common Cuckoo	*Cuculus canorus*							
A*	Black-billed Cuckoo	*Coccyzus erythrophthalmus*							
A	Yellow-billed Cuckoo	*Coccyzus americanus*							
A	Barn Owl	*Tyto alba*							
A	Eurasian Scops Owl	*Otus scops*							
A	Snowy Owl	*Nyctea scandiaca*							
A*	Northern Hawk Owl	*Surnia ulula*							
C	Little Owl	*Athene noctua*							
A	Tawny Owl	*Strix aluco*							
A	Long-eared Owl	*Asio otus*							
A	Short-eared Owl	*Asio flammeus*							
A	Tengmalm's Owl	*Aegolius funereus*							
A	European Nightjar	*Caprimulgus europaeus*							
A*	Common Nighthawk	*Chordeiles minor*							
A*	Chimney Swift	*Chaetura pelagica*							
	Sub total								

A*	White-throated Needletail	*Hirundapus caudacutus*						
A	Common Swift	*Apus apus*						
A*	Pallid Swift	*Apus pallidus*						
A	Alpine Swift	*Apus melba*						
A*	Little Swift	*Apus affinis*						
A	Common Kingfisher	*Alcedo atthis*						
A*	Blue-cheeked Bee-eater	*Merops superciliosus*						
A	European Bee-eater	*Merops apiaster*						
A	European Roller	*Coracias garrulus*						
A	Hoopoe	*Upupa epops*						
A	Eurasian Wryneck	*Jynx torquilla*						
A	Green Woodpecker	*Picus viridis*						
A	Great Spotted Woodpecker	*Dendrocopos major*						
A*	Lesser Spotted Woodpecker	*Dendrocopos minor*						
A*	Calandra Lark	*Melanocorypha calandra*						
A*	Bimaculated Lark	*Melanocorypha bimaculata*						
A	Greater Short-toed Lark	*Calandrella brachydactyla*						
A*	Crested Lark	*Galerida cristata*						
A	Wood Lark	*Lullula arborea*						
A	Sky Lark	*Alauda arvensis*						
A	Horned Lark	*Eremophila alpestris*						
A	Sand Martin	*Riparia riparia*						
A*	Eurasian Crag Martin	*Ptyonoprogne rupestris*						
A	Barn Swallow	*Hirundo rustica*						
A	Red-rumped Swallow	*Hirundo daurica*						
A	House Martin	*Delichon urbica*						
A	Richard's Pipit	*Anthus novaeseelandiae*						
A*	Blyth's Pipit	*Anthus godlewskii*						
A	Tawny Pipit	*Anthus campestris*						
A	Olive-backed Pipit	*Anthus hodgsoni*						
A	Tree Pipit	*Anthus trivialis*						
A	Pechora Pipit	*Anthus gustavi*						
A	Meadow Pipit	*Anthus pratensis*						
A	Red-throated Pipit	*Anthus cervinus*						
A	Rock Pipit	*Anthus petrosus*						
A	Water Pipit	*Anthus spinoletta*						
A*	Buff-bellied Pipit	*Anthus rubescens*						
A	Yellow Wagtail	*Motacilla flava*						
A	Citrine Wagtail	*Motacilla citreola*						
A	Grey Wagtail	*Motacilla cinerea*						
A	White/Pied Wagtail	*Motacilla alba*						
A*	Cedar Waxwing	*Bombycilla cedrorum*						
A	Bohemian Waxwing	*Bombycilla garrulus*						
A	White-throated Dipper	*Cinclus cinclus*						
A	Winter Wren	*Troglodytes troglodytes*						
A	Hedge Accentor	*Prunella modularis*						
A*	Alpine Accentor	*Prunella collaris*						
A	European Robin	*Erithacus rubecula*						
A	Thrush Nightingale	*Luscinia luscinia*						
A	Common Nightingale	*Luscinia megarhynchos*						
A*	Siberian Rubythroat	*Luscinia calliope*						
A	Bluethroat	*Luscinia svecica*						
A*	Siberian Blue Robin	*Luscinia cyane*						
A	Red-flanked Bluetail	*Tarsiger cyanurus*						
A	Black Redstart	*Phoenicurus ochruros*						
Sub total								

			Phoenicurus phoenicurus						
A	Common Redstart		Phoenicurus phoenicurus						
A	Whinchat		Saxicola rubetra						
A	Stonechat		Saxicola torquata						
A*	Isabelline Wheatear		Oenanthe isabellina						
A	Northern Wheatear		Oenanthe oenanthe						
A	Pied Wheatear		Oenanthe pleschanka						
A	Black-eared Wheatear		Oenanthe hispanica						
A	Desert Wheatear		Oenanthe deserti						
A*	Rufous-tailed Rock Thrush		Monticola saxatilis						
A*	Blue Rock Thrush		Monticola solitarius						
A	White's Thrush		Zoothera dauma						
A*	Siberian Thrush		Zoothera sibirica						
A*	Hermit Thrush		Catharus guttatus						
A*	Swainson's Thrush		Catharus ustulatus						
A	Grey-cheeked Thrush		Catharus minimus						
A*	Veery		Catharus fuscescens						
A	Ring Ouzel		Turdus torquatus						
A	Common Blackbird		Turdus merula						
A	Eyebrowed Thrush		Turdus obscurus						
A*	Dusky Thrush		Turdus naumanni						
A	Dark-throated Thrush		Turdus ruficollis						
A	Fieldfare		Turdus pilaris						
A	Song Thrush		Turdus philomelos						
A	Redwing		Turdus iliacus						
A	Mistle Thrush		Turdus viscivorus						
A	American Robin		Turdus migratorius						
A*	Cetti's Warbler		Cettia cetti						
A	Pallas's Grasshopper Warbler		Locustella certhiola						
A	Lanceolated Warbler		Locustella lanceolata						
A	Common Grasshopper Warbler		Locustella naevia						
A	River Warbler		Locustella fluviatilis						
A	Savi's Warbler		Locustella luscinioides						
A	Aquatic Warbler		Acrocephalus paludicola						
A	Sedge Warbler		Acrocephalus schoenobaenus						
A	Paddyfield Warbler		Acrocephalus agricola						
A	Blyth's Reed Warbler		Acrocephalus dumetorum						
A	Marsh Warbler		Acrocephalus palustris						
A	Eurasian Reed Warbler		Acrocephalus scirpaceus						
A	Great Reed Warbler		Acrocephalus arundinaceus						
A*	Thick-billed Warbler		Acrocephalus aedon						
A*	Olivaceous Warbler		Hippolais pallida						
A*	Sykes's Warbler		Hippolais rama						
A	Booted Warbler		Hippolais caligata						
A	Icterine Warbler		Hippolais icterina						
A	Melodious Warbler		Hippolais polyglotta						
A*	Marmora's Warbler		Sylvia sarda						
A*	Dartford Warbler		Sylvia undata						
A	Subalpine Warbler		Sylvia cantillans						
A	Sardinian Warbler		Sylvia melanocephala						
A*	Rüppell's Warbler		Sylvia rueppelli						
A*	Orphean Warbler		Sylvia hortensis						
A	Barred Warbler		Sylvia nisoria						
A	Lesser Whitethroat		Sylvia curruca						
A	Common Whitethroat		Sylvia communis						
A	Garden Warbler		Sylvia borin						
Sub total									

A	Blackcap	*Sylvia atricapilla*							
A	Greenish Warbler	*Phylloscopus trochiloides*							
A	Arctic Warbler	*Phylloscopus borealis*							
A	Pallas's Leaf Warbler	*Phylloscopus proregulus*							
A	Yellow-browed Warbler	*Phylloscopus inornatus*							
A*	Hume's Leaf Warbler	*Phylloscopus humei*							
A	Radde's Warbler	*Phylloscopus schwarzi*							
A	Dusky Warbler	*Phylloscopus fuscatus*							
A	Western Bonelli's Warbler	*Phylloscopus bonelli*							
A*	Eastern Bonelli's Warbler	*Phylloscopus orientalis*							
A	Wood Warbler	*Phylloscopus sibilatrix*							
A	Common Chiffchaff	*Phylloscopus collybita*							
A	Willow Warbler	*Phylloscopus trochilus*							
A	Goldcrest	*Regulus regulus*							
A	Firecrest	*Regulus ignicapilla*							
A	Spotted Flycatcher	*Muscicapa striata*							
A	Red-breasted Flycatcher	*Ficedula parva*							
A	Collared Flycatcher	*Ficedula albicollis*							
A	Pied Flycatcher	*Ficedula hypoleuca*							
A	Bearded Tit	*Panurus biarmicus*							
A	Long-tailed Tit	*Aegithalos caudatus*							
A	Marsh Tit	*Parus palustris*							
A	Willow Tit	*Parus montanus*							
A	Crested Tit	*Parus cristatus*							
A	Coal Tit	*Parus ater*							
A	Blue Tit	*Parus caeruleus*							
A	Great Tit	*Parus major*							
A	Wood Nuthatch	*Sitta europaea*							
A	Eurasian Treecreeper	*Certhia familiaris*							
A	Eurasian Golden Oriole	*Oriolus oriolus*							
A*	Brown Shrike	*Lanius cristatus*							
A	Isabelline Shrike	*Lanius isabellinus*							
A	Red-backed Shrike	*Lanius collurio*							
A	Lesser Grey Shrike	*Lanius minor*							
A	Great Grey Shrike	*Lanius excubitor*							
A*	Southern Grey Shrike	*Lanius meridionalis*							
A	Woodchat Shrike	*Lanius senator*							
A	Eurasian Jay	*Garrulus glandarius*							
A	Black-billed Magpie	*Pica pica*							
A*	Spotted Nutcracker	*Nucifraga caryocatactes*							
A	Red-billed Chough	*Pyrrhocorax pyrrhocorax*							
A	Eurasian Jackdaw	*Corvus monedula*							
A	Rook	*Corvus frugilegus*							
A	Hooded Crow	*Corvus cornix*							
A	Carrion Crow	*Corvus corone*							
A	Common Raven	*Corvus corax*							
A	Common Starling	*Sturnus vulgaris*							
A	Rosy Starling	*Sturnus roseus*							
A	House Sparrow	*Passer domesticus*							
A*	Spanish Sparrow	*Passer hispaniolensis*							
A	Eurasian Tree Sparrow	*Passer montanus*							
A*	Red-eyed Vireo	*Vireo olivaceus*							
A	Chaffinch	*Fringilla coelebs*							
A	Brambling	*Fringilla montifringilla*							
A	European Serin	*Serinus serinus*							
Sub total									

A	European Greenfinch	*Carduelis chloris*							
A	European Goldfinch	*Carduelis carduelis*							
A	Eurasian Siskin	*Carduelis spinus*							
A	Common Linnet	*Carduelis cannabina*							
A	Twite	*Carduelis flavirostris*							
A	Lesser Redpoll	*Carduelis cabaret*							
A	Common Redpoll	*Carduelis flammea*							
A	Arctic Redpoll	*Carduelis hornemanni*							
A	Two-barred Crossbill	*Loxia leucoptera*							
A	Common Crossbill	*Loxia curvirostra*							
A	Scottish Crossbill	*Loxia scotica*							
A	Parrot Crossbill	*Loxia pytyopsittacus*							
A*	Trumpeter Finch	*Bucanetes githagineus*							
A	Common Rosefinch	*Carpodacus erythrinus*							
A*	Pine Grosbeak	*Pinicola enucleator*							
A	Common Bullfinch	*Pyrrhula pyrrhula*							
A	Hawfinch	*Coccothraustes coccothraustes*							
A*	Evening Grosbeak	*Hesperiphona vespertina*							
B*	Black-and-white Warbler	*Mniotilta varia*							
A*	Tennessee Warbler	*Vermivora peregrina*							
A*	Yellow Warbler	*Dendroica petechia*							
A*	Chestnut-sided Warbler	*Dendroica pensylvanica*							
A*	Blackburnian Warbler	*Dendroica fusca*							
A*	Cape May Warbler	*Dendroica tigrina*							
A*	Yellow-rumped Warbler	*Dendroica coronata*							
A*	Blackpoll Warbler	*Dendroica striata*							
A*	American Redstart	*Setophaga ruticilla*							
A*	Ovenbird	*Seiurus aurocapilla*							
A*	Common Yellowthroat	*Geothlypis trichas*							
A*	Hooded Warbler	*Wilsonia citrina*							
A*	Savannah Sparrow	*Passerculus sandwichensis*							
A*	Song Sparrow	*Melospiza melodia*							
A*	White-crowned Sparrow	*Zonotrichia leucophrys*							
A	White-throated Sparrow	*Zonotrichia albicollis*							
A*	Dark-eyed Junco	*Junco hyemalis*							
A	Lapland Longspur	*Calcarius lapponicus*							
A	Snow Bunting	*Plectrophenax nivalis*							
A*	Black-faced Bunting	*Emberiza spodocephala*							
A	Pine Bunting	*Emberiza leucocephalos*							
A	Yellowhammer	*Emberiza citrinella*							
A	Cirl Bunting	*Emberiza cirlus*							
A	Ortolan Bunting	*Emberiza hortulana*							
A*	Cretzschmar's Bunting	*Emberiza caesia*							
A*	Yellow-browed Bunting	*Emberiza chrysophrys*							
A	Rustic Bunting	*Emberiza rustica*							
A	Little Bunting	*Emberiza pusilla*							
A	Yellow-breasted Bunting	*Emberiza aureola*							
A	Reed Bunting	*Emberiza schoeniclus*							
A*	Pallas's Bunting	*Emberiza pallasi*							
A	Black-headed Bunting	*Emberiza melanocephala*							
A	Corn Bunting	*Miliaria calandra*							
A*	Rose-breasted Grosbeak	*Pheucticus ludovicianus*							
A*	Bobolink	*Dolichonyx oryzivorus*							
Sub total									

SUBMITTING RECORDS

THE SCOTTISH HIGHLANDS cover a massive area and the number of active birders is low. Huge swathes of the Highlands are totally unrecorded or under-recorded. For that reason alone, it is helpful if you send details of your sightings to the appropriate recorder at the end of your holiday.

The recorders are not just interested in rare birds. Details of common birds are just as important. Details of first dates and last dates for migrants, flock counts and seawatching records etc are particularly welcome. To give you a better idea of what's needed, check out http://www.birdinghighland.com/

All the areas publish an annual bird report and you would be supporting the cause immensely if you bought one for your favourite areas.

SCOTTISH BIRD RECORDERS AND REPORTS

CAITHNESS

Local Recorder
Stan Laybourne, Old Schoolhouse, Harpsdale, Halkirk, Caithness KW12 6UN.
E-mail: stanlaybourne@talk21.com

Caithness Bird Report
Available from: Julian Smith, St John, Broch, Dunnet, Caithness

HIGHLAND

Local Recorder
Alastair F McNee, Liathach, 4 Balnafettack Place, Inverness, IV3 8TQ. 01463 220493.
E-mail: aj.mcnee@care4free.net

Highland Bird Report
Editor: Alastair McNee, Address as above

MORAY AND NAIRN

Local Recorder
Martin Cook, Rowanbrae, Clochan, Buckie, Banffshire AB56 5EQ
E-mail martin.cook9@virgin.net

Moray And Nairn Bird Report
Editor: Martin Cook, Address as above

NORTH-EAST SCOTLAND

Local Recorder
Andy Thorpe, 30 Monearn Gardens, Milltimber, Aberdeen, AB13 0EA.
01224-733296.
E-mail:
Andrewthorpe4@aol.com

North-East Scotland Bird Report
Editors: Editors: Andrew Thorpe, Ian Francis and Richard Schofield
Address for purchases: Dave Gill, Drakemyre Croft, Cairnorrie, Methlick, Aberdeenshire AB41 0JN

PERTH AND KINROSS

Local Recorder
Ron Youngman, Blairchroisk Cottage, Ballinluig, Pitlochry, Perthshire PH9 0NE. 01796 482324
E-mail blairchroisk@aol.com

Perth And Kinross Bird Report
Editor: Ron Youngman
Address as above.

SCOTLAND ON THE INTERNET

THE WEBSITES featured here are among the most useful I've discovered. If you want to explore further, it is worth checking out the community websites for the small towns and villages in the area that interests you most. They often have a section on local wildlife. Similarly, some of the hotel and bed and breakfast websites can also provide an unexpectedly rich source of information.

However, be aware that the quality and topicality of sites can wane. Many sites run by university bird clubs lapsed as the students graduated and moved away and this is certainly true of a lot of Scottish sites. There is a lot of useful information around, but you notice that some sites were last updated some considerable time ago.

ORGANISATIONS

http://www.forestry.gov.uk/
It is not the easiest website in the world to navigate, but the Forestry Commission's site has details of all its woods, together with access details and wildlife notes.

http://www.rspb.org.uk/
The RSPB has a massive website. As well as information about all its reserves, look out for the webcam pages in summer. There is usually footage from the Loch Garten Osprey nest and, if the birds oblige, from a Hen Harrier nest at Forsinard.

http://www.snh.org.uk/
Scottish Natural Heritage's site has recently been revamped, but is still fairly user-unfriendly. Content here is largely technical and of minimal interest to the casual visitor. For more information on the reserves, visit http://www.nnr-scotland.org.uk/ Details are fairly sketchy and there isn't any feeling of enthusiasm for these fantastic places.

http://www.swt.org.uk/
The Scottish Wildlife Trust's site has information on all its reserves and 20 key species, as well as plenty of organised walks and other events. Layout is friendly and this is a site the kids may well want to explore.

http://www.the-soc.fsnet.co.uk/
The Scottish Ornithologists' Club has an excellent website. Details of recent sightings are restricted to members only, but there are some good 'where to watch' guides, a Scottish checklist and general news about the Scottish birding scene.

MAILING LISTS

There are a couple of groups that discuss Scottish birds. Once you sign up for a group, you automatically receive e-mails of any messages posted.

ABZ covers birds in North East Scotland, especially the Aberdeen area and coastal sites.
To subscribe to this group, send an email to:
ABZ-Rare-Birds-subscribe@yahoogroups.com
Or visit http://groups.yahoo.com/group/ABZ-Rare-Birds/

Highland and Moray Birds deals, as you might expect, with birds in those two areas. To subscribe to this group, send an email to:
Highland_and_Moray_Birds-subscribe@yahoogroups.com
Or visit http://groups.yahoo.com/group/Highland_and_Moray_Birds/

One other bird group that is worth looking at is Bird Forum (http://www.birdforum.net/) More than 23,000 members at the time of writing discuss anything to do with birding. If you have a particular query, are looking for information in general or just to want to tell everyone about your brilliant day out, then this is the place to go.

PERSONAL SITES

http://www.allanbantick.net
Allan is heavily involved in Scottish wildlife conservation, especially in the Speyside area. You can read his diaries here and find a good assortment of related links.

http://www.roydennis.org
There is plenty of information here (including maps) about satellite tracking Scottish Ospreys, Marsh Harriers and Honey Buzzards. Articles still under construction will discuss various mammalian reintroduction projects.

REGIONAL SITES

http://www.birdinghighland.com/
This has an online bird report of sightings in the Highlands, but is dragging its heels a bit. A very useful section details the sorts of records the recorder would love to receive from visitors.

http://www.skye-birds.com/
A relatively new site and an excellent one, too. Bang up to date with details of latest sightings on Skye, there is a comprehensive 'where to watch' section, species list and hints on watching eagles.

http://www.wildcaithness.org
A lot of interesting information about the wildlife of Caithness, but needs to be updated more regularly in terms of forthcoming events.

http://cgi.wildlifeweb.force9.co.uk/news/guestbook.htm
This page has details of all the latest sightings from the Grampian region. This page is updated daily, but there is no obvious way to get back from here to the main site, so if you want to see some 'where to watch sites' for the whole of Scotland, visit http://www.wildlifeweb.co.uk/menu/scotmap.html though large chunks still remain unwritten after several years.

TRANSPORT

http://www.calmac.co.uk/
If you plan to visit one of the islands, the Caledonian MacBrayne website has all the timetable details for the inter-island ferries.

FURTHER READING

Bird books

Birds in Scotland (Thom, Poyser 1986, ISBN 0 85661 040 2) A typically scholarly Poyser book covering the status of birds across the whole of Scotland. A new edition is apparently in preparation, but won't be ready for another few years yet.

The Birds of Badenoch and Strathspey (Dennis, Colin Baxter 1995 ISBN 0-948661-62-3) An avifauna covering the area from Loch Laggan in the west to Lochindorb in the east.

A Guide to the Breeding Birds of Caithness (Dickson, Palanquin Books 1996, ISBN 0 948122 12 9) An avifauna of a sort, strangely arranged by habitat rather than systematically.

Sutherland Birds (Angus, Northern Times Ltd 1983 ISBN 0 9501718 3 2) More for historical interest, data now superseded by Vittery – below)

The Birds of Sutherland (Vittery, Colin Baxter 1997, ISBN 1-900455-18-8) An up-to-date and, strangely for this type of book, eminently readable avifauna.

Island Eagles (Crane and Nellist, Cartwheeling Press 1999, ISBN 0 9536033 0 X) An account of years of observations of Golden Eagles on Skye.

Scottish Birds – Culture and Tradition (Hull, Mercat Press 2001 ISBN 184183 0259) A fascinating look at the history of Scottish birds together with their folklore and various dialect names.

Highland Birds (Nethersole-Thompson, Highlands and Islands Development Board, ISBN 0 00 411157 5) A profusely illustrated guide to many of the region's speciality birds.

The Birds of Moray and Nairn (Cook, Mercat Press 1992, ISBN 1873644051) Another avifauna covering many of the sites mentioned in this book.

Where to Watch Birds in Scotland – 4th edtion (Madders, Helm, 2002, ISBN 0-7136-5693-X) A long-standing where to watch guide covering the whole of Scotland rather than just the Highlands.

Other natural history

Highland Country Diaries (Collier, Colin Baxter 1997, ISBN 1-900455-28-5) An absolutely delightful series of articles taken from the author's column in the *Guardian*. Guaranteed to make you want to head north again as soon as possible.

Torridon, the Nature of the Place (Lowe, Wester Ross Net 2000, 0 9538765 0 0) Includes sections on the geology of the area as well as the flora and fauna.

Wild Scotland (McCarthy, Luath Press 1995, ISBN 0-946487-37-5) A mini where to watch guide covering all wildlife, not just birds, with extra chapters on conservation etc.

Scotland's Nature and Wildlife (Taylor, Lomond Books 2002, ISBN 1-84204-025-1) A large format where to watch guide, albeit with limited number of sites. Plenty of colour photos and hints for general wildlife watching.

Song of the Rolling Earth (Lister-Kaye, Time Warner, 2003, ISBN 0-7515-3383-1) How one man had the vision and determination to establish the Aigas Field Centre (near Glen Strathfarrar) and the wildlife he found there.

Guidebooks

Blue Guide to Scotland 12th edition (Wills and Wills, A&C Black 2001, ISBN 0-7136-4998-4) An all-round general guidebook including hotels and restaurants. Good for history and archaeology. Wildlife sections are dodgy.

The North West Highlands: Roads to the Isles (ISBN 0 946487 54 5)
The Northern Highlands: The Empty Lands (ISBN 0 946487 55 3)
The West Highlands: The Lonely Lands (ISBN 0 946487 56 1)
All by Tom Atkinson, published by Luath Press are the best guides to the respective areas I have come across, featuring a good mix of description, history, legend and natural history. They achieve what every guidebook should do; make you want to go there.

Out of print books

Many of the titles listed above are no longer in print. To find copies, visit www.abebooks.co.uk - a massive database of hundreds of second hand bookshops across the world.

OSPREYS

THE STORY of the Ospreys' return to the Scottish Highlands has been well documented and is one of the great conservation success stories. The last pair bred in 1916 before a pair returned to Speyside in 1954.

Truth to tell, they are not difficult birds to see, with the Scottish population heading towards the 200 mark and the species now establishing a toe-hold in England. No matter how often you see them though, there is always a sense of great excitement when you see one hovering over water before plunging feet first in pursuit of a trout or flounder.

Ospreys arrive in April though there is always the occasional sighting in late March. The eggs are laid in late April and the young hatch from late May before fledging from mid July to mid August, spending about a few weeks near the nest before starting to venture further afield. Adults leave for West Africa from mid August, leaving the young birds to both feed themselves and then find their own way to their wintering grounds. It is fascinating following the progress of radio-tagged birds on the internet, as they try a few practice flights, maybe into the Irish or North Seas before heading off south. (see www.ospreys.org.uk)

Identification shouldn't pose too much of a problem. The birds have a hunched appearance when perched. In flight, the combination of dark plumage above and white below is pretty diagnostic. Even if you only see the bird in silhouette, you shouldn't have too much trouble; look for the four fingers showing on the wing tips and the bowed shape of slightly drooping wings if you see the bird head on.

If you want to see Ospreys at the nest, then visit either Loch Garten or Loch of the Lowes. To see them feeding, try Inverdruie Fish Farm, Spey Bay, Findhorn Bay or Loch Fleet.

This index lists all the site names, other relevant places and all birds listed in the 'Likely bird species' lists in the site guide section. The number of entries listed under each species should not be seen as an indication of how common or otherwise the bird is in the Scottish Highlands.

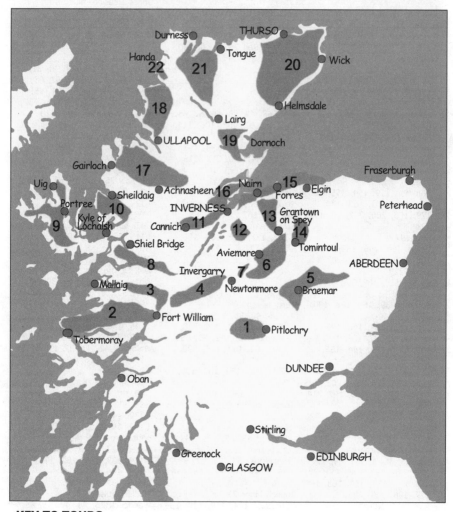

KEY TO TOURS

1. Perthshire Tour
2. Ardnamurchan Tour
3. Loch Arkaig Tour
4. Loch Laggan Tour
5. Upper Deeside Tour
6. Speyside Area
7. Insh Marshes
8. Loch Hourn Tours
9. Isle of Skye Tours
10. Applecross Peninsula
11. Inverness Glens
12. Findhorn Valley Tour
13. Lochindorb Tour
14. Glenlivet Estate
15. Moray Firth Tour
16. The Black Isle Tour
17. Beinn Eighe Tour
18. Inverpolly Tour
19. Loch Fleet Tour
20. Caithness Tour
21. Lairg and Tongue Tour
22. Handa Tour